An Impossible Livin

AN IMPOSSIBLE LIVING
in a Transborder World

Culture, Confianza, and Economy of
Mexican-Origin Populations

CARLOS G. VÉLEZ-IBÁÑEZ

The University of Arizona Press   Tucson

The University of Arizona Press
© 2010 The Arizona Board of Regents
All rights reserved

www.uapress.arizona.edu

Library of Congress Cataloging-in-Publication Data

Vélez-Ibáñez, Carlos G., 1936–
   An impossible living in a transborder world : culture,
confianza, and economy of Mexican-origin populations /
Carlos G. Vélez-Ibáñez.
      p.   cm.
   Includes bibliographical references and index.
   ISBN 978-0-8165-2634-5 (cloth : alk. paper) —
ISBN 978-0-8165-2635-2 (pbk. : alk. paper)
   1. Rotating credit associations—Mexico.   2. Rotating credit
associations—Southwest, New.   3. Mexican Americans—
Southwest, New—Economic conditions.   4. Mexican-American
Border Region—Economic conditions.   5. Mexican-American
Border Region—Social conditions.   I. Title.
   HG2039.M4V443 2010
   306.30972′1—dc22   2010017946

15   14   13   12   11   10   6   5   4   3   2   1

Portions of *Bonds of Mutual Trust: The Cultural Systems of
Rotating Credit Associations among Urban Mexicans and Chicanos*
(Rutgers University Press, New Brunswick, NJ, 1983) were
integrated into this manuscript.

A mis padres
Los primeros que me enseñaron confianza
A Mari Luz y nuestra hija Nayely, que me enseñan lo mismo todos
los días con su afecto y amor
A mis hijos Carmelita, Damian, Miguel, Lucy, Mariel, y Carlos y a
los nietos preciosos, mi cariño y calor

Contents

Illustrations

Figures

Tables

Acknowledgments

I conducted my original research on rotating savings and credit associations (ROSCAs) in 1978 and 1979, and I have continued my work on this topic from 1980 to the present. The most recent research concentrated on the Mexican states of Sinaloa and Baja California and on the U.S. states of Arizona, California (both northern and southern), New Mexico, and Washington. I wish to thank Fausto Vásquez Flores, an extraordinary researcher in Sinaloa; Paloma, in whatever state you really live in; and a great graduate student, Irene Vega, who carried out original research on the Arizona-Sonora border. Great appreciation is also owed to Camilo García Para, who is now a faculty member of the University of Veracruz, Xalapa. He carried out invaluable research for my first book on this topic, *Bonds of Mutual Trust* (Vélez-Ibáñez 1983). I would be remiss if I did not thank Andrea Perusquía, a graduate student at Arizona State University, whose magnificent artwork graces the book's cover page. She is the future of original Mexican creative works.

I especially would like to thank the Motorola Company for their generosity in supporting my endowed Chair, which provided me the support needed to publish this manuscript. I laud my colleague, Dr. Guillermina Nuñez, for her finely honed field research in New Mexico, which afforded me the opportunity to gain insight into true transborder living.

Most of all, I would like to thank the hundreds of people who had enough *confianza* in this work to provide me with information and crucial insights into ROSCAs, these simple but invaluable human inventions.

An Impossible Living in a Transborder World

Introduction

At first light, this book may seem to be merely about some economic practices shared by mostly Mexican-origin populations on both sides of the border. However, it is much more about the manner in which these populations are part of greater economies and polities and how such populations manage to use their social and cultural capital to engage in, as well as suffer through, this moment in the twenty-first-century global and transnational economy. In this global arena, it seems there is no place to hide from the very broad schemes and scripts by which the process of extracting labor and value is made unending and is rationalized. Transborder peoples, especially, are subject to unbelievable pressures to fit themselves into ongoing, and apparently normal, cultural "megascripts," which are couched in the language of values such as "achievement" or "success."[1] Despite the reality of great sacrifices, sometimes-tragic circumstances, and incontrovertible exploitation of limbs and brains, these megascripts push all populations to extreme measures in different ways. They are pushed to excel for their children without internal protest and, regardless of often-rapid aging and failing physical and mental health, to create home and hearth upheld by debt and borrowing, and to develop social and cultural platforms filled with contradictions and oppositions for succeeding generations. Individuals certainly succeed, but in the process, groups get left way behind, paying the price for the few to achieve. Jules Henry (1963) long ago suggested that these processes were almost pathological quests for success. He termed this quest "driveness," in which especially modern, and now much of postmodern, *Homo sapiens* suffer and desire simultaneously.[2] This book is about that struggle, and I use frequently unrecognized, yet ordinary, behaviors and frequently unmentioned cultural understandings to lay out the narrative and the lenses through which we can see those practices unfold in this struggle.

An Impossible Living in a Transborder World: Culture, Confianza, and Economy of Mexican-Origin Populations is a narrative about Mexican populations caught in an accelerated and dizzying transborder world of economy while struggling to make a living made almost impossible. Twenty-first-century populations are forced to dig deeply into their cultural reservoirs to develop, manage, and operate within ever-more-restrictive global demands for their labor and energy. They struggle valiantly to expand their ability to protect their progeny, yet simultaneously they engage in the very economic actions that both figuratively and in reality guarantee the next generation's participation in the same impossible processes. This narrative is about that, but it is a roundabout tale told through very specific lenses.

Eric R. Wolf, the great American anthropologist, who positioned himself theoretically to fundamentally understand these processes, wrote the foreword (appendix A) to an earlier version of this book (Vélez-Ibáñez 1983). He stated, in his usual erudite manner, that "anthropology was always at its best when it was able to locate seemingly ordinary behaviors in daily life in a new light, and deduce unforeseen implications from that examination" (xiv). Operating in transborder cultural systems, rotating savings and credit associations (ROSCAs) are just such ordinary behaviors. This book digs into new, previously unconsidered areas; draws new, unforeseen implications; and presents new and important findings. Coupled with work previously accomplished, it shows how ROSCAs are integral to the culture and economy of Mexican-origin populations of the Southwest North American Region, which includes the U.S. and northern Mexican border states, and beyond, and how they contribute to the very contradictions of culture and economy that these practices seek to resolve. Additionally, this work continues to contribute to the world literature on ROSCAs, since they appear in many populations around the world, as further discussions will illustrate.[3]

This seemingly very ordinary behavior in its most simple form consists of a savings-and-lending operation organized among friends, neighbors, relatives, or fellow workers. As a simple example, a hypothetical ROSCA might consist of an organizer and four other persons who agree to contribute a set amount of $10 a week. The order in which these monies are distributed is decided by lot or by the order in which the members joined. Each person, including the organizer, receives a one-time payment of $50 from the ROSCA. Thus, each person contributes to the others' $50 payments, at the rate of $10 dollars per week. The total lifespan of this hypothetical ROSCA would be five weeks. Or, as Shirley Ardener, one of the pioneers in the study of this phenomenon, explains, a ROSCA consists of "a core of participants who agree to make regular contributions to a fund which is given, in whole or in part, to each contributor in rotation" (1964, 201). As will be shown, this simple model has evolved into much more complex structural and institutional types, which vary in their formality, their borders, and even their classes.

This book focuses on ROSCAs, but its scope goes far beyond this "ordinary behavior." The ROSCA serves as a lens through which we become much more familiar with the manner in which culture and political economy interact throughout the great region that includes all the Mexican and U.S. states along the border and, many times, beyond those places, both north and south. It provides us with a means and measure for cultural change at this point in time when broad demographic and economic dynamics move people, redefine spaces, and transnationalize places beyond national boundaries. Multiple sources and fonts of cultural identity derive from this juncture. Yet the ROSCA also lets us track how great cultural megascripts—like "individualism," "success," and "mutual trust"—that undergird these dynamics become embedded in the daily lives of people. These are learned and distributed without conscious recognition of their presence, their contradictions, or their disastrous consequences in the lives of individuals, as revealed in chapter 4.

Lastly, it also provides us with a lens through which to understand how everyday persons tackle global processes at local levels to deal with over-indebtedness, lack of opportunity, poverty, and the struggle to provide stable social platforms for their families and households. Cultural megascripts are not only embedded within practices but also articulated and reproduced increasingly in the hands of women. They bear the brunt of provisioning households and emotionally supporting their families, and it is they who must seek out all possible means of stability, including the behaviors described in this book.

In order to ensure that these lenses provide the right magnification, it is imperative to understand why and how these behaviors emerge as part of much larger transnational and transborder economic, ecological, political, cultural, and social contexts and processes. It is also necessary to explain how these function in multiple places and spaces as well as within and between different classes. Throughout the book, these variations in context require the articulation of a number of theoretical positions, of a high order as well as of middle and lower levels, in order to understand the whys of the great variation in ROSCAs and the multiple cultural and social contexts in which they are embedded. However, in the final analysis, like most social science books, this work attempts to provide an understanding of how human beings adjust, adapt, and create innovative ideas and practices in the midst of broader economic dynamics and demographic movements that are usually deleterious to most individuals, even as they support a handful of others. These will be articulated and unfold as the book progresses.

In the transnational and transborder arenas where Mexican ROSCAs operate, they are known by a variety of names, but basically these can be reduced to two terms: *cundina*, which is the term commonly used in the Southwest North American Region, and *tanda*, which is the term more common in central and southern Mexico. These practices have spread with the transnationalization of the Mexican and U.S. economies and workforces, but as will be seen, such practices are in fact worldwide. They have numerous names, but at their most simple level, they operate basically as described above.

Regardless of place, however, ROSCAs still seem quaint to some, obvious to others, and certainly unimportant to many. When I explain them to different sectors among the Mexican-origin population in the United States or to Mexicans in Mexico, they look askance, puzzled that anyone would be interested in these obvious behaviors that so many engage in on a daily basis. For many, participating in them is as common as creating fictive kinship relations with each other. To those so engaged, there is no real mystery. But like all human behaviors, these, albeit seemingly trivial, mean something beyond the obvious. Sometimes the meanings are so transparent that they are invisible until someone such as an anthropologist begins asking, out of anthropological curiosity, about the whys, the whens, and the whats. In other words, the very common is so much on the front stage of life that people assume that there is no backstage—nothing hidden underneath; nothing masked by its commonness; nothing to be explained because everyone already knows about it.

This book is an expanded, revamped, and rethought-out version of *Bonds of Mutual Trust: The Cultural Systems of Rotating Credit Associations among Urban Mexicans and Chicanos*, published in 1983. At first glance, it seemed like a dip into a common and unremarkable practice that mostly went unnoticed at the time. Although the underlying theoretical and methodological templates that I used in the original version partially still stand, this work develops new theoretical and methodological frameworks that travel far beyond those suggested in the 1983 work. It also offers new data that illustrate the rapid economic impact of global and transnational processes. Among these is the demographic explosion of Mexican-origin and other Latino populations throughout the United States, which has necessitated an entirely new approach and explanation of ROSCAs and their spread instead of diffusion.[4] Another impact has been the rapid transformations of Mexican localities and regions, whose inhabitants have been forced to migrate to the "north," be it to northern Mexico or to the United States. A third impact is the formation of the amazing transportation, trade-and-exchange, and communication links, cross-border human traffic and processes, and the extensive cultural transformations that create entirely new landscapes of cultural creation and interaction in what I would regard as a central economic and ecological region, which I term the Southwest North American Region. This region is discussed in Chapter 4, but it is basically comprised of the southwestern United States and northern Mexico, and many times beyond. Therefore, this work, like the expanding populations and the processes in which they are involved, is transnational and transborder in that it crosses physical, political, social, economic, cultural, and cognitive borders.

As we will also see, the spread of the Internet has been one of the true boons to the appearance of ROSCAs and their commercial versions, rotating credit associations (RCAs). Although much of the twenty-first-century literature has discarded the term "rotating credit association," I revive it to indicate commercially organized and directed businesses, on a small and large scale, that utilize the practices of ROSCAs to provide long-term credit. Some RCAs are transborder and transnational as well as being local. I will analyze these in chapter 1.

Like all inventions, an underlying cultural value supports ROSCAs and, to some degree, RCAs regardless of place. It is the cultural concept of *confianza*, or mutual trust. It is paramount, and it designates a type of a relationship that is built around the idea of reciprocity involving persons who trust each other sufficiently to form a select circle or network in which all have agreed to rotate money without external legal oversight. At more complex and formal levels, institutions, agencies, and companies depend on contracts and agreements to achieve an equivalent function. Unlike the confianza-based informal ROSCAs, these arrangements require little social maintenance. Yet they tap into the cultural basis of confianza, as the major value to attract customers, even as they guarantee that trust through legal means.

Rotating savings and credit associations represent attempts to reduce the uncertainty of people's lives and as far as possible create wealth and security. However, they also respond to much larger and intertwined global, national, and local economic changes, which are expressed in diverse ways at each of these levels. In a sense, many local-level practices of different sorts are the immediate versions of much broader global processes and megascripts that permeate the entire gamut of human economic, social, political, and cultural expectations, behaviors, and ideologies in the twenty-first century and beyond.

These massive changes can be appreciated through just two examples: one simple and economic, and the other much more transculturative. In the first instance, transmigration and transborder travel have led to the founding of six start-up Mexican airlines since 2002. They offer no-frills service from central and southern Mexico to Mexican border cities, and their customers—some with, but most without, documents—then cross the international border. These planes usually are filled going north and almost empty going south.[5] Second, more intense processes of transculturation penetrate formerly Anglo and African American spaces in the United States, including many rural areas of the southern United States. These processes change the demography and social foundations of declining agricultural towns while simultaneously, on a daily basis at local and regional levels, creating contested social and cultural grounds. This "transculturation" of American towns by Mexican-origin populations in places like Alabama, Mississippi, North Carolina, and many others includes the introduction of ROSCAs into the social discourse of daily life in rural areas. These changes are part of the "transnational" local spaces created by migrating and settling populations due to great economic shifts and changes occurring especially since World War II, and the ever-increasing penetration of transnational capital and the assembly and disassembly of human localities.

Yet there are negative economic and political punctuations. We might perceive that certain temporary economic changes seem to slow this process down (such as the 2009 recession and global shocks felt around the world). But these developments may very well accentuate the need for populations to migrate from their point of origin to greener pastures. Undocumented Mexican migration to the United States increased from 8.5 million in 2000 to 11.6 million in 2006.[6] Even with billions spent on "border security" and increased apprehensions and deportations, Mexican towns continue to be vacated of cohorts of younger people, with mostly the older generations taking care of children left behind. And while 9/11, the turndown in the U.S economy, and stricter border control reduce the numbers of Mexicans overstaying their visas or facing horrific crossing conditions along the desert entries to "El Norte," there is also no doubt that such migratory processes will continue.

The post-2000 global period is yet another version of global and local processes that extend back into antiquity, but today, electronic communications and transactions, massive movements of populations, and rapid economic synergies and asymmetries between national economies accentuate them. Rotating savings and credit associations spread not just as the result of "diasporic" populations, but of "diasporic" economic transnational economic institutions such as the North American Free Trade Agreement (NAFTA), the General Agreement on Tariffs and Trade (GATT), and World Bank expansions that have created both opportunities and income disparities for millions of populations. This has meant that the Southwest North American Region, encompassing the southwestern United States and northern Mexico, is rapidly becoming a center of economy, polity, social structure, culture, linguistic variance, and expression more intense than at any time in history. I will elaborate on this later (it is really a subject for another book), but suffice it to say that Mexican-origin populations spreading out from this region to other parts of the United States (the East Coast, the South, the Midwest, and even Hawaii and Alaska) are peripheral populations to those in the region.

Thus, this new book theoretically and empirically disassembles and reassembles the previous work. In doing so, it focuses further on the cognitive, social, economic, and cultural transborder and transnational features of ROSCAs and highly commercialized RCAs important to populations in Mexico and to Mexican-origin populations in the United States.[7]

The book is divided into six chapters. Chapter 1's discussion of theoretical issues and transborder cultural constructs is certainly problematic because of the expansion of ROSCAs with the swelling of Mexican-origin populations throughout the United States and in all six Mexican border states. The chapter articulates a number of major theoretical positions as the bases for discussion, and it discusses the basic methodological and technical approaches used in the work.

Chapter 2 develops the underlying cultural construct of confianza, which is central to social exchange and the operation of ROSCAs. It also analyzes their class characteristics, their basic mechanisms and structures, and their characteristics within local, regional, national, and transnational contexts. Chapter 3 focuses on the social and cultural dimensions and dynamics of the class situations and sectors in which

ROSCAs occur and on new dimensions of risk and safeguards. It also discusses RCAs, the corporate form of ROSCAs. Chapter 4 develops how ROSCAs become embedded within the transborder centrality of the Southwest North American Region and in an individual's "calculus" of economic and political strategies. Two detailed case studies illustrate how border populations maneuver and create "slantwise"[8] approaches to daily life in order to gain an edge in the highly competitive and often repressive necessities of simple survival. Chapter 5 offers an intensive discussion of the multiple functions served by ROSCA practices and the important implications for learning that manifest as "deutero-learning" phenomena.

The final chapter ties together the various themes of the work within a discussion of how the uncertainty arising from the rapid global and transborder dynamics of economy, polity, and culture are partially mitigated by ROSCAs and similar practices. In the final analysis, these are simultaneously respites from, but also contributors to, the transborder cultural scripts that arise in this new century, when the commoditization of entire populations is continuously rationalized and made acceptable.

I have developed a bibliography to illustrate the sheer explosion in the literature on ROSCAs as a reflection of their continuing and increasing importance worldwide for developmental policies and as a means to improve the lives of people in extreme poverty in Africa, Asia, and Latin America. As well, the bibliography provides a partial record for those interested in the topic to more systematically place the various types and practices within larger theoretical frameworks. This bibliography can be requested from the author.

1

The Transborder and Transnational Dimensions of Culture and Political Economy

On Theorizing

Although a tiny but significant comment hidden in a footnote twenty-seven years ago declared that there were indications of the existence of "transnational commuter rotating credit associations" (Vélez-Ibáñez 1983, 26, table 1.1, n. 4), I failed to develop this in my thinking or focus on it in either in an empirical or cognitive sense. When I use the word "transnational," I mean multiple things. First, I am referring to people's actual participation in a rotating savings and credit association (ROSCA) on one or both sides of the U.S.–Mexico border. Second, I also mean the introduction of very useful practices, which are either brought from the communities of origin to a new national setting by people already accustomed to those practices or which arise as new knowledge learned in the new setting. But there is also a spatial sense that is not located in a single place. People live out "transnational lives," so their "citizenship" is not the main locater for their existential sense of self. Rather, it is tied to myriad points of physical spaces, emotional places, and cultural references. For Mexican-origin populations living in the United States and for those migrating to Mexico's northern border, this last facet has been increasingly important, especially because of the great demographic transitions between Mexico and the United States that have taken place from 1980 to the present, with much of these transitions the aftermath of the North American Free Trade Agreement (NAFTA).[1]

However, ROSCAs serve as connectors to people's transnational lives. These associations function as transnational reminders and actions, but within a local context, combining with countless daily social, cultural, and economic relations and nexuses as well as with electronic, media, and personal communications. This is especially so in the southwestern United States and northern Mexico. The phrase "the global is in the local" is apt here since ROSCAs are probably the result of much larger economic processes that have emerged, in the Mexican case, since the nineteenth century. However, there is recent evidence that ROSCAs were developed by Mexicans in the United States as early as the mid-nineteenth century by Juntas Patrióticas Mexicanas (Mexican Patriotic Councils), which were benevolent associations in Los Angeles, California, supporting Mexican patriots fighting against the French intervention in Mexico of 1864.[2] However, I take a broad view of transnationalism and transborder phenomena, especially given the special nature of the history of the region. The territorial conquest of parts of the Southwest by the United States,[3] the Gadsden Purchase at the point of a gun,[4] the economic integration of the border region,[5] the continued linguistic and cultural exchange throughout the southwestern United States and northern Mexico, and the continuous movement of populations from south to north and north to south all constitute the basis of a regional history that people certainly experience and remember to varying degrees.[6] Thus, regional historical memory is distributed among individuals, groups, and networks that for decades largely comprised mixed cohorts of citizens, residents, and undocumented individuals, sometimes in the same household and, most certainly, in many Mexican-origin communities on both sides of the border. For some, such memory has depth stretching back to the founding of Santa Fe, New Mexico, by their ancestors in the seventeenth century. Borders were later imposed, and great tracts of land lost but not forgotten by, among others, the land grantees.[7] For others more recent, another historical memory of the region is the recollections by waiters and busgirls of having to hide in their Mexican restaurant's refrigerator when U.S. Immigration and Customs Enforcement (ICE) agents enter the establishment, sniffing around for the presence of undocumented workers. Yet both memories are of the region—different, special, but constituted by the crossing of the border by Americans in the nineteenth century, in one case, and by present-day Mexicans in the other—and thus form some aspects of the complexity of the transborder region.

Other Points of View

There are points of view that ignore the regional historical development of what I term the "transnational" or the "transborder." Portes (2001a, b; 2002) restricts the transnational and transborder phenomena to those individuals who are regularly and constantly engaged in transnational behaviors, and Itzigsohn et al. (1999) distinguish between narrow and broad transnationalism. In contrast, I agree with Kim (2003), Levitt and Glick-Schiller (2004), Mahler and Pessar (2004), R. Smith (2006), and especially with Morawska (2004) and Glick-Schiller (2003a, b) that contemporary transnationalism and transborder analysis must connect all levels of social experience. I would say this is especially so in the Southwest North American Region in that transborder and transnational phenomena are complex and multilayered and cannot be reduced to how many times a person in the United States interacts with an individual in Mexico or vice versa.[8] Rotating savings and credit associations are one important, but nevertheless only one, medium by which transnational and transborder practices, ideas, feelings, emotions, materials, and values are articulated daily, frequently, and constantly in this region.

When we consider the weight of the hundreds of institutions that constantly cross borders or that are created to thwart their crossings, then transborder definitions cannot be reduced to the number of individuals who have relatives across the border or only know relatives on one side or the other. Given the increasing importance of transnational political organizations, both indigenous and mestizo, that are often supported by Mexican state institutions like those described by M. Smith and Bakker (2008) for Guanajuato and by Kearney (2004) for Mixtecs, then institutionalized transborder relations utilizing local actors must be included in the transborder constructs. Thus, new social and cultural dynamics have emerged in which transnational organizations have become influential sources in both the United States and Mexico in their respective political systems, beyond only social relations, and contribute further to the creation of a transborder region.[9] Even the militarization of the border and increased border vigilance have created much more sophisticated methods for crossing and for hindering discovery. This has created entire industries of surveillance and its opposite, and in so doing, millions of dollars are invested in the region not only to keep it apart but also to narrow the differences of polity within an integrated economy.[10] Numerous transborder spaces are not even located at the border. One example is the Mexican flag waving next to the U.S. flag on poles in front of banks, state buildings, and businesses in Tucson, Albuquerque, Las Cruces, San Diego, and El Paso. Others are the hundreds of small events that occur daily along the immense expanse of the region, such as a lunch hour in southeastern Arizona where uniformed men—UPS drivers, Border Patrol agents, and sheriff's deputies—sit chatting together in Spanish and English in a gas station parking lot as they eat a lunch of *mariscos* (shrimp) or tacos sold from his food cart by Pancho, who may or may not be documented. We can thus assert that the region is a trans-border and transnational space and place to varying but certain degrees. Nourished by myriad museum showings of the art, music, and films of the borderlands on both sides of the border, cultural forms unique to the region and their syncretic forms emerge in transborder and hybridic ways.[11] Rotating savings and credit associations are yet another local and regional cross-border practice that joins all other cultural forms.

ROSCAs as Transborder Local and Regional Institutions

In these transnational senses, the increasing use of ROSCAs has led to the rise of rotating credit associations (RCAs), which I use as the term to designate institutionalized formal mechanisms of credit and savings, especially in Mexico and the northern border areas. Today, nongovernmental organizations (NGOs) and U.S. banking, sales, and lending institutions are also paying serious attention to them. This specific development provides us with a new theoretical opportunity to decipher how transnational capitalist expansion appropriates the cultural scripts of local populations to advance its own abilities to extract ever-greater value by extending credit to localities where banking institutions would have little opportunities to extract value. In a very contradictory but rational manner, such institutional expansion also eliminates local competition for the same money that is lent without interest through ROSCAs. Now, using RCAs, it is possible to create a totally market-driven and -gained structure that looks familiar culturally, but is totally immersed within the market economy and extracted from local control. Importantly, ROSCAs, even at the local level, are not "forms of resistance," but rather mechanisms that allow individuals to access and accentuate their participation in a market economy through the use of nonmarket forms of exchange in a "slantwise" manner.[12] For millions of people worldwide who have no access to resources or power domains that can facilitate such access, ROSCAs are a local means of generating social capital to make possible an initial, "slantwise" entry into investment avenues, savings venues, and economic domains. Rotating credit associations ease access to credit for bigger expenditures, like automobiles and homes, and simultaneously, the credit market captures those participating.

I have previously stressed the diffusionist and transformational aspects of the rise of such practices, and although the diffusion of human inventions among different populations has been the bread and butter of anthropology, it does not explain why they should be diffused. I now consider that sort of explanation a highly limiting one that does not extend our theoretical understanding beyond description. Similarly, I suggested transformational reasons, such as middle-class populations having to expand their creditworthiness or economically marginal populations, like migrants, having greater "structural" incentives to participate in ROSCAs. Although these assertions are true, they do not extend our understanding much beyond a limited level of analysis.

Culture and Political Economy

Whether middle class, working class, or a member of an economically marginal population, people in the twenty-first century are subject to the same global economic forces that dig deeply for additional sources of value as part of a much larger capitalist project. Each class sector is created by multitudes of transnational market economic forces, but all are subject to their continuing degradation in one way or another. This may manifest in a middle-class person investing longer hours at work, or in an economically marginal population being forced to accept state subsidies. At the highest levels of political and economic privilege, these forces emerge and gain further control and influence over existing labor, land, and productive value. Both ROSCAs and RCAs are means to slightly balance in a "slantwise" manner the resulting economic disadvantage by using alternative means of engaging the political economy at the local level. Thus, "political economy" and culture intersect, as populations seek to cope with the continuous degradation of their ability to deal with transnational market forces through practices built around cultural values. These attempts to fend off the worst aspects of deeply penetrating market pressures can succeed only in a minimal sense, as will be shown.

So, at the local level, ROSCAs are not "resistance" forms nor do they eventually make people more "independent" of formal markets. Instead, they are built on culturally expected values of reciprocity and exchange and of mutual trust. Their practices are more like social exchange and less like market exchange. Although "individuals" engage in ROSCAs, they can only do so as part of a social compact built on nonmarket values of *confianza* (mutual trust) that are engineered within webs of social networks and groups. As Cruz Torres (personal communication, n.d.) showed, even in the most competitive of market environments—such as that for shrimp-vending women in the Mexican state of Sinaloa where each is engaged in a daily war of selling and buying shrimp—the entire market edifice is built on reciprocity and exchange, each person with the others, with their creditors, and even with their customers, despite incessant disputes about prices and competitive advantages taken during the course of selling their products.[13] At the local level, the use of this social capital is the currency by which ROSCAs are able to operate in the absence of access to formal institutions. More importantly, this capital is often the only available source of balancing the extreme pressures of a globalizing political economy and its scrapping of value at local and regional levels.

The Portability and Adaptability of Transborder ROSCAs and RCAs

As is the case for many who operate within an amazingly complex series of economic market and nonmarket transactions of borrowing, credit, investment, and profit-making, participation in ROSCAs and RCAs is often long term. This participation can stretch into years and move across regions, nations, and even borders. These organizations may end in one site, only to be taken up quickly in the new one and begun all over again. Their very transnationality, portability, and adaptability make them amenable to their continued development and expansion as part and parcel of very complex decade-long strategies of economic and social mobility. For example, "Paloma," who originally used *tandas* (as ROSCAs are called in central and southern Mexico) to save and eventually purchase a home in Mexico City, also used the same practice in rural California (where a ROSCA is called a *cundina*) as one of the central mechanisms to accumulate investment properties worth hundreds of thousands of dollars. Many people like Paloma, living as undocumented workers, may accumulate sufficient money in combination with other economic activities to enter housing markets as investors, when only a few years earlier they had been working seventy hours a week for minimum wage. As I will show in chapter 4, however, U.S. judicial systems misunderstand ROSCAs. Judges either are completely confounded by their efficacy and efficiency and are incredulous that someone like Paloma could successfully accumulate investment properties without also participating in illegal activities, or they deem them pyramid schemes. From the point of view of some judicial authorities, it would be impossible for "illegals" to devise such complex logistics without resorting to extra-legal means. In that same chapter, I detail the "transborder economic calculus" of border survival and success in "Valentina's" case. She and her entire family engage in border trade, ownership, and entrepreneurial tactics and strategies and utilize rich cultural "slantwise" behaviors to filter the juridical demands of border regulations, interventions, and trade. These practices are possible because borders both stop and simultaneously facilitate economic opportunities, and when symmetries of economy are especially uneven, as is the case along the two-thousand-mile border, then local border populations take advantage of every social, juridical, and economic nook and cranny that they can identify. Where none exists, they will create one. Yet they are truly transborder in the sense that the border is a place where ROSCAs, and their commercial brethren RCAs, also cross—rather than only a site that somehow stops them from emerging.

Gender, ROSCAs, and Social Capital and Reproduction

I cannot emphasize too strongly that the majority of the literally thousands of tandas or cundinas operating throughout northern Mexico and the southwestern United States—and now in parts of the Midwest, the South, and on the East Coast—are in the hands of women. They are both participants and managers in formal, semiformal, and informal settings. As the world literature shows, most ROSCAs were largely in the hands of men and originally had developed from forms of agricultural exchange. This was the case in rural India, Asia, Africa, the Cape Verde Islands, and many other places. In contrast, contemporary monetized economies—whether rural, urban, developing, or developed—seem largely to be in the hands of women.[14] In part, I hypothesize that two conditions are necessary for women's participation. First, women in traditionally land-based economies were excluded from holding lands, and except for their labor, they had access to few resources. In a monetized economy, women's access to income-generating activities was and is largely restricted to petty market- or home-based economic transactions. In the case of women in the U.S. Southwest, the same condition holds, except that it is exacerbated by transnational migration. Women have very few resources other than limited wage labor to develop capital for consumption, investment, or saving. With credit markets initially very limited—because of low wages, lack of collateral, or attitudinal or market conditions—thousands of women in the region must use all available means in order to provide subsistence support for their families. Among these are ROSCAs, which are a means for generating savings in order to create income-producing enterprises. The one existing strength that is present within many networks of women worldwide is social capital and the willingness to extend it to others in many forms. This makes the rise of ROSCAs run by women possible.

However, an important cultural reproductive dynamic also develops: female offspring, especially within the context of small-business enterprises, learn the basic processes. As young as nine or ten years of age, they begin to fashion their own limited but nevertheless important tandas integrated within other income-generating activities. These "tanda" children themselves in time become quite accustomed to handling and managing accounts, collecting and dispensing monies, and ensuring that all participants fulfill their obligations. These children have an amazing confidence and self-assurance, even at this young age, and they literally learn to learn how to be successfully independent. At the same time, to gain legitimacy, they draw on the social capital of their networks of relatives and others. They not only build their own confidence but also gain the confidence of others. In this way, they establish a basis for long-term social contracts regardless of where they may be situated in time and space. In this special sense, these children engage in actions and behaviors that are transnational in time and space, and like all well-learned, practiced, and positive behaviors, they are carried and extended in time and space as well.

In relation to gender, however, two central concerns in the original work bear repeating here from a more psychocultural point of view.[15] In my original work, I noted that ROSCAs were highly adaptive forms that meet many needs, and while this is self-evident, it does not add much to our understanding of why they emerge in so many different circumstances, among so many different people, and in a variety of class and social sectors. I also emphasized the indeterminacy of social life as highly determinate for people to be engaged in ROSCAs. That is, these practices assist in reducing indeterminacy and uncertainty, whether because of the lack of credit and savings or simply because there are few other means by which to accumulate small capital. Although true, this does not explain why persons are motivated to join a ROSCA.

I suggest strongly that although ROSCAs are exceedingly helpful for both long- and short-term needs and strategies, they are especially important for women as "one way out" of their economic situation, whether the consequence of desperation, created opportunity, relatively stable but precarious income, or balancing middle-class status with working-class income. The "economic calculus" that mainly women have to invent to balance almost successfully the margin of debt, credit, and resources, although highly admirable, is often illusory. Capitalist inclusion is a hydra-headed proposition at best. Eventually, no matter how successful the tanda participant, her very activity contributes to a kind of frantic and fanatical participation, as she tries to keep up with the newest symbol of consumption, or save to make investments, which will cost her a part of her labor, wages, land, or production. No person is an isolate from the chains of production and labor, so every decision impacts and costs someone not present or not even in mind. Women worldwide are in the most precarious of positions. Nevertheless, women who engage in ROSCAs and myriad other calculated economic enterprises gain limited independence at the level of the household. As will be seen in chapter 4, the way in which women manipulate the social and economic algebras, the sheer courage they display, and their high levels of risk taking are all pyschocultural learning patterns that encourage even more risk taking, economic calculation, and the ability to lay out long-term, intentional strategies. Rotating savings and credit associations contribute strongly to these skills and practices. Thus, women who participate in tandas and cundinas can count more reliably on their own skills and make predictive insights about the future.

Background

In 1971, I first became familiar with rotating savings and credit associations in Ciudad Netzahualcoyótl—a city of more than a million persons seventeen kilometers from the center of Mexico City. Known in central urban Mexico as tandas (turns or rotations) and sometimes *vaquitas* (small cows or calves colloquially), ROSCAs now appear throughout urban and semirural Mexico and throughout the U.S. South, Midwest, and East Coast, almost wherever Mexican-origin populations reside. They are known by a variety of names, and they appear in many class, residential, and institutional sectors. Although the literature is now much more extensive than when I first wrote about ROSCAs, their progressively more-complex economic, political, and social functions and their increasingly variable degrees of formality and commercialization are not quite yet appreciated. Beyond what is presented in the current literature, ROSCAs have many intended and unintended consequences. Additionally, the cultural construct of confianza continues to play a role as the adhesive for reciprocal obligations within ROSCAs, and it has expanded much beyond what is presented in the existing literature. Confianza, as the central practice and the tool for creating relations not yet established, spreads out as the globalizing processes have spread the distribution of ROSCAs throughout the Southwest North American Region and in other parts of Mexico and the United States.[16]

As I indicated previously, a ROSCA consists of "a core of participants who agree to make regular contributions to a fund which is given, in whole or in part, to each contributor in rotation" (Ardener 1964, 201).[17] Since the publication of *Bonds of Mutual Trust* (Vélez-Ibáñez 1983), the literature expressing appreciation for the ROSCAs has exploded, especially regarding the possibility that they might offer a solution to poverty in Asia and Africa. The Global Development Research Center, a virtual network developed in 2001 out of a number of research and bibliographic programs, has compressed the myriad forms of ROSCAs into a list of the practices worldwide.[18] As in most of the development literature, these are part of the "microfinance" and "microcredit" practices, which help to alleviate poverty. They are such an important topic that the United Nations declared 2005 the International Year of Microcredit, and the 2006 Nobel Peace Prize was awarded to Muhammad Yunus, Bangladeshi banker and economist, and the Grameen Bank, which he founded and which makes small loans for self-employment to Bangledeshi.

With many other small-scale practices, including Papa and Mama Cards in Zaire, Moneyshops in the Philippines, Mobile Banks in Western Africa, Syndicate Bank's Pigmy Deposit Scheme in India, and Flash Cash in Cameroon, ROSCAs become part of a complex of lending, borrowing, and savings initiatives often tied to NGO interventions. However, in the face of great global and transborder commercial and economic expansions and connections, microenterprises seem to also expand in light of the ever-increasing demand for cheaper goods, easier market entries, and small-scale participation. Globalization and transnational penetration increases the likelihood of penetration of localities through the increased demands of required supply chains for non-local markets. Thus, from chilies grown by small farmers in Sinaloa for the U.S. market to the capitalization for their migrating sons and daughters, monies from many sources are required to feed the supply chains necessary for cheap produce that flows into the United States and to feed the millions of middle-class people and the low-waged labor supply chains for the hundreds of jobs available for documented and undocumented workers in the United States. In this sense, microenterprises, including ROSCAs, are mechanisms that arise and emerge outside of the "poverty-focused" explanation, but they are often tied to development schemes.

However, much of the "development-oriented" literature focuses on the manner in which ROSCAs seem to play an increasingly important role in the capitalization of individuals where credit sources are weak or unable to provide needed resources for investment for the development of local markets or goods (Ardener and Burman 1995, 2). Nongovernmental organizations of many types also seem to appreciate the cultural congruence of such practices in Africa and in Asia, especially after events have overturned existing civic and civil institutions, such as, for example, the cultural revolution in China, the Vietnam War, or other such political upheavals especially common in sub-Saharan Africa (Ardener and Burman 1995, 2).

In accordance with my own broader perspective, in which globalization is the key feature accounting for the spread of ROSCAs and the culture of confianza, I also stress the participation from a transborder perspective of lower-middle-class and working-class people and those from the professional sectors in ROSCAs in the region and beyond. I also pay particular attention to documented and undocumented working-class Mexicans and lower-middle-class, first-generation Mexicans living in the United States. Thus, "poverty" is not the most important variable for the participation for a great deal of the Mexican-origin population either in Mexico or in the United States. Instead, people's participation in ROSCAs is driven by the need to stay up with and balance the debt-credit-income cycle, rather than the engine being simple poverty, cultural congruence, or a penchant for savings.

At the same time, specific enterprises also lock into such processes by inventing methods to take advantage of these conditions. They can appropriate the tanda or cundina term to organize what is in effect a credit mechanism rather than a savings and credit mechanism. Again, these commercialized inventions emerge simultaneously with informal tandas, but these can no longer be understood as ROSCAs: they are instead rotating credit associations (RCAs). I will illustrate their differences in a later part of this chapter.[19]

Previously, I had considered that ROSCAs were generally confined to urban areas, but since my original work was published, I have found that not to be the case.[20] They show up in many rural places wherever markets have penetrated deeply, such as in *ejidos* in Sinaloa and elsewhere.[21] As with many other rural areas in Mexico, people have multiple jobs: farming an ejido; working as a migrant in other regions of Mexico or in the United States; working as an agricultural wage earner on other ejidos, in coconut and mango groves, or in chili fields; and working in aquaculture, either tending shrimp farms or fishing in cooperative shrimp fisheries. And it is women, especially, who organize and participate in ROSCAs and who also are employed in multiple enterprises. They combine many income-generating activities together with their employment as field hands, broom makers, and copra sorters, and the work they do on their own ejido land. Additionally, they are responsible for all of the household tasks.[22] Thus, these products—from brooms to copra and from chilies to mangos—are each part of the supply chain leading to transnational markets, to the border, and to national markets, like Guadalajara, where copra, for example, is used as the basis for cosmetics and face soaps, which themselves are then exported north and nationally (Cruz Torres 2004, 87). In a similar manner, Mexican-origin populations are treated as labor commodities in Mexico and in the United States, and especially in the Southwest North American Region, and these become links in the chain of production in many other industries. Rotating savings and credit associations are one of the few relatively independent means around those wage chains because, although they are dependent on wages, ROSCAs provide participants with a method of savings and investment outside of the commercial-market credit chains.

However, even within the same region, multiple explanations may be necessary. In the United States, different versions of ROSCAs coexist, which were brought to just Los Angeles alone from the Caribbean, China, India, Japan, Korea, and Mexico, together with sundry other practices.[23] Yet their points of origin were at entirely different stages of industrialization and modernization when these practices were brought in by migrating populations. In the nineteenth century, China and Japan were both agricultural societies, and the migrating populations were made up of peasants. The Mexican versions, on the other hand, were carried to the United States by twentieth-century and now twenty-first-century urban and rural migrants to border cities and states. Combining causal explanations and diffusion analysis is especially efficacious if the latter can be related to proven cross-cultural theories. Learning theory, for example, might be included as a construct within diffusion analysis and might provide insights contributing to the discovery of theoretically sound principles. But in the twenty-first century, and particularly since 1980, transnational necessities created by NAFTA and other transborder economic policies penetrating into local markets have accelerated the movement of populations from south to north at a level never before observed in the history of economic relationships between Mexico and the United States. The same can be said for transborder markets, institutions, and production.[24]

An important discovery made in the first phase of my research is that Mexicans have generated a variety of different forms of these practices, which the literature covering Mexico, the United States, Africa, or Asia has never before reported. In the post-1983 research, the increasing importance of commercial versions has necessitated my differentiating ROSCAs from RCAs, since the latter have appropriated the format, organization, and cultural equivalents regarding confianza as well. Some of these are transnational in scope, for example, automobile RCAs situated in Mazatlán, Sinaloa, that cater to those who live in the United States. On the one hand, for the twenty-first century, mutual trust continues to be the underlying bond that holds people together sufficiently to participate in a somewhat risky practice. On the other hand, as will also be discussed, the post-1980s have also seen a rise in slightly more fraud and failures, given the radical demographic shifts and decontextualization of social relations due to migration. Yet it is the case that even in such indeterminate conditions, participating in ROSCAs and other social cohesive practices, like rituals, contribute to groups and networks developing broader circles of trust as well as developing a positive attitude toward savings even in modest economic circumstances. Even RCAs serve as mechanisms for saving, because people delay immediate gratification that would have come from purchasing large commercial items, like automobiles, homes, or whole kitchens.

Methods and Techniques

This book is based on data collected in the field over a thirty-year period, from 1971 intermittently through 2008. I developed the first extensive database in 1978 and 1979, based on ROSCAs I had identified in Mexico and the United States. Snowball and opportunistic samples generated the data on 65 informal and intermediate ROSCAs, 4 of which I now term formal RCAs. I based my 1983 book, *Bonds of Mutual Trust*, on that information. The data were trustworthy on 56 ROSCAs; data on the remainder are questionable. From 2000 to 2009, two intensive field studies used opportunistic and snowball sampling to gather additional data. This work was concentrated in Arizona, Southern California, Washington, the Arizona-Sonora border, Baja California, Sonora, and very intensively in Sinaloa. This database includes 65 new informal ROSCAs and 7 RCAs. The data en toto prior to 1983 and through 2009 cover 137 informal, intermediate, and formally institutionalized ROSCAs and RCAs.[25] These represent approximately five thousand people, and the data were gathered from more than ninety informants, ten web pages, countless e-mails, and numerous "quick" conversational exchanges between me and at least forty people, covering an area from Seattle, Washington, all the way to Xalapa, Veracruz, and other parts of Latin America. I have also participated in three ROSCAs: two in Phoenix, Arizona, and one in San Luis Río Colorado, which straddles the Arizona-Sonora border. The latter one was a complex transborder type, with the participants living on both sides of the border and using both pesos and dollars as the currencies.

Two techniques were used for the field studies. One involved personal contacts from previous fieldwork, friends, and established professional and kin networks. The other entailed more formal engagement by two students: Irene Vega in the border area and Fausto Vásquez Flores in Sinaloa. I thus gained entry into very heterogeneous social sectors throughout Mexico, the southwestern United States, northern California, and Washington State. I also drew on information gathered during fieldwork on other projects in the Hatch Valley in New Mexico and the Coachella Valley in Southern California.

It should be emphasized that ROSCAs appear anywhere Mexican-origin populations in the twenty-first century also appear. Therefore, methodologically, to capture the full distribution of such practices in either the United States or Mexico, and in the region, the "representativeness" and the distribution of ROSCAs is technically not amenable to the usual random or stratified sampling techniques.

Nevertheless, opportunistically, each personal contact point led to numerous ROSCAs, which in turn led to many others. A broad spectrum of these were sampled, and when specific types were uncovered that were organized formally—such as company-organized ones used to

sell cars, homes, appliances, home products, and other merchandise—
they were treated to more intensive research.

I tapped into people encountered in taxis; during commensal and
ritual occasions; in entertainment and recreational centers; in hotels and
restaurants; in queues at banks, food centers, and bus stops; in commercial institutions and public spaces; and at professional meetings and
informal gatherings. For example, a chance encounter with the psychia-
trist of a neighbor in Mazatlán, Sinaloa, provided access to information
on middle-class ROSCAs. Speaking casually to a waitress at a Mexican
restaurant in Scottsdale, Arizona, led to her recruitment to help clean a
friend's home, and she later revealed that she had organized ROSCAs in
Phoenix and Mexico for twenty years. A fortuitous conversation with a
taxi driver in Ensenada, Baja California, introduced me for the first time
to a disrupted ROSCA, in Los Angeles, California, in which a near relative had absconded with the money and fled to Mexico.

Thus, this work derives from an extensive range of universes that
may represent almost all social sectors in which ROSCAs operate. As a
result, I can make some general statements concerning the main theoretical issues, which cross geographical, social, political, and economic
boundaries.

Geographic Distribution: The Transborder Dynamic

Lewis (1959, 68, 148; 1961, 453; 1968, 214) first reported the Mexican
version of the ROSCA, the tanda (turn), in Mexico City's *vecindades*
(neighborhoods). Unfortunately, he did little analysis of the practice
or its distribution. From fieldwork data collected among Mexicans in
San Ysidro, California, and Tijuana, Baja California, during 1968–1969,
Kurtz (1973) reported on the existence of two types of ROSCA, the cundina (from the verb *cundir*, to spread) and the *rol* (list). Interestingly,
Lomnitz gathered data on the tanda at roughly the same time, in Cerrada
del Condor in Mexico City, which she reported later in her outstanding
work *Networks and Marginality* (1977).

My first glimpses of the ROSCAs in the early 1970s, including some
research into them that I did at the National Library of Anthropology and the National Library of Mexico in Mexico City, gave no hint
of their widespread geographic distribution. In 1978, Kurtz and Showman (66) reported that the tanda was common in the city of Puebla

and its suburbs, and in the municipalities of San Felipe Hueyotlipan and San Jerónimo Caleras. The participants in the tandas came from a wide spectrum of social backgrounds: blue- and white-collar workers (factory workers, bank employees, seamstresses, store clerks) as well as house-wives, food vendors, and so on.

The early published literature and personal research in Ciudad Net-zhualcoyótl and the Federal District of Mexico also turned up other ROSCAs. One informant who had been a traveling salesman indicated that such practices were also common in San Cristobal de las Casas and Tuxtla Gutiérrez, Chiapas; Oaxaca, Oaxaca; Puebla, Puebla; and Tonalá, Jalisco. The associations Kurtz (1973) identified in Tijuana and San Ysidro were verified in my research.

I also tested the hypothesis that where Chinese contract workers established residence in Mexico after 1899, a Chinese version of the ROSCA, termed *hui*,[26] would also appear. I hypothesized that in places where the Chinese were not expelled,[27] the hui would take root as it had in other parts of the world, such as New Guinea, Britain, and the United States.[28] According to Ching Chieh Chang (1956, 56–59), Chinese labor eventually settled in the major cities of the extreme southern areas of Mexico, such as Tapachula, Chiapas, and Mérida, Yucatán; and in the north in Tampica, Tamaulipas; Monterrey, Nuevo León; Mexicali, Baja California; and Chihuahua, Chihuahua. I did research in all these cities and states except Tampico and found a number of ROSCAs in each city. Only one definite relationship could be established with the Chinese hui, but it was insufficient to verify the original hypothesis.

My research from 2000 forward shows that ROSCAs are distributed extensively throughout urban and rural Mexico, parts of the urban and rural U.S. Southwest, and almost anywhere Mexican-origin populations reside. They have also been reported in Peru and Guatemala, and I con-firmed their use in Antigua and Guatemala City in 2007.[29] Guatema-lan workers living on the West Coast of the United States had told me about a Guatemalan version known as a *cuchuval*, from the Quiche word *cuchu*, meaning congregation or reunion, and *val*, to raise (de Bour-bourg 1862: 174; 229). These informants indicated that in Tecún Umán (in the department of San Marcos), low-paid workers in factories and large commercial concerns organized such associations. They also said that they participated in Mexican ROSCAs in Los Angeles, where they were known as cundinas. This was not the term used in Guatemala and was specific to the Mexicans with whom they associated at work, in the neighborhood, and in recreational activities. It is significant that these Guatemalan workers participated with Mexican workers in ROSCAs and that both groups were undocumented immigrants. Both groups thus suffered from a high degree of uncertainty.

New and past research also uncovered ROSCAs in Guanajuato, Guanajuato; Guadalajara, Jalisco; Hidalgo, Hidalgo; Papantla, Poza Rica, and Xalapa, Veracruz; Ciudad Júarez, Chihuahua; Ensenada, Baja California; Saltillo, Coahuila; Concordia, Culiacán, El Cerro, Esquinapa, and Mazatlán, Sinaloa; and in many of the ejidos and fish cooperatives throughout coastal Sinaloa. They were also discovered in El Paso, Texas; Chula Vista, Hollywood, La Jolla, National City, San Diego, Beverly Hills, San Pedro, Wilmington, West Los Angeles, unincorporated East Los Angeles, and much of metropolitan Los Angeles, California. Phoenix, Arizona, a center for Mexican migrants crossing through to other destinations, has numerous ROSCAs. In Rio Rico, Arizona, a small community close to Tucson, someone advertised on the Web, offering a cundina of ten numbers that would distribute numerous articles.[30] One informant also reported the existence of ROSCAs in Chicago. In addition, I would predict that St. Louis, Detroit, and urban centers in Indiana and other Midwestern regions that attract large numbers of Mexican workers or where Latinos from other countries converge, such as Paterson, New Jersey, will also have such associations.[31] I would venture to suggest that ROSCAs also appear in New York City, given the recent influx of populations from the Mexican states of Puebla, Mexico, and Veracruz, but this has not yet been confirmed. On the other hand, their absence has been reported in one study of Latino entrepreneurs in Virginia.[32] Certainly, both sides of the border are key junctures for the distributions of populations and ROSCAs (for example, El Paso, Texas–Ciudad Juárez, Chihuahua; Nogales, Sonora–Nogales, Arizona; San Luis Río Colorado, Sonora–San Luis, Arizona; San Diego, California–Tijuana, Baja California; as well as Yuma, Arizona, and the Mexicali/Calexico/Imperial and Coachella Valley corridors in California.

Transborder Distribution

From the primary data collected in my original (pre-1983) and latest (1983–2008) research and the references of other researchers, I have found that ROSCAs operate in 130 urban, suburban, and rural municipalities in Mexico and the United States—up from the original 30 reported in

1983. Informants also reliably identified 5 other urban, suburban, and rural municipalities, towns, and villages as having ROSCAs. Of the 146 sites I investigated, 97 were Mexican urban, suburban, or rural communities, and 49 were in U.S. communities (table 1.1).

In addition to Mexico City and the Federal District, 18 of the 31 Mexican states can be reliably said to have such associations, up from 13 in 1982. North of the Río Bravo, the practice is quite well established in California and Texas. The original literature had not reported them in Arizona, New Mexico, or Colorado, nor did personal inquiries prove fruitful.[33] However, the 2000–2008 research found them in Casa Grande, Chandler, Coolidge, Gilbert, Mesa, Nogales, Phoenix, San Luis, Tucson, and Yuma, Arizona.

In New Mexico, ROSCAs were found in Las Cruces, Mesilla, and throughout the Hatch Valley, including the *colonias* (townships of Milagro, Placitas, Rincon, Rodey, Salem, and the town of Hatch). Nevada, Illinois, Michigan, Mississippi, North and South Carolina, Florida, New Jersey and New York also have both northern (cundina) and southern (tanda) versions of the ROSCAs. Nevada has seen a quantum jump in the Mexican-origin population since 1980, who are drawn especially by the construction industry, which has meant a rise in the number of tandas or cundinas there. On the other hand, the spread of ROSCAs to the southern U.S. states is primarily the consequence of agricultural workers from New Mexico, Arizona, and California, originally migrants from Mexico, moving east into the southern states.

California probably has the most extensive distribution of ROSCAs in the United States because of the heavy migration of Mexicans into that area, especially since 1980.[34] The greatest concentration of ROSCAs seems to be in the San Diego area, which includes, among others, the cities of San Diego itself, Chula Vista, National City, and San Ysidro. In the Los Angeles area, the greatest concentration seems to be in San Pedro, Wilmington, East Highlands, East Los Angeles, and portions of central Los Angeles.

The geographic distribution discussed above illustrates that ROSCAs are truly transborder and transnational and that they emerge in urban, suburban, and rural areas in Mexico and the United States. They are not "contained" by rurality or urbanity or national boundaries. In rural areas, such as the Río Grande Valley in southern New Mexico, tandas or cundinas are prevalent. From there, they are easily carried to urban centers, such as Albuquerque or Las Cruces to the north. They can also travel from Ciudad Juárez north to El Paso and then to the colonias

Table 1.1 Site Identification of ROSCAS in Mexico and
the United States

Northern Mexico
  Monterrey, Nuevo León

Northwestern Mexico
  Ensenada, Mexicali, Tijuana,[1] and Baja California
  Colima, Colima
  Chihuahua and Ciudad Juárez, Chihuahua
  Concordia, Culiacán, El Cerro, Esquinapa, Mazatlán, Nogales, and San Luis Río
    Colorado, Sonora

Central Mexico
  Ciudad Netzahualcoyótl and Mexico City,[2] Federal District, State of Mexico
  Guanajuato, Guanajuato
  Hidalgo, Hidalgo
  Puebla,[3] San Felipe, and San Jerónimo Caleras, Puebla
  Zacatecas, Zacatecas

South-Central Mexico
  Guerrero, Guerrero
  Chapala, Guadalajara, and Tonalá, Jalisco

Southern Mexico (Gulf of Mexico side)
  Papantla, Poza Rica, and Xalapa, Veracruz
  Mérida, Yucatán

Southern Mexico (Pacific Ocean side)
  Guatemala, San Cristóbal de las Casas, Tapachula, and
  Tuxtla Gutiérrez, Chiapas
  Oaxaca, Oaxaca

Southwestern United States
  Casa Grande, Coolidge, Gilbert, Mesa, Nogales, Phoenix,
  San Luis, Tucson, and Yuma, Arizona
  Chula Vista, unincorporated East Los Angeles, Hollywood and Beverly Hills,
    Los Angeles,[4] National City, San Diego, San Pedro, San Ysidro,[5] Wilmington,
    California
  Las Vegas, Nevada
  El Milagro, Hatch, Las Cruces, Mesilla, Placitas, Rincon, Rodey, and Salem, New
    Mexico; 27 other New Mexico *colonias* (Galan 2000a)
  El Paso, Texas; 1,500 other Texas *colonias* (Vélez-Ibáñez 2004b)

(Continued)

Table 1.1   *(Continued)*

Midwest
   Illinois, Indiana, Michigan

South and East
   Florida, Mississippi, North and South Carolina
   New Jersey and New York

Source: Vélez-Ibáñez 1982 and post-1983 fieldwork.

[1] Reported by Kurtz (1973) and verified by this research.

[2] Reported by Lewis (1959, 1961, 1968) and Lomnitz (1977) and verified by this research.

[3] Reported by Kurtz and Showman (1978) and Cope and Kurtz (1980).

[4] Includes West Los Angeles.

[5] Reported by Kurtz (1973) and verified by this research.

of the Hatch Valley. The enormous cross-border traffic of people and material from Ciudad Juárez, Chihuahua, to El Paso, Texas, facilitates and even pushes the movement of ROSCAs. As Morse (2007) has stated, "The El Paso and Juárez metropolitan area includes some 2.6 million people and represents North America's fourth-largest manufacturing hub," which gives rise to huge exchanges of goods and services.[35] When one adds the flows of Mexican agricultural labor into the Hatch Valley, it is clear that there is an intense transborder dynamic of constant movement of people and their practices of cundinas or tandas.

Nomenclature

The names of the associations vary by geographical area. Sometimes the names are used interchangeably to denote similar practices of saving or cooperative pooling. For example, ROSCAs are known as tandas (turns) in Monterrey, with local variants being *ronda*, *quiniela*, or *quincela*. A ronda is usually a round of a game or drinks, or contributions to pay for the same, while a quiniela is more strictly a betting pool. Quincela is a derivative of the word *quincena* (fortnight), a reference to the distribution of money in the associations after each semimonthly payday. However, some informants in Monterrey consistently used the term *quiniela* for *tanda*, while only one made a distinction between a quiniela as a betting pool and an RCA or a tanda. Another informant stated that *quiniela* and *ronda* were used interchangeably with *tanda*, but during the course of the interview, she consistently used the term *tanda*.

Because of the problem of variation in usage, it is necessary to pinpoint the location of variants. This discussion will provide a general guide for other researchers, and their findings may vary, add to, or provide alternative interpretations for the sources and locations identified here.

In Ciudad Juárez, the local variations of nomenclature became particularly interesting since there were so many varieties of savings and lottery practices. *Quiniela* seemed to be the preferred term. There were various versions of lotteries such as the vaquita (small cow or calf) in which people bought a share of a national lottery ticket. Some informants referred to the standard tanda as vaquita or *vaca* (cow), but the vaca was usually reserved for RCAs in El Paso, Texas, which is the border city to Ciudad Juárez.

Female employees in the maquiladoras (labor-intensive light industry) and government offices in Ciudad Juárez preferred the term *quiniela*. At times, informants used the phrase *cajas de ahorros* for the RCAs, but most agreed that the cajas were more like credit unions formally established by the firm or government agency for which they worked or informally by the workers themselves. In the cajas, unlike the RCAs, no set amount had to be contributed. On the other hand, in some offices, women and only women combined quinielas (RCAs) with the practice of *regalos* (gift giving, especially on saints' days and birthdays), and with monthly commensal activities, in which cakes and pies were also exchanged. All three practices, however, operated unrecognized within these institutions as being anything but givens. In the same way that hundreds of informal mechanisms function within institutions without the institutions themselves formally recognizing them, so also function ROSCAs and their accompanying practices.

One informant who had extensive knowledge of savings and lottery practices in Ciudad Juárez distinguished between quinielas, cajas de ahorros, and tandas. He stated that the quiniela was a type of lottery in which one hundred or so people participated in a drawing in which there was only one winner. The caja de ahorros was an informally organized credit union, and he had seen it operating among bartenders and waitresses. Tandas, the standard informally organized ROSCA, were restricted to those who earned higher wages. In contrast, however, five people interviewed in an industrial park were not familiar with the term *tanda*, but knew the practice as *quiniela*. Two of these five people had been organizers of ROSCAs and were most reliable informants. Of those interviewed, all but one agreed that *quiniela* was preferred. A taxi driver said that his chauffeurs' association used *quiniela*.

The data on ROSCAs in the city of Chihuahua are limited to informants. However, they had lived there for many years, knew it extremely well, and had organized ROSCAs not only in residential areas but also in a variety of places of employment and recreation. They stated that in Chihuahua the preferred term was *tanda* and that other terms were inappropriate since *quiniela* referred to a lottery and *cajas de ahorros* to types of credit unions. Independently, informants agreed that tandas were quite widespread in the state of Chihuahua, and that many people were familiar with them, even though not everyone participated. It seems fair to state that the term *tanda* is the standard one for ROSCAs in the city of Chihuahua. Informants independently agreed that *tanda* was a term that had been diffused from the south of Mexico and was not limited to or original in northern Mexico. This suggests that migrants from the south could have introduced the practice to northern Mexico, which is in keeping with the general diffusion of the practice northward.

In Sinaloa, however, one of Mexico's northwestern states, informants used the term *cundina*. In Culiacán and Mazatlán, they stated that *cundina* had been used by the previous generation, so the practice must have been operating for at least sixty years at the time our data were gathered in 1979. *Cundina* is also used in Concordia, Sinaloa, a small rural town between the cities of Culiacán and Mazatlán. This was also true in other rural towns populated by people who had migrated from other more southern states such as Nayarit. However, some informants made an important differentiation in that they used the term *ahorros* (savings) to describe cundinas in which the organizer charged a fee by taking a number (that is, she took a turn without contributing). This was mentioned by a network of shrimp-market women as well as white-collar office workers in Mazatlán.

In central Mexico, which includes the Federal District, Mexico City, and Ciudad Netzahualcoyótl, the popular term is *tanda*. Our informants—including a government economist, a labor organizer, a sociology graduate student, low-level government employees, museum employees, upper-class housewives, upper-middle-class retirees, hotel employees, taxi drivers, and people in numerous queues in banks, subways, and movie houses—all verified the preference for the term *tanda*. *Vaca* or *vaquita* was, however, used synonymously by some informants. Some tandas in this area were known specifically by their purpose. In *tandas de Volkswagen*, for example, a Volkswagen Beetle is distributed as the share, and *tandas de casa* (home RCAs) as well as *tandas de Datsun* were also mentioned. These latter formal RCAs I will discuss separately.

In the Lecumberri prison, Mexico's most infamous jail for political prisoners, a vaca or vaquita was a cooperative savings group organized to buy larger amounts of marijuana (cannabis of whatever species), which was sold within the prison for a discount. Unlike the standard tanda, the vaca or vaquita was not necessarily made up of individual equal shares, although this was the preferred form. If equal shares were not possible, then the amount of marijuana doled out was equal to the amount contributed. Thus, *cannabis mexicana vacas* seem to have been the most specialized.

In Guadalajara, *tanda* was preferred. Informants who had lived in the city and who had participated as organizers and participants for more than thirty years all indicated that *tanda* was the only term used, but the term *rifa* (raffle) was also used by an ex-organizer to describe rotating credit associations. One informant, a saleswoman who traveled extensively between Guadalajara and Chihuahua, verified that *quiniela* was used in Ciudad Juárez and *tanda* was used in Chihuahua. A sample of ten other people—university student, bank clerk, proletarian housewife, secretary, anthropologist, ceramicist, hotel employee, petty merchant, businessman, and high school student—all indicated that *tanda* was the preferred term. Nearby, in Tonalá and Chapala, *tanda* was again the term used.

To the southeast, in the state of Veracruz, the informants in the cities of Papantla, Poza Rica, and Xalapa also preferred *tanda*, although specialized uses required more specific nomenclature. Thus, a *tanda de cuates* (an RCA of pals) is a very small one, for no more than five persons. Its specific goal is to purchase alcoholic beverages, from which results an unintended consequence: prestige for the person who can consume the most alcohol without becoming intoxicated.

The term *bolita* (little ball) was used occasionally by informants, generally to describe ROSCAs in which forty or more participated. The term came from the numbered balls used in randomly selecting the order of distribution of the share fund to the members.

Regardless of the term used, informants who had participated and organized tandas for fifteen years all agreed that the term *tanda* was used in Veracruz and that it was strictly an urban practice and not known to *gente de rancho* (persons from rural areas).

In Tapachula, Chiapas, *tanda* is most frequently used, although one informant used *quiniela* interchangeably, as well as *rol* and *poya* (share or amount due). This should be considered exceptional. In Tapachula, informants of Chinese descent admitted to being familiar with the Chinese hui. Most stated that their forebears had participated in China, but did not recall such associations in the Chinese colony in Tapachula. Yet the reticence of the informants does lead one to suspect that the local associations of *paisanos* (fellow fellow citizens), as the Chinese refer to themselves in Mexico, do in fact have huis in operation. Others of Chinese descent indicated very strongly that the Chinese were assimilated into Mexican life. The local Chinese benevolent association met to consider cooperation with this research. The strength of their denial and the fact that organizations based on Chinese descent exist suggest that a great deal of fear of Mexican chauvinism may still be felt and for very good historical reasons (see n. 27 this chapter).

Although material collected in this research substantiated Kurtz's findings of the ROSCA in the San Diego–Tijuana area (1973), it showed transnational characteristics not explored by Kurtz. In addition, cundinas were found in Ensenada and Mexicali, Baja California. Our informants, however, did not use the word *rol*, as Kurtz indicated his did, but instead used only *cundina*. Informants did refer to newspaper articles in which the term *tanda* was used. These findings do not negate Kurtz's original discovery: our informants simply were not familiar with the term *rol*.

The term *cundina* is widespread in the San Diego area, and the data in part were generated from the city of Chula Vista, which is between San Diego and San Ysidro–Tijuana. There are even commuter cundinas that cross the borders between Tijuana and Chula Vista. Our informants in Chula Vista had participated in these for more than twenty years in both the United States and Mexico. All agreed that the preferred term was *cundina*, and some were familiar with the word *tanda*. They nevertheless made careful distinctions between cundinas and *mutualistas*. The latter were strictly funerary associations and not rotating credit associations.

In San Pedro, Wilmington, and Hollywood, which are incorporated into Los Angeles City, *cundina* was the preferred term. This was also the case in Beverly Hills, central Los Angeles City, and West Los Angeles. Nevertheless, there were informants who were familiar with *tanda* as the proper nomenclature, and it is more likely that these people had come from the central or southern areas of Mexico. (Two informants stated that in their state of Guanajuato in central Mexico, *tanda* was the normal usage, while *cundina* was used exclusively in downtown Los Angeles.)

On the other hand, one informant who had learned the practice in the United States simply called it *ahorro*.

This ahorro, however, should not be confused with the savings cooperatives formed by Chicano steelworkers during World War II. Such noninstitutionalized savings cooperatives were modeled after the Liga Obrera Mexicana (see n. 33, this chapter), but the steelworker cooperatives dissolved because so many participants were drafted into the army.

People in Arizona, New Mexico, and Texas used both terms—*cundina* and *tanda*; national origin and specific geographic area determined which one was used by a given individual. People from Guatemala, working in Phoenix restaurants, would use the term *cuchuval* among themselves, but they would use *tanda* or *cundina* if the organizer or most of the participants were Mexican. Regardless of the term used, all participants knew the expectations and rules governing behavior and conduct when participating in a ROSCA.

Table 1.2 summarizes the nomenclature discovered in my original and latest research and that reported previously by others. This table includes four terms: *muerta* or *viva* (dead or alive) and *fuerte* or *pequeña* (strong or weak). The former pair, as will be discussed shortly, refers to the more commercial RCAs, as opposed to noncommercial, informal ROSCAs. The latter pair refers to those in which the fund share and the contributions are large (fuerte) or small (pequeña).

As the table indicates, *tanda* appears in northern, central, and southern Mexican states, and it is more frequently used than *cundina*. *Cundina*, the second most frequently used term, is restricted to some northern Mexican states and the southwestern United States. For unknown reasons, *quiniela* has taken root in Ciudad Juárez, even though the city is only a few hundred miles away from Chihuahua, where *tanda* is the most popular term. Equally curious is the fact that *vaca* is the preferred term in El Paso, which is directly across the border from Ciudad Juárez. On the other hand, *mutualista*, which has long been a term associated only with funerary associations, is the major term used in Mérida, and *caja de ahorro* is used infrequently.

Types of ROSCAs

Fuerte and Pequeña

Kurtz and Showman (1978, 67) analytically distinguished repeating tandas from episodic ones in San Felipe and San Jerónimo Caleras, Puebla.

Table 1.2 Nomenclature by Area[1]

Principal Term	Area	City	Variants
Tanda: muerta–viva fuerte–pequeña	northern Mexico	Monterrey, Nuevo León	ronda, quiniela, quincela, rol
Tanda	northern Mexico	Saltillo, Coahuilla	none known
Cundina: fuerte–pequeña	northern Mexico	Ensenada, Mexicali, and Tijuana, Baja California; Nogales[3] and San Luis Río Colorado, Sonora	rol, tanda[2]
Quiniela	northern Mexico	Ciudad Juárez, Chihuahua	caja de ahorros
Tanda: fuerte–pequeña	northern Mexico	Chihuahua, Chihuahua	none known
Cundina	northern Mexico	Colima, Colima; Concordia, Culiacán, El Cerro, Esquinapa, and Mazatlán, Sinaloa	none known
Tanda: muerta–viva fuerte–pequeña	central Mexico	Ciudad Netzahualcoyótl, Mexico City,[4] Federal District, State of Mexico	vaca, vaquita
Tanda	central Mexico	Guanajuato, Guanajuato; Hidalgo, Hidalgo	none known
Tanda	central Mexico	Puebla,[5] San Felipe, and San Jerónimo Caleras, Puebla	none known

Table 1.2 (*Continued*)

Principal Term	Area	City	Variants
Tanda	south-central Mexico	Guerrero, Guerrero; Chapala, Guadalajara, and Tonalá, Jalisco; Zacatecas, Zacatecas	rifa
Mutualista: informal–formal	southern Mexico (Gulf of Mexico side)	Mérida, Yucatán	caja de ahorros
Tanda: muerta–viva	southern Mexico (Gulf of Mexico side)	Papantla, Poza Rica, and Xalapa, Veracruz	bolita
Tanda	southern Mexico	San Cristóbal de la Casas, Tapachula, and Tuxtla Guitiérrez, Chiapas	none known
Tanda	southern Mexico (Guatemala side)	Oaxaca, Oaxaca	none known
Vaca	southwestern United States	El Paso, Texas	vaquita
Cundina	southwestern United States	Chula Vista, National City, San Diego, and San Ysidro,[6] California	rol, tanda
Cundina	U.S.–Mexico border region	Nogales, Tucson, and Yuma, Arizona; Tijuana–San Diego area, Baja California; San Luis Río Colorado, Sonora; El Paso, and 1,500 other colonias, Texas	tanda
Cundina	southwestern United States	Beverly Hills, unincorporated East Los Angeles, Hollywood, Los Angeles,[7] San Pedro, and Wilmington, California;	tanda, ahorro

(Continued)

Table 1.2   (*Continued*)

Principal Term	Area	City	Variants
		Casa Grande, Coolidge, Gilbert, Mesa, and Phoenix, Arizona; Las Vegas, Nevada; El Milagro, Hatch, Las Cruces, Mesilla, Rincon, Rodey, Salem, Placitas, and 27 other colonias of New Mexico	
Cundina	U.S. Midwest, South, and East	Illinois, Indiana, Michigan; Florida, Mississippi, North and South Carolina; New Jersey and New York	tanda
Cuchuval	northern Guatemala	Guatemala City, San Marcos, Tecúnuman	none known
Pandero	Peru	Lima, Huancayo	junta

Source: Prepared by the author.

[1] Not all sites are represented in this table.

[2] Reported by Kurtz (1973) and, except for the term *rol*, verified by this research.

[3] Reported by Lewis (1959, 1961, 1968) and Lomnitz (1977) and verified by this research.

[4] Reported by Kurtz and Showman (1978) and Cope and Kurtz (1980).

[5] Reported by Kurtz (1973) and verified by this research, with the added discovery of transnational commuter associations.

[6] Includes West Los Angeles.

[7] The large influx to New York from the Mexican state of Puebla makes this a certainty.

The repeating tandas were organized by one person on an ongoing basis; the episodic tandas disbanded after a single cycle. The repeating tandas were embedded in neighborhoods, and long-term residents participated, whereas peers from a place of employment, as well as neighbors and relatives, could participate in episodic tandas.

Most of our informants distinguished between *tandas fuertes* (strong tandas) and *tandas pequeñas* (small tandas). This research found that both can operate in neighborhoods, workplaces, or familial networks, and long-term residents, coworkers, or relatives participate. In some long-term or repeating tandas, the organizer inherited the tanda from a previous organizer in the same neighborhood or workplace, or from a lineal or consanguineous family member. The passing on of tandas provides a cultural cement that generates confianza and imbues the practice with a legitimacy lacking in episodic or short-term tandas. Higher contributions are more likely in strong tandas than in small ones. In addition, the dense social relationships accumulated among participants in small tandas may arise from their long-term association with the same organizer and other RCA participants. One informant had participated in an ROSCA that operated with the same organizer and with about 75 percent of the original membership for more than twenty years. Density can also accumulate through the existence of multiple ties, such as friendship, fictive kinship, and residence in the same area. The strength and durability of the strong tandas is supported by this density.

Strong tandas are usually organized to meet short-range goals, such as a pressing economic need or a forgotten ritual obligation. These may also consist of people with dense social relationships, but the density of relationships is unlikely to have been generated by tanda participation itself. Contributions and the number of participants are likely to be small, since immediate goals must be fulfilled. Tandas with strong relationships will tend to have characteristics associated with repeating tandas, whereas small tandas exhibit characteristics associated with episodic ones.

Informal and Intermediate

The least complex ROSCA is the informal association, in which participants are tied by confianza, and the associations are embedded within the participants' neighborhoods or workplaces or within familial networks. Sanctions, accounting processes, and contributions and collections are all accomplished face to face. Informal associations are of two subtypes, commercialized and noncommercialized (see chap. 2).

A more formal ROSCA organizationally, which can also be either commercialized or noncommercialized, is the intermediate type, in which an accountant or bookkeeper of a company handles the contributions and fund shares. For example, in Tapachula, the cashier of a small factory is in charge of deducting the tanda contribution from a participant's pay. In addition, all members are provided a document showing that they belong to the tanda, and that they agree to abide by its rules. The cashier keeps a formal record of payments and disbursements (see chap. 2 for an expanded discussion of this type).

Commuter

Among the more intriguing types are the commuter cundinas in the Tijuana–San Diego and the Yuma and San Luis, Arizona–San Luis Río Colorado, Sonora area. These are very similar, so I will discuss only the former. Two subtypes exist, both tied to variations in the exchange rate and the profit-making possibilities rate variations present (see chap. 5). One is composed of people who work in one place but live in another. The organizer, who usually lives in Tijuana, commutes back and forth across the border, collecting and dispensing money on paydays in San Diego. In the second subtype, people organize associations in the San Diego area that include participants from Tijuana, with the organizer living in either city. Commuter cundinas operate very similarly all along the border between the United States and Mexico, and they may number in the hundreds, if not thousands.

Specialized Commercialized RCAs

In Yucatán, the term *mutualista* (mutual societies) is used to describe both informal and formal commercial associations. (The term is also used to describe funerary associations, which are not rotating credit associations.) The state's commercialized mutualistas are organizationally the most complex and formal RCAs. A corporation, licensed by the state of Yucatán, runs them, and it is responsible for the simultaneous functioning of pools of different amounts. Both informally organized ROSCAs and formally organized RCAs are prevalent in Mérida, which also has the most elaborate and commercialized RCAs.

The crucial differences between RCAs lie in the potential sanctions and the degree of complexity and commercialization. A corporation sanctioned by the state runs the Mérida mutualista, whereas the intermediate RCA is embedded within the accounting system of a private firm, but is not organized or formally sanctioned by the firm. It lends its machinery, but is not responsible for the operation of the RCA. In contrast, for the informal mutualista, records are kept even in the most informal association, but it operates with only the moral sanction derived from the confianza enjoyed by the organizer vis-à-vis the participants and the participants vis-à-vis each other.

Specialized formal RCAs were reported in my original work and most recently in the Mexican literature by Mansell Carstens (1995). Schreiner (1999), researching Argentina, states that banks and car dealers organize RCAs, and, significantly, the members lack social capital and do not know each other. Moreover, the Argentine RCAs are government regulated.[36] Highly commercialized credit-oriented automobile RCAs include one initiated by Volkswagen of Mexico's finance arm in 1977, and ones started by Nissan, Ford, and Chrysler, according to Mansell Carstens (1995, 119). Through the Internet, I have also found various finance companies such as SICREA México Autofinanciamento offering tandas for Nissan; Planfia, for Chrysler; and Alfin for Honda.[37]

After intensive credit checks as well as collateral promises, 40 to 50 people (in some cases up to 125) contribute designated amounts of money each month for between forty to sixty months, depending on the number of people participating. Each month, one or more of the group is selected by lottery to receive a new automobile. Regardless of when the person receives his/her car, he or she must eventually contribute the total amount of his/her purchase. It is obvious that the longer the rotational cycle has been in operation, the greater the likelihood of being selected, since those having received an automobile are removed from the lottery, although they continue to pay contributions.

Mansell Carstens (1995) reports RCAs for animals (120), businesses (63), and automobiles (119–120); she also reports that Dormitandas are used by Dormimundo, a mattress company, which allow a buyer to pay for one mattress for three months before it is delivered, protecting the client against inflation. This is a kind of insurance, and it has the potential of saving money if prices should rise. Similarly, using the Internet, I have found commercial firms selling perfumes; companies selling hundreds of different household items, from bed sheets to vacuum cleaners; and Alfin, which finances Hondas and Toromex motorcycles. Additionally, individual entrepreneurs "rotate" computers, and the savings come in the price protection offered the buyer.

A very interesting transborder version is that offered by SICREA México. Run from an office in Los Angeles, the firm launched an auto-finance

program in 2006 for Mexicans living in the United States, called Plan Paisano (paisano, as noted earlier, means fellow citizen). People can finance
the latest-model vehicles to be delivered to relatives in Mexico. According to SICREA México, "the main objective is to provide an opportunity
to provide a patrimony for their relatives in Mexico through the purchase and financing of an automobile in Los Angeles."[38] One of our key
informants occupied a house acquired by means of a house tanda, which
operates in a similar manner. People also participate in kitchen tandas,
in which a carpenter makes cabinets and shelves, and the participants
pay for two months, and then, by lottery, one of the participants receives
a remodeled kitchen in each subsequent month. In book RCAs, children
in the same elementary school contribute money toward the purchase of
books, which are then rotated by lot to participants.

The drinking-bout RCAs have already been described. Equally as
specialized are the "birthday" tandas formed by wealthy matrons, who
contribute one thousand pesos a month and purchase birthday gifts for
each other with the accumulated contributions. In the same class sector are variants called *canasta tandas*, in which card games are played,
and the pot is accumulated to purchase gifts. In the following chapters,
more types will be described, including the details of their operational
complexity.

The rapid spread of RCAs is primarily due to the use of the globalizing Internet to spread electronic advertisements and promote network
"clubs." MexicaNet is an electronic subsidiary of Banamex and Banorte,
two of the largest banking consortiums in Mexico. MexicaNet offers
"Tandas Mexicanas" on its web page. The tanda lasts three months, and
a person can join through the Internet with a voter registration card
(issued by the Instituto Federal Electoral, IFE) or a student credential.
Each contribution is one hundred pesos, and participants are charged
a commission of twenty pesos if they fail to make their contribution or
if they would like to withdraw from the tanda before their turn. A life
insurance plan in case of death is available, along with a bank guarantee
of solvency. A record is available via the Internet, and payments can be
made through PayPal, by postal order, or by telegraph.[39]

A new, highly patented and protected version of the cundina known
as the Moneypool, in Phoenix, Arizona, has been organized through
the Internet which will soon enable university students to participate
in a network of cundinas. Within this commercialized format, students
and other interested individuals will be able to save at low interest rates

of 5 percent, and they will be eligible for loans at lower-than-market rates. In fact, they will be creating their own network of savings, borrowing, and investment participants through close acquaintances with whom they have established confianza. By using contractural agreements to which all will abide and by offering protection through funding insurance, this service will initially appeal mostly to Latino students on both sides of the border who are already familiar with ROSCA versions. Two enterprising transborder Mexicanos, former university students, have worked diligently to create their business with the logo eMONEYPOOL. Their Web site is http://emoneypool.com/, and their e-mail address is Fco@eMoneyPool.com. After a very long period of development of the business structure, it will go online as this book goes to press.

As well, the Mission Asset Fund (MAF) recently founded Cestas Populares, viable alternatives to high-cost predatory loans offering a hybridic version of the commercialized type, but with a sense of social responsibility. This program helps participants establish or improve their credit scores simply by recognizing, recording, and reporting financial activity that occurs in peer lending circles commonly practiced by immigrant communities. Indeed, by formalizing these financial activities, MAF is helping immigrants improve their credit history by valuing their cultural assets: their participation in peer lending circles with their family, friends, and co-workers. In just twelve months, MAF made eighty-seven *cesta* loans to seventy-nine participants, totaling $105,200, with an average loan amount of $1,209.[40]

Finally, in a recent development in Paterson, New Jersey, Latinos from other Latin American countries may use their "Susu" or "Sociedad" contributions as collateral for loans by showing documents that verify the client's regular participation in the fund; provide evidence that the funds are deposited in a financial institution; and state the number of weeks in the rotation, the date of disbursement to the client, and the remaining amount of obligation remaining. We have not found this to be the case in the border region.[41] In contradistinction to Kurtz and Showman (1978), we found these commercial versions in many regions in Mexico as well as in parts of the southwestern United States. If one accepts the argument of modernization theory that commercial practices can serve to educate people in commercial attitudes (Geertz 1962), then certainly the commercialized RCAs described here would serve that function. Yet the commercialized practices found in this research, as well as the acquisition of commercial attitudes, antedate modernization theories. The formally organized mutualista was a late-nineteenth- and early-twentieth-century practice, as newspapers of the period demonstrate.[42] Some of our informants reported having participated in RCAs before modernization notions existed. Two informants placed the beginnings of fee-type cundinas in Tijuana–San Diego between 1936 and 1938. Another informant in Mérida had participated in a mutualista in 1943. He had been appointed agent in the government department where he worked and has been responsible for mutualistas in which 365 fellow employees participated. I have already alluded to an informant from the state of Sinaloa whose parents had participated in cundinas sixty years prior to my original research.

Mutualistas, cundinas, and RCAs in general were in existence and commercialized long before notions of modernization became popular. This indicates that people had learned to save long before it was thought fashionable, and in the process, they had learned commercial attitudes. These are the very indicators thought important for development, and they indicate movement toward the very goal developmentalists seem to appreciate most: the dynamic use of funds. On the other hand, such "developmental" models simply cannot account for contemporary transnational and transborder processes because these trump any developmental schematic. Instead, ours is a more analytical and nonlinear theoretical assumption: the people most involved in these practices are themselves highly entrepreneurial. This is the case for networks of businesspeople, ranging from shrimp-market women in Mazatlán, Sinaloa, to restaurant owners in Los Angeles. Therefore, the "commercializing" developmental model is neither sufficient nor necessary to explain the emergence of ROSCAs and RCAs. Rather, multiple, interpenetrating global, national, and regional economies—whose main function is to extract value from any source—pushes individuals and groups to form these associations as a result of their indebtedness, lack of access to credit, and desire to be able to predict when expenditures can be made in the near or distant future.

Thus, this survey of practices, places, and types all point to the way ROSCAs are clearly not just embedded within national borders but also are, by design, highly portable, highly adaptable, and widely and decidedly used by many classes and groups. In particular, women in many different circumstances use them and find them valuable. Yet ROSCAs do not appear merely because populations of individuals move from one place to another. I contend that they are strongly associated and connected to the much larger phenomena of transnational economies in the southwestern United States and northern Mexico, and north and south of that center, which penetrate multitudes of localities as these economies seek to extract value from products and labor. That center is the Southwest North American Region.

2
Confianza
Building Block of Social Exchange and the Operational Cycles of ROSCAs

Confianza: A Transborder Construct

Rotating savings and credit associations (ROSCAs) cannot operate without confianza (mutual trust), and this mutual trust has to be understood as truly a transborder construct operating since Mexican-origin populations have lived in the Southwest North American Region and in the Americas. Confianza has certainly been present and been a crucial part of the culture since the Spanish colonial period, when the nonindigenous populations became known as "españoles mexicanos."[1] One informant referred to the ROSCA as "una unión de confianza" (a bond of mutual trust), which is highly significant because, despite the occurrence of specific economic transactions, social exchange is the basis for the associations.[2] This is emphasized in the exchange relationship, and it is a widely understood and valued requirement for the smooth operation of ROSCAs among Mexicans north and south of the Río Bravo. The term *confianza* (see Lomnitz's excellent discussions, 1971, 1977) signifies a cultural construct containing numerous factors, among them people's willingness to be in a reciprocal relationship with one another. Like any other human construct, it expands in use and evolves along with the social networks in which it occurs. Thus, confianza will be variable in function across social sectors. Yet this willingness to initiate reciprocity is crucial to understanding the potentialities of ROSCAs and their widespread geographical distribution and transborder mobility.

The cultural construct of confianza is a subjective, descriptive understanding analogous to Polanyi's (1957) analytical idea of the reciprocal exchange mode and Sahlins's (1969) notion of "generalized reciprocity." Among Mexicans, confianza designates generosity and intimacy as well as a personal investment in others; it also indicates a willingness to establish such generosity and intimacy. This general construct is projected and sought, and it even includes those with whom no actual intimacy has been established. This last assertion contradicts Lomnitz;

however, in this book, confianza indicates more than relationships in which favors, confidences, or assistance have actually been exchanged. Lomnitz has described confianza's key elements in the following way:

> A person feels confianza in another when he trusts the other to have the ability, the desire, and the good disposition to initiate a personal relationship of reciprocity exchange, or when his own familiarity with the other would encourage him to make the first approach himself. Such an initial move usually consists of requesting a favor or in offering to perform a favor without risking a misinterpretation of this gesture. Another form of expressing *confianza* is the act of volunteering an item of personal information of an intimate character, thus implying faith in the discretion and friendly disposition of the other person (1977, 196–197; emphasis added).

Lomnitz uses Sahlins's definitional contrasts between "generalized reciprocity" and "balanced reciprocity" to flesh out the degree and intensity of confianza. Generalized reciprocity is an exchange in which people give each other material items, favors, or labor without expecting anything in return at that time or in the immediate future. Balance reciprocity is an exchange in which the items, favors, or labor have a precise worth, and the reciprocated exchange is equivalent to the item received and is made without delay (Sahlins 1969, 147–148). Rotating savings and credit associations are balanced reciprocity relationships because their duration and the money or other items to be exchanged are explicitly stated in advance. Although this definition may provide a valid analytical boundary between generalized and balanced reciprocity, the cultural construct of confianza that allows the ROSCA to emerge and function is actually generalized mutual trust. Negotiations, transformations, compacts, conviviality, and specific needs ultimately determine the actual nature of confianza in specific contexts, but the construct of confianza as a core expectation begins as a generalized reciprocal construct. While ROSCAs may be engaged in balanced reciprocal exchanges, these could not occur without the presence of more general, diffuse expectations of mutual trust (confianza). These have a variety of culturally constituted safeguards, as later analysis will demonstrate.

Confianza, then, is the psychocultural construct organizing expectations for intended relationships. It patterns social and political interpersonal and exchange networks, and it is transborder in its flexibility. It is basic to such Mexican social categories and types of relationships as *compadrazgo* (co-godparenthood), *amistad* or *cuatismo* (friendship or palship), *padrino político* (political godfather; Carlos and Anderson 1981), *asesor* or *coyote* (consultant or broker), and *cacique* (political figure and broker; Carlos and Anderson 1981; Lomnitz 1977). Above all, this imperative cultural glue gives adhesion to "dense relationships" (as chap. 3 and figs. 3.1–3.6 illustrate).

Although varying in organizational influence, the confianza construct does provide a formula for reciprocity for each of these social categories and their relationships. As these unfold in social processes and events, the relationships—equal and unequal—express the reciprocal exchange mode to varying degrees. Whether used in exchanges involving power or affection, the construct of confianza patterns the initial willingness to reciprocate not only between dyads but also in contacts that go far beyond known and established relationships.

As an organizing principle, confianza shapes the expectations for relationships within broad networks of interpersonal links, in which intimacies, favors, goods, services, emotion, power, or information are exchanged. Whether such exchanges are expressed in political domains between patrons and clients, in intimate relationships between friends, or between coworkers, confianza is the core principle underlying the development and stability of these exchanges. In the case of ROSCAs, however, it is insufficient to always protect all participants from fraud or to prevent someone from leaving without contributing his or her share. Finally, confianza selects for an organized means of forming predictable expectations about relationships. How such relationships are actually transformed and negotiated is a processual and structural matter.

Open, Processual, and Closed Confianza

Cultural expectations are not usually maintained unless they are given life in social relationships. In the case of ROSCAs, the economic motivation to participate is paramount, and everyone has the opportunity to benefit at least once. However, economic interest, although necessary, is not sufficient for participation. On the one hand, no social relationship is ever tidy or totally coherent. The processual reality for most social relationships is that they are initially "open" in the sense that little has been settled by the actors that would define the exchanges as being of one sort or another. Even once defined, however, other relationships, from other contexts, affect those being established between any two actors.

On the other hand, some relationships, such as kinship, are "givens." In these "closed" relations, expectations are well defined and exchanges are relatively predictable. Yet a host of other relationships from other contexts still influence closed relations.

Confianza as a cultural construct is an expectation about relationships. It takes its open or closed character from the sorts of exchanges in which any two actors engage, the duration of these exchanges, the social and economic context in which such relations are articulated, and, very importantly, the effect other relationships have on those being established, already established, or being dissolved. For example, office workers who participate in ROSCAs have a lot on the line if confianza is not maintained. A breakdown would affect their job functions, their relationships with people with whom they must cooperate in fulfilling tasks, and their predictions about who deserves advancement, rewards, and bonuses. All those things might be denied to a person who does not fulfill his or her ROSCA obligations. The person might even be fired from the job. No matter how closed a confianza relationship might appear, a host of other relationships still affect it.

Importantly, although confianza is a psychocultural expectation, it is given life by the state of existing social relationships, the nature of the relationships being transacted, and the stability or instability of any set of relationships for a set of actors who share confianza. These relationships, however, are not fixed in a totally predetermined or certain pattern. Although confianza is a construct for organizing predictable expectations about relationships, the construct is sufficiently flexible and inclusive to allow the reality of social living to change its boundaries for any actor or set of actors.

When relationships are first initiated, they will be marked by "open" confianza, in which so much is indeterminate and uncertain that actors give each other great latitude in the face of mistakes and faux pas. For example, recent urban migrants will seek out others with whom to establish confianza, and they will try out and experiment with many different contexts and types of exchanges. Those contexts and exchanges that prove to be most rewarding will be retained as proper for the type of confianza established between any two actors. Once established, however, that confianza is not necessarily embedded perpetually, for the reasons given. Nevertheless, as confianza articulated between friends, for example, becomes expected, and the nature of the exchanges becomes relatively defined, these relationships are introduced into already established, closed confianza relationships. Thus, any two friends who have established confianza will in turn establish that friendship with other friends and kinfolk. During the process of contacting other networks of relationships, confianza becomes a "processual confianza" in that others are commenting upon and evaluating the persons engaged in the friendship. It is during the period of processual confianza that the politics of exchange will occur, that claims of worthiness or unworthiness are made, and that friendships become articulated within previously established, relatively close confianza relationships.

For a time, these relationships will be part of the actors' relatively closed networks of relationships, and confianza between those two actors will be closed to others, at least at the conscious level of exchange. However, closed-ness is illusionary, since even the most closed relationships are open to the unintended consequences of the actions of others, to changing economic and social conditions, and to the failure of expectations to be met.

There is no necessary continuum between open, processual, and closed confianza. At any stage of development, open confianza can be disrupted by the unintended consequences mentioned. Processual confianza can be interrupted by the judgments of those in closed confianza or by the appearance of other open confianza relationships that might appear to be more rewarding. Closed confianza relationships can be disrupted by an immigration raid in the United States, or as the case discussed in chapter 4 illustrates, the density of confianza may very well lead to terrible, unintended consequences beyond the participants' control.

Confianza, then, is a dynamic psychocultural construct in that its boundaries change with changing conditions. It is therefore ultimately very selective for the populations who share it. For Mexicans, confianza is a transborder concept that is an especially positively selective construct given the pressures of mobility, economic conditions, and racialized statuses, as chapter 4 will show. In a predictable manner, confianza fixes and establishes expectations about relationships in uncertain and indeterminate contexts, but it is a sufficiently flexible construct to change as contexts become more certain or social relations more determinate.

Conditions for Confianza and Reciprocity in the Transborder Context

Lomnitz has suggested that confianza is especially prevalent among large urban populations, such as the economically marginal poor, in which institutionalized means are inadequate for establishing security (1977, 198). However, an important discovery in my original research was that confianza and the reciprocal exchange mode transcend the class sectors that concerned Lomnitz. Lomnitz and Pérez (1974) have analyzed reciprocal exchange used by Mexican upper-class sectors to preserve or increase corporate interests, and Carlos (1973) and Carlos and Anderson (1981) have analyzed the dynamic penetration of reciprocal interpersonal relationships and networks into institutional domains. Definite data also show that various class sectors in rural and urban settings develop confianza. No research prior to *Bonds of Mutual Trust* (Vélez-Ibáñez 1983) has used a single mechanism, as the ROSCA is used here, to illustrate the existence of reciprocity, in which confianza is the cement for social relations in a variety of class, residential, and institutional sectors.

On the other hand, the transborder context of migration, class movement, many-sourced enculturation influences, institutional inaccessibility, and, at times, ethnocentrism and racialized statuses create indeterminacy in Mexican-origin populations. Many people in this population, and their progeny, experience indeterminacy, conditions of distrust, instability, and the inability to predict certain outcomes. One of the most important findings in the post-1983 study of ROSCAs is that a certain number of people were defrauded or suffered a loss when participants did not fulfill their obligations. Nevertheless, these occurrences are very minimal in contrast to the many well-served participants. Yet despite conditions of indeterminacy, Mexican-origin populations continue to use the construct of confianza as the basis for creating social relations and reciprocal interactions, and for investing their hard-earned monies in ROSCAs.

The issue here is that there are underlying conditions that give rise to practices like the ROSCA, their reciprocal mechanisms, and the cultural construct of confianza. For Lomnitz (1977, 191), "a condition of balanced scarcity [is] assumed to persist indefinitely for both partners." She has also stated that these conditions are present when persons "live beyond their means," as in middle-class sectors. I would argue that these are sufficient, but not necessary, conditions for the rise of the reciprocal mode and practices like the ROSCA. The necessary and sufficient conditions are uncertain contexts, undetermined relationships, scarce resources, or ambiguous statuses. In uncertain contexts, a lack of information makes it impossible to form coherent expectations (Orbach 1979). Undetermined relationships refer to the manipulative or negotiable aspects of all relationships.

Most contexts have some degree of uncertainty, and all relationships have room for negotiation and manipulation. However, even small differences in debt and solvency are accentuated for working-class people, white-collar workers, and professionals, especially in the Southwest North American Region. This is certainly the case among immigrants, owners of small businesses, and second-generation working-class individuals, as well as among those in professional arenas, such as teachers and white-collar workers whose income has never been sufficient to avoid reliance on credit for either daily consumption or its bigger brother—conspicuous consumption.

Yet, for all ROSCAs, confianza is the cultural glue that holds steady all relationships between participants. The reputation of the organizer, the recruitment of participants, and the manner in which the organizational mechanisms play out and their conclusion are all dynamically integrated to the concept of confianza. They could not operate without its explicit and implicit understanding and presence.

Thus, although the basic mechanisms for the sampled associations' operations are generally the same, differences in the amount contributed, the number of persons participating, the number of permissible contributions per person, and the amount of time for a full cycle of operation all generate permutations. Without confianza, the heterogeneity of operation could not unfold. The introduction of other variables—such as splitting a single contribution, borrowing money on a share, or the political considerations of deciding the order in which people receive their fund share—increases the complexity of operation. Nevertheless, the sampled associations in all of my original studies show how confianza is the major cultural capital in the development of ROSCAs.

Organizing, Joining, and Recruiting: Confianza in Operation

The manner in which ROSCAs begin is related to their contexts. Episodic associations begin spontaneously. People form them when they are hard pressed to pay a debt, want to accumulate cash to make an investment, want to buy a major consumer good, or want to to purchase sumptuary items. At the informal level, the initiator will usually ask coworkers, relatives, friends, and neighbors to join a new association. Each person invited to participate may ask another to join, even though the organizer does not know that person. In any case, the willingness to establish confianza must exist before establishing the ROSCA. Confianza can be based on, for example, the longevity of employment or the age of the person, or it may have been established in other ways. Participants do not establish the same degree of confianza with all members, but minimal confianza is expected between the organizer and the participants and among some of the participants. Confianza then expands to everyone in the association through various links. Confianza links will be both direct and indirect and will vary in quality and density. Regarding completing the obligations of the ROSCA, members must trust in the trustworthiness of others they know little about. As one informant put it, "Mutual trust is lent."

All ROSCA organizers sampled in the study had an established reputation. They had organized or participated in associations that lasted as long as fifteen years. (In that particular case, this was unusually long, but it was attributable to the large number of people who participated.) Some ROSCAs maintain a continuous membership. These tend to be characterized by allotments of more than one share per person, a membership of fewer than twenty people, and the involvement of a full-time organizer. The organizer will have prestigious characteristics, such as age, reputation, and political connections. Some regularized tandas have been inherited through friendship or consanguineous relations. The new organizer inherits the founder's reputation when the founder ritually introduces the person, by taking him or her to each household for an extended visit, with the formal introductions made over some commensal activity. After the introductions have been completed, the new organizer holds a dinner for the participants and the former organizer, at which confianza and the new organizer's reputation are ritually sealed.

In contrast, in some cases, the participants who organized an association will turn it over to an individual, because they cannot agree on the person who is to be responsible for collecting money, keeping records, allocating numbers, and dispersing funds. In one case, there was disagreement among the male participants, so they turned to the only female participant, who came from the same hometown as the men. Since there seemed to be an unspoken understanding that women were generally trustworthy, they saw her as the person of greatest confianza.

People can also establish a ROSCA as part of more complex reciprocal relations, originating in familiar, friendship, institutional, or residential contexts. The ROSCA is an economic extension of other dense relations, like those reported by Lomnitz (1977, 131–158), but it develops in other contexts as well. Intense interactive networks appear, for example, among female government office workers who combine ritual gift giving, commensal activities, and economic assistance. The origins of their exchange complexes, of which the ROSCA is a crucial reciprocal mechanism, lie not in subsistence needs, as reported by Lomnitz, nor in the drives of individual organizers. Instead, the total complex of dense relations among these office workers provides the impetus for the establishment of a regular method of distributing money. These are "normal social relations" (Goffman 1961, 6) replicated within such partial institutions as government agencies or private corporations.

In a different example, the people involved are heterogeneous, but contextualized by the institution of which they are a part: in this case, a university in northwestern Mexico. Thus, as the Sinaloa sample of table 2.1 shows, class, age, and education are heterogeneous across the forty people sampled. Only five were men, which illustrates the cultural congruence of the practice with two probable factors. First, women are less likely to earn as much as men, and they are, therefore, in greater need, while also more adept in utilizing social relations as a means of stabilizing their incomes. Second, there is a broader, culturally defined and expected propensity for sociability among women.[3]

These institutional ROSCAs are of interest since the participants themselves organize them. The person responsible for collecting the contribution is not an organizer, but rather the person whose turn it is to receive a share of the fund. The rotation, collection, and dispensation of money are cooperatively accomplished, but they are tied to ritual gift giving (birthdays, feast days, and saints' days) and sharing donated pies and cakes during lunch hours. Three levels of exchange emerge: the ROSCA, gift giving, and eating together. None is necessarily related to subsistence needs, but these activities nevertheless express and reinforce confianza.

In the more pecuniary ROSCAs, confianza is an important means of entrée. For example, in one border city, an organizer is responsible for strictly upper-middle-class cundinas of $1,000. Over a period of forty-four weeks, ten people weekly contribute $25, plus a 10 percent fee. The fee amounts to $25 weekly (10 percent $\times$ $25 = $2.50 $\times$ 10 persons = $25). This is placed in reserve in case one of the participants, for whatever reason, cannot contribute the agreed-upon amount. Even with this reserve as a cushion, the organizer usually does not allow a person to join one of the cundinas she operates unless an established confianza relationship is already in place. In five cundinas sampled, of the fifty members,

Table 2.1. Cundina Heterogeneity

Name	Gender	Age	Civil Status	Educational Level
Andrea	Female	40	Married	Middle school
Adrian	Male	33	Married	Professional
Adriana	Female	41	Married	Not known
Agueda	Female	24	Single	University student
Chuya	Female	51	Divorced	Technical
Cindy	Female	24	Single	
Claudia	Female	26	Single	Professional
Consuelo	Female	49	Unknown	Professional
Cristina	Female	27	Single	Professional University
Delia	Female	43	Divorced	Secondary
Dora	Female	45	Divorced	Technical
Esther	Female	37	Married	Secondary
Evelia	Female	23	Single	Preparatory
Fabiola	Female	24	Single	University student
Gaby	Female	22	Single	Preparatory
Gladys	Female	27	Single	Professional
Hortencia	Female	45	Married	Professional
Iris	Female	29	Divorced	Primary
Isadora	Female	46	Married	Primary
Jazmin	Female	22	Single	University student
Josefina	Female	58	Married	Primary
Juan	Male	53	Married	Not known
Leti	Female	45	Married	Professional
Lupita	Female	42	Single mother	Technical
Maria	Female	47	Married	Primary
Maria de Jesus	Female	41	Divorced	Technical
Marisol	Female	25	Single	Professional
Martin	Male	45	Married	Secondary
Meili	Female	23	Single	Professional
Miguel	Male	32	Married	Professional
Mirella	Female	47	Married	Not known
Nadia	Female	25	Single	Professional
Nicolasa	Female	49	Married	Secondary
Rogelio	Male	36	Single	Preparatory
Rosa	Female	42	Married	Not Known
Rosy	Female	52	Married	Primary

(Continued)

Table 2.1. *(Continued)*

Name	Gender	Age	Civil Status	Educational Level
Sary	Female	25	Single	Professional
Selene Castillo	Female	25	Married	Preparatory
Selene Hernandez	Female	27	Single	Preparatory
Viridiana	Female	28	Single	Technical

Source: Prepared by the author.

forty-two were long-term participants and only eight were "new." This particular organizer recruited solely from upper-middle-class social networks, to which she gained access through her membership in various voluntary service clubs (see the section "Contexts and Sectors," chap. 3, for more details.)

Class and Origin Dimensions: Confianza and Its Distribution

Most organizers indicated that no invitation is extended to people whose status is not fixed either occupationally, residentially, consanguineously, affinally, fictively, or by friendship. On the other hand, people may initially be reluctant to join because they know about saving accounts or harbor doubts about the validity of the rotation process, and the organizer must overcome this resistance. The organizer's success is based on establishing confianza and on his or her status, and it does not depend on the newcomer establishing confianza with the other participants. There are class-specific stimuli that encourage people to participate in the ROSCAs.

Working-class and economically marginal members often contrasted ROSCAs to formal institutions like banks or savings and loan offices. People interviewed stated that while formal institutions demanded intimate knowledge ("everything in one's life from top to bottom"), no reciprocal personal relationships were generated. Mutuality was absent in commercial relations. On the other hand, confianza in ROSCAs arose from intimate personal knowledge and a public reputation, and it was privately secured through the organizer's established, personal relationships of trust and the context in which they occurred. Since intimate knowledge and personal relationships are the basic ingredients of confianza that generate mutual trust, formal institutions were in fact the antithesis of the informal rotating credit associations in the eyes of these populations.

Thus, in a Mexican chain restaurant, La Parilla Suiza, in Phoenix, Arizona, a ROSCA with eleven members was organized by a person who had already managed five tandas or cundinas. Her reputation had been the necessary condition that made it possible to organize this ROSCA since there was turnover among the employees. Of the eleven participants, five were from Mexico City; two from Sinaloa; and one each from Veracruz, Puebla, and Sonora (Mexico) and El Salvador (Central America). Their only relationship was as fellow employees. The organizer's status was such that everyone trusted her to collect and distribute the contributions in a timely manner. One member was continuously late, and when the organizer started a new ROSCA, she did not invite him to join since she and the participants did not regard him as a person of confianza.

In other words, in the ROSCA, personal relationships must exist, and the needed personal information serves as precious currency that defines the relationship. Nevertheless, it is the case that not everyone has the same information. In constrast, in public institutions or private entities like restaurants, participants may or may not want personal relationships, but personal information, although needed, is unknown. Although the reputation of both participants and the organizer is public knowledge within the networks people join or are recruited from, reputations are variable and open to interpretation. Thus, necessary personal information—about reliability and past and present behaviors—forms the basis of the reputation of the person invited to or wishing to join a ROSCA. From this information, the personal relations between participants and organizers are mated to form the basis of confianza, which glues the person joining to the organizer. On the other hand, public institutions have no privately generated reputations within limited private social domains (put differently, a customer does not care about the bank clerk's private reputation, only about the reputation of the bank itself). Instead, the relations generated in those domains are primarily "single-stranded" types (Boissevain 1974, 30) in which people engage in a single-role relationship, such as that between a bank officer and a depositor or borrower. For those in working-class and economically marginal sectors, an inherent contradiction exists. The institutions need clients' personal information to justify the establishment of a single-stranded relationship for market purposes, yet they demand this information without expressing any personal-level exchange. In other words, no confianza is established.

However, once ROSCA participants have built up sufficient capital to open an account in a formal institution that requires personal data, some seem to regard themselves as sufficiently "respectable" to enter into market-exchange relations with public institutions. Importantly, for these classes and sectors, money is necessary to establish themselves as bona fides. Middle- and upper-class sectors can, if they wish, join traditional banking or saving institutions, so the impetus to participate in a ROSCA is not the same.

Professionals

Changes in economic fortunes for professionals on either side of the border depend on the health of the border economies. In 2008, for example, the U.S. economic downturn directly affected the purchasing power of Mexican professionals buying goods in the United States, because buying power acquired through participation in tandas or cundinas declined as the exchange rate worsened. In the reverse, cundinas in U.S. border towns in which Mexican-origin professionals participate are affected by the declines in purchases of goods and services (at clinics, restaurants, clothing stores, and for many other economic ventures, such as packing houses, warehouses, trucking, and import-export businesses). But, just as importantly, the 1982, 1985, and 1995 downturns in the Mexican economy forced Mexican professionals especially to join tandas or cundinas on both sides of the border.

Equally so, the purchase of an automobile at high interest rates, private school tuition, the limitations imposed by a single income, the buying of a fashionable home, and the recreational activities standard in such sectors place very real strains on inflation-ridden budgets.[4] These people find it difficult to maintain class-specific expectations without relatively large amounts of money. A ROSCA, because it sets up an obligatory savings scheme within a same-class network and does not require any collateral, may provide a desirable way to have access to funds at regular intervals. Informants suggested that the pressures to consume or to pay debts immediately made it almost impossible to save, but that ROSCAs are a scheme of forced savings that circumvents that. The saving takes place within the context of other relations of confianza, and the threat of losing prestige if obligations are unmet reinforces the stability of ROSCAs.

The forced savings aspect was repeatedly mentioned by all classes, but especially by the middle classes. They seem more prone to living beyond their means and very much prone to economic impacts when border economies shift downward. The importance of the ROSCA is related to these factors more than to values of thriftiness.

Since the upper-middle-class and some upper-class sectors have ready access to resources, and profit-making ventures, ROSCAs do not serve as forced-saving vehicles for them. Among some women in upper-middle-class or upper-class residential areas, the associations are a means for entering prestigious residential networks. Thus, in the wealthy residential area of Lomas de Chapultepec in Mexico City, a fifteen-woman network uses a ROSCA to screen newly arrived residents. Embedded within commensal, gift giving, and card-playing activities, ROSCAs are used as recruiting mechanisms. The high cost of the contributions (one thousand pesos per month in 1982) indicates status and a willingness to share with other women who are on the same economic level. Over three to six months, between forty-five thousand and ninety thousand pesos accumulate. The contributions are usually not reallocated by lot or by chronology. Instead, the women spend the funds on luxury birthday gifts for each other. Since some of the fifteen women will have birthdays in the same month, the organizer makes a special effort to include women whose dates of birth are not too close to others. Therefore, no more than eight women will have birthdays during any six-month period, so each gift will be worth approximately twelve thousand pesos. Here, the emphasis is less on the price of the gift than on the imagination shown in its purchase. "Sumptuous consumption" and network recruitment, not balanced scarcity or spending beyond one's means, are the primary motives for joining this type of ROSCA.

High-stakes ROSCAs are also common among lawyers, doctors, businesspeople, and other professionals, even heads of bureaucracies, corporate banking officers, and directors of economic planning offices. All these individuals are familiar with savings institutions and other forms of interest-bearing investments, so the motive for participation is not connected to a desire to circumvent formal savings institutions. This type of ROSCA is usually part of larger voluntary associations, such as a chamber of commerce or the Lions Clubs International. Each member contributes 10,000 pesos per month in a fifteen-member cundina, and so the fund share would be worth 150,000 pesos. Here, clearly, this cooperative activity is not initiated because of economic need or because the members live beyond their means. A desire for sumptuous consumption is also not a motive. Rather, political stresses on individuals within the various social domains in which their professional activities take place select for ROSCA participation, as further analysis will illustrate.

In addition, retired, elderly, upper-middle-class cosmopolitans have formed associations as part of their recreational life, alongside such activities as playing canasta, giving parties, going on excursions, and attending recreational painting classes. Here the impetus for joining ROSCAs does not lie in a scarcity of resources, living beyond one's means, a desire for sumptuous consumption, or political stress. Instead, the desire is to fill in the final days of the life cycle.

Recently, Franziska Castillo (2009), a reporter writing an article on tandas, provided invaluable information on a professional "coperativa" composed of professionals in Washington, D.C.—mainly Latina and Latino lawyers, administrators, and consultants—who, although having IRAs and savings accounts, nevertheless had organized, over the two previous years, tandas specifically oriented toward first-time home buyers, which is especially crucial in the high-priced Washington, D.C., area. They incorporate a combination of formal and informal rules: they send a formal letter of invitation to a perspective participant and provide documentary agreements, but invite or reject new members through a process of election, with confianza playing an overriding role in their acceptance.

Sorting out the numbers by lot, most participants were acquainted with similar practices by their parents, but have incorporated new techonology with the use of e-mail and the development of a Yahoo! Group for this purpose. What is uniquely interesting is that their contributions can be made online, with a due date and a grace period of three days, or through ING Direct checking. Each has a customer number to transfer funds online, or participants can deposit their contribution directly into their account, or they can use PayPal. Others can enter the "coperativa" as teams, as couples, or as a small group with the same accounting rules as for individuals. As the organizer concludes in the interview, "This is really a twenty-first century tanda."

Basic Mechanisms and Structures: Confianza in Operation

As has been stated, the structures and mechanisms involved in the Mexican ROSCAs vary in complexity. Among the simplest is the leaderless one with a small contribution and fund share. It is socially dense and cooperatively run, occupational or residential, with neither a part-time nor a full-time specialist, and confianza is the main cultural medium for its development. Usually five to ten people agree to form this type of ROSCA. They decide the amount to be contributed, how often the money is to be collected—weekly, semimonthly, or monthly, depending on the source of income—and how often the money is to be allocated. In private corporations, in both Mexico and the United States, weekly contributions tend to be the norm, with semimonthly or monthly contributions usual in public corporations or government offices. For example, five restaurant service workers at the Beverly Hills Hotel in Los Angeles were paid semimonthly at a rate of $75. Four would contribute a semimonthly paycheck to the current recipient of the fund share. After drawing paper slips marked from one to five, number one would be designated to receive $300 at the first turn. The following month number two would receive the amount, and so on until four months after the first turn, when all five would have received $300, and the rotation would be complete.

Participants in simple ROSCAs do not necessarily contribute their whole salary. Often, the contributions are smaller and can be as low as the equivalent of US $2.24 in peso-denominated ROSCAs, or, depending on the period of study, between $25 and $100 in dollar-denominated ones. Contributions and the allocation of fund shares have to occur at the same time. For example, contributions can be made weekly, and the fund share allocated monthly.

In the simple ROSCAs, two intervening factors play important parts in defining the complexity of operation: the number and class sector of participants. Most simple ROSCAs, operating without an organizer, have ten members, and the amounts contributed are relatively small, with no fees or interest charges. High-level managers and professionals participate in ROSCAs of about the same size, but with higher contributions. Thus, within a national government agency in Mexico responsible for economic agricultural forecasting, a one-thousand-peso contribution for a ten-thousand-peso share was operated without a leader by ten economists, geographers, rural sociologists, and demographers. The glue of confianza in this case had been established among five of the ten, since they had attended the same preparatory school and university courses and had been students of the same internationally famous Mexican economist. The other five enjoyed varying degrees of confianza among those classmates.

Similarly, participants in a ROSCA in Yuma, Arizona, led by one of the teachers and operating within the local school district, communicate via the Internet concerning the date of payment, collection, issues, and any problems that may arise. The ROSCA consists mostly of female teachers, with only occasionally a few men. From the organizer's point of view, gender is an issue because the male participants were less likely to make their contributions on time, since they were sports coaches who often traveled and were not always in town when a contribution was due. The organizer also stated that they had tried to include participants who did not work in the institution, but it had not worked out because it was a "hassle." It was easier to have members who worked in the school district since they were paid at the same time, and to limit participation to women.

In the case of the Beverly Hills Hotel and the Mexican economic forecasting agency, both examples of the simplest type of ROSCA, participation was relatively closed according to class and occupation, and dense social relations were generated among the participants. Therefore, two factors must be kept in mind in considering the complexity of the informal ROSCA. First, those with fewer members will have fewer organizational problems of control or difficulties in collecting and dispensing money since confianza is the primary vehicle for all participants. Second, the number of members and their class sector determine the frequency of collection, as well as the probable completion of the full cycle.

In a working-class ROSCA, contributions are made on a payment plan, with records kept, accounts maintained, and interest charged for tardy payments, so the operation is more complex and formalized. On the other hand, people with resources are generally not going to pay on a payment plan, and the collection of money is certainly much simpler.

Permutations

Permutations emerge, however, with variations in the amount contributed, the number of members, the number of contributions allowed, and the duration of a full cycle.

In Ciudad Netzahualcoyótl, a ROSCA of thirty turns worth 100 pesos each was available to six participants (appendix C). Membership was thus restricted. Participants selected as many turns as they could afford. Thus, one person selected turns 1–10; another, 11–15; another, 16–20; another, 21–25; another, 26–29; and another, turn 30. For thirty weeks, an exchange of money occurred with the fund for each person ranging from 2,900 pesos to 20,000 pesos. Person 1 had selected turns 1–10, each worth 100 pesos, and contributed 1,000 pesos weekly. Person 2 (turns 11–15), Person 3 (turns 16–20), and Person 4 (turns 21–25) each contributed 500 pesos weekly. Person 5 selected turns 26–29 and contributed

400 pesos weekly. Finally, Person 6 with turn 30 contributed only 100 pesos each week.

During the first ten weeks, Person 1, who had the first ten turns, did not contribute and only received shares. Beginning in the eleventh week, the first person paid 1,000 pesos a week until the end of the rotation of all members, which is equal to 100 times the number of shares he requested. Person 2, who had turns 11–15, paid 500 pesos a week for the first ten weeks to Person 1; Person 3, who had turns 16–20, paid 500 pesos a week for the first ten weeks to Person 1; Person 4, who had turns 21–25, paid 500 pesos a week for the first ten weeks to Person 1; Person 5, who had turns 26–29, paid 400 pesos a week for the first ten weeks to Person 1; and the last person, who had only turn 30, 100 pesos a week for the first ten weeks to Person 1. Thus, Person 1 received 2,000 pesos per week from the other five in the tanda for ten weeks for a total of 20,000 pesos.

After the tenth week, Person 2, who had turns 11–15, began to receive money: from Person 1, who had ten turns (1–10), 1,000 pesos a week for five weeks; from Person 3, who had five turns (16–20), 500 pesos a week for five weeks; from Person 4, who had five turns (21–25), 500 pesos a week for five weeks; from Person 5, who had four turns (26–29), 400 pesos a week for five weeks; and from Person 6, who had one turn (30), 100 pesos a week for five weeks. Thus, Person 2 received 2,500 pesos a week from the other five members for five weeks for a total of 12,500 pesos.

Persons 3 and 4 went through exactly the same process as Person 2, being paid the same total weekly amount since they also held five turns. In each case, they received 2,500 pesos weekly for a total of 12,500 pesos. After Person 4 had received her turn, twenty-five weeks had elapsed.

Person 5, who had four turns (26–29), received 2,600 pesos for four weeks: 1,000 a week from Person 1; 500 a week from Persons 2, 3, and 4; and 100 pesos a week from Person 6. This totaled 10,400 pesos for the four-week period, and the elapsed time was twenty-nine weeks. Person 6, who had turn 30, received one lump sum of 2,900 pesos at the end of the tanda. In each case, no person received more than what he or she had contributed.

The number of possible permutations for this sort of informal ROSCA is quite large, although some versions are more widespread than are others, especially among people who have not only a qualitative but also a long-term dense relationship. On the other hand, commercialized informal ROSCAs exactly like the one just described also operate, but each weekly contribution requires paying the organizer a 10 percent fee.

Thus, each person contributes more than what he or she receives. In the example just discussed, the last individual would pay 110 pesos weekly for a total of 3,190 pesos, but would receive only 2,900 from the other members. The organizer's earnings would be 10 percent of the total contributions paid (10 percent of 70,800, or 7,080 pesos).

In another version of the simple ROSCA, disbursement is delayed so that fund shares increase. Thus, for example, ten people will contribute 1,000 pesos per week for five weeks. In the fifth week, one person is allocated 50,000 pesos (10 people × 1,000 pesos × 5 weeks = 50,000 pesos), and every fifth week thereafter, one member will receive 50,000 pesos. The cycle of collection and allocation thus takes fifty weeks. Not uncommonly, people choose a ten-week period. In a ten-person tanda, 100,000 pesos would be allocated every tenth week for a total cycle of one hundred weeks. The allocation period can also be shortened. In one case, the amount contributed was enlarged so that in a 30,000-peso fund, ten people collected and received all the money in ninety days.

When the agreed-upon mechanisms for rotating the money are altered, problems can arise. For example, participants may want to double or split their shares, exchange numbers, or borrow against the share fund. If these changes have not been agreed to previously, it is more than likely that intense local-level political hassles will ensue. Negotiations to alter the mechanisms of the ROSCA will generate a host of claims and counterclaims between the organizer and the participants. In those ROSCAs where alterations are possible, the political maneuvering will take place before the operations begin. In both cases, local-level political struggles may intensify as the ROSCA evolves under changing circumstances and unforeseen factors that create uncertainty for organizers and participants.

We can see this clearly in the case of an informal ROSCA with an organizer but without an objective mechanism to determine the order of turns, like a lottery. Instead, old favors are cashed in, claims of proximity made, and feelings played upon. In those informal ROSCAs in which the order of turns is negotiated, intense political claims and counterclaims emerge. For example, an organizer may save the first turns for close relatives or friends and inform all other participants that those turns are taken, or the organizer may claim to have taken the first turn and then negotiate for that first turn with someone else shortly before the beginning of the ROSCA cycle. When fellow participants learn of such intrigues, feelings will be hurt and further claims will be made against both the organizer and the person for whom the favor was done.

For those who have participated in ROSCAs with the same organizer for years, seniority determines who receives the first turn. For example, a person may have begun with turn 16 in her or his first ROSCA and, after having participated in thirteen ROSCAs, be given the opportunity to select turn 3 in a new ROSCA. However, long-standing participants sometimes claim greater seniority than what they actually have in order to receive a turn sooner, or the organizer may understate one participant's seniority in order to give someone else with greater confianza an earlier turn. In these cases, the organizer may give her or his own first turn to the long-standing participant and give the other contested turn to the person with greater confianza, or vice versa. However, if that strategy is followed, much more intense political problems with the long-standing participant will follow, since he or she will claim one of the first turns in the next ROSCA. In either case, the selection of turns in formal ROSCAs can be made much more complicated by the introduction of intense local-level politics. Thus, it is extremely important to keep records.

Intermediate ROSCAs and Formal RCA Structures

Although intermediate ROSCAs and the formal institutionalized RCA *mutualistas* are also subject to local-level political maneuvering, both types operate relatively consistently, and their mechanisms remain largely unchanged. The intermediate ROSCAs are relatively stable because they are set within the context of a formal accounting system in, for example, a factory, a bureau office, or a service company. The turns are selected only once, contributions are deducted through the payroll system, a written agreement of participation is included, and the turns and the shares allotted are recorded. One must remember the distinction between ROSCAs that are formally integrated into a company's accounting system and those that only use the accounting system to keep the ROSCA records. In the informal type, the bookkeeper or accountant is the organizer or a prominent member, but the company's accounting system is used without managerial sanction. An informally organized ROSCA can become a management-controlled association when conflict over the mechanisms of the ROSCA leads the management to "take over" the ROSCA from the employees. The accounting practices for informal intermediate ROSCAs are impressive, since three sets of books are kept: one for the company, one for the ROSCA members, and one for the accountant. This type of ROSCA numbers in the hundreds in both the United States and Mexico, and they are especially common among employees in movie theaters, governmental offices, mid-sized restaurants, and schools.

The Mutualistas

These RCAs are strictly profit-seeking organizations. In the pre-1983 sample, the formally organized mutualistas of Mérida were the most complex of all the RCAs. However, multiple formally organized tandas have emerged since then in both the United States and Mexico. In the most commercialized ones, collateral has replaced confianza, although the language of confianza may be utilized when advertising the formation of the association. Anyone wishing to join must agree to a lien being placed over movable property or real estate, must put up collateral, and must agree to have his or her credit history checked. Market exchange is the central mechanism, so that only those with a substantial amount of accumulated property are eligible to join. Confianza, in this scenario, is limited to the reputation of the company or institution that operates the RCA.

Corporations with officers and other formal institutional characteristics are responsible for transactions in the mutualistas. Although fund shares vary from 20,000 to 150,000 pesos (10,000-peso shares were discontinued in 1978), the structural elements and processes are the same in all of them (table 2.2).

A new mutualista is usually announced in the local newspapers. This announcement includes a description of the amount of the "savings fund" (*fondos de ahorro*), the number of shares (*acciones*), each of the shares' individual worth, the cycle's duration, the age restrictions (15–60), the legal sponsor (the corporation), and the objective (obligatory savings).

Table 2.2.   Mutualistas of Yucatán

Number of Participants	Contribution (in pesos)	Number of Weeks	Fund Share (in thousands of pesos)
50	320 + 190	393	150
50	212 + 128	394	100
50	106 + 64	394	50
40	54 + 26	327	20
40	27 + 13	327	10

Source: Vélez-Ibáñez 1983.

Each person is required to sign a contract of agreement (see appendix D) and a lien equal to the amount of the advertised fund share. Each also provides an initial deposit and fee that varies with the amount of the share. In return, the person receives a certificate of participation and association and insurance against death or permanent disability during the life of the mutualista.

At the beginning cycle of the mutualista, each person is given a number registered solely in her or his name. That number will be on one of the forty or fifty (depending on the number of participants) lottery balls placed in a large wire hopper. Every ten weeks, the winning numbers are randomly selected. The lottery process shifts according to computational tables, as fewer and fewer persons continue to be eligible. A new cycle of operation begins when fifty new people register as members. As a result, three or four months may pass between the end of one mutualista and the beginning of a new one. Because of the difference in amounts (20,000 to 150,000 pesos), four and five mutualistas may operate simultaneously on different cycles with an entirely different set of people participating in each one.

The terms for payment and receipt of money are more complicated than this description would suggest. Those selected first during the course of the cycle in fact pay more than they receive for the privilege of using the money first. Those whose numbers are selected last pay less than what they receive as compensation for allowing others the use of their money.

To see how a mutualista works, consider a 20,000-peso, forty-person version. Each individual pays an initial contribution of 54 pesos for 326 weeks. After the person has received his or her 20,000 pesos, a premium of 26 pesos is added weekly for an 80-peso total. The person selected first in the lottery pays 80 pesos weekly for 326 weeks for a total of 26,080 pesos. The twentieth person pays 54 pesos for the first 163 weeks and a premium of 26 pesos for the next 163 weeks, for a total of 21,842 pesos. The fortieth person pays only 54 pesos for 326 weeks for a total of 17,604 pesos. The totals include interest charges not computed in these figures, so that each total in fact is greater than the figures given here. All participants will receive at least 20,000 pesos, the amount originally announced for the mutualista.

At this complex level of operation, the mutualista, by making its investors' funds available for use by others, functions exactly like a commercial lending and borrowing institution. The crucial difference between mutualistas and traditional savings and loan institutions is the element of chance that is the result of using a lottery, which determines whether a person will be a lender or a borrower.

As in commercial institutions, the lenders' and borrowers' funds are used to maintain the organizational structure of the corporation, including the overhead costs of the mutualistas. These are calculated at 6 percent of each payment made. Eight percent of the fund share is allocated for "collection and administration," which includes salaries to the collectors who ride out daily on their motorcycles to gather payments; rent and utilities; supplies and materials; and the salaries of fiscal and corporate accountants.

These costs include honorariums for the corporate officers. In one corporation, the officers receiving salaries and honorariums included the president of the mutualista, who was the corporation's secretary's son; the secretary, who was the president's mother; and the director-treasurer, who was the secretary's brother and the president's uncle. It would seem that confianza, while not a factor between the corporation and mutualista participants, was in fact highly valued within the corporate organization.

FYGO: A Transborder Version

David G. Farias, of Phoenix, Arizona, began a ROSCA version located in the United States, which he termed "peer lending." He had first simulated an American version of an RCA in one of his managerial economics courses at Arizona State University (2004). It was an exact replica of a tanda, but it was commercialized with fees, projected earnings, and long-term economic benefits for both the commercial enterprise itself and for the RCA's participants. He later utilized the model for an online version he labeled FYGO and introduced in 2007 in the Phoenix area. He calls it an "Internet Social Lending Network."[5]

This person-to-person lending network is sponsored by FYGO, a private "holding company." When an individual needs a loan, he or she can set up a network of friends and family who are willing to lend the money. Alternatively, a lender can set up the network with other potential lenders, or there can be a combination of the two. The names and legal addresses of the people in the network are registered and verified by FYGO. Physically, the network can be either a private or public one, but it has to be built up before lending or borrowing can take place.

The network organizer must submit to a credit check and obtain the permission of the other members to join the network. The person's identity from his or her credit file is then verified by FYGO. Finally, after verification, the person can offer to make a loan to, or request one from, anyone in the network, and people can accept or negotiate. Once the network is in place, the loan or offer to make a loan can be extended to anyone in the network, and people can accept or negotiate.

Farias cites Mexican tandas or cundinas, and their organization and the concept of confianza, as the model that ensures the benefits of social networking. According to Farias, access and reach to friends and family through FYGO are guaranteed in an emergency. Larger amounts may be leveraged, with ten persons in the networks lending $500 each for a $5,000 loan. According to Farias, the best financial guarantee is fairness and the lender's integrity.[6] This format is unlike the Zopas, Prosper, and International Kivas in the United Kingdom, all of which function as micro-lending institutions, which are based on an open market and FICO scores because lending and borrowing is done through the institution and not from the network itself.

Basic Characteristics of ROSCAs and RCAs: The Sample

Number of Participants

As will be recalled, in our sample of 146 ROSCAs and RCAs in which money is the medium of exchange, 130 were informally organized and the remainder were intermediate ROSCAs and formal RCAs. Data were collected on 5 intermediate ROSCAs that are formally or informally integrated into the accounting system of companies but not as the major business venture. There are truly hundreds of formal commercialized RCAs, including the Mutualista de Yucatán (a pseudonym), distributed among automobile, sumptuary-item, household-goods, cosmetics, computer, kitchen, and house tandas. Finance companies, for example, have no limits on the number of participants, except for allowing only a set number of participants for each automobile or motorcycle.

However, FYGO has almost unlimited potential in terms of the number of participants, since the size of the social network determines this. Most social networks have natural limits in terms of the number of trusted relatives, friends, or colleagues at any one time, so that paths leading to and from individuals are limited to two or perhaps three steps of communication to reach any one individual to ascertain his or her reliability. Thus, the denser the relationship, the higher the probability for trust and for participation in a FYGO.

The discussion below does not reflect the characteristics of all 130 informal ROSCAs. I base the discussion on reliable and complete data, so the number of ROSCAs varies with the specific topic being considered.

The categories of informal, intermediate, and formal commercialized RCAs are used as convenient distinctions. "Peso" and "dollar" refer to the currency used in the associations, but it should be understood that this does not automatically indicate the physical location of the association, since many ROSCAs in northern Mexican border states use dollars as the medium of exchange. The opposite, however, does not occur. The use of pesos in ROSCAs in the United States has never been reported.

Figure 2.1 illustrates the frequency of the number of participants in informal and intermediate associations. In the 135 informal and intermediate ROSCAs analyzed, the most frequent were ten-person ROSCAs, which continued to be the case throughout my research; the next most frequent were twelve- and fifteen-person ROSCAs; and the third most

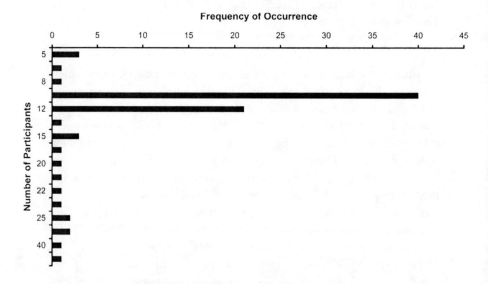

Figure 2.1 Number of participants in informal and intermediate ROSCAs (N = 135). *Source*: Prepared by the author.

frequent were five- and fifteen-person ones. With slightly different frequencies, an assorted number of people participated in other ROSCAs.

Informal and intermediate ROSCAs (N = 135) of ten members occur twice as often as those of twelve and twenty, and slightly more than six times as often as those of five and fifteen (fig. 2.1). This indicates that ten-person ROSCAs are the preferred size for informal and intermediate types. Care must be taken in making such a generalization, however, since many ROSCAs have eleven or twelve members or fewer than ten, depending on circumstances. Nevertheless, the evidence seems to indicate that the ten-person ROSCA is more manageable; it corresponds to a relatively short period (usually ten weeks or ten months), and it increases the probability that confianza has been established among the participants. Having only ten participants reduces the distance traveled by an organizer in residential ROSCAs, and ten probably corresponds closely to the maximum number of colleagues with friendship ties in an office, factory, or business concern. With ten participants, the certainty that funds will be properly allocated increases, since some of the participants will be part of other networks of relationships. It is more likely that in a ROSCA of this size, a larger portion of the participants will have developed multiple relations.

My finding that informal ROSCAs most frequently have ten members agrees with Kurtz's (1973) and Kurtz and Showman's (1978) findings for San Pedro, San Felipe, and San Jerónimo Caleras. However, Kurtz and Showman also report membership sizes ranging from three to twenty-six in San Felipe and San Jerónimo Caleras, and Lomnitz (1977, 88) reports groups of four to ten. I did not find any informal ROSCA with fewer than five members nor any with twenty-six or more members. All the research, including that through 2008, shows that the largest membership was sixteen, in a university cundina in northwestern Mexico, and sixteen in a Phoenix, Arizona, ROSCA. The latter was embedded in a Mexican restaurant where the organizer had operated six "tandas," keeping one number for herself in each of them.

My findings conflict with Kurtz and Showman's suggestion that there is "no necessary correspondence between the number of memberships and number of members" (1978, 67). I believe that it is more likely that correspondence exists, unless a participant splits one membership in two. In all the data studied, most ROSCAs normally have only one number split between two individuals, while everyone else took whole numbers. Thus, a ROSCA may have twelve memberships with fourteen members since two or more members have split the same number. However, in general, the membership and the number of members correspond one to the other.

There are indications that in the more commercialized informal ROSCAs directed by specialists, care is taken to limit the number of memberships to the number of members, for reasons of organizational convenience.

Amounts Contributed

Between 1983 and 2008, the size of the contributions doubled from those of the pre-1983 research at the lower end of the spectrum in peso and dollar amounts in both the United States and Mexico. However, the size of contributions depends on context. For example, in Mazatlán, Sinaloa, in a sample of forty-four participants in various cundinas that included primarily university students, professors, and administrative personnel, the contributions varied from 100 to 1,000 pesos every fifteen days, which coincided with university pay periods.

On the other hand, twenty-five market women in the same city contributed much higher amounts. However, this scheme entailed a very complex calculus of borrowing, selling, and saving that utilized cundinas, *prestamos* (loans),[7] and personal savings in banks. The savings were intended to allow for the purchase on credit of seafood products—fish, shrimp, and scallops—followed by their same-day sale. This maintained the women at a low margin of profit, but how they managed this against fees and license taxes, and the hundreds of daily expenses—plastic bags, ice, towels, meals, and the required purchase of a trinket or an item from the vendors who came to buy shrimp—determined future investments and profit margins. Then, the cundinas play a key role in balancing all these. When this calculus is integrated with daily household needs, the rearing of children, transportation, housing, rituals, and the hundreds of other aspects of daily living that cost money, how all this is balanced out is indeed a mathematical wonder. Only eight of the twenty-five women practice the 100,000-peso cundina, along with one supplier and one packing house manager.

The sums contributed in informal and intermediate peso-denominated ROSCAs varied from 50 to 10,000 pesos in 1983 and 100 pesos to 100,000 pesos in 2008. As an average from all samples from the 1970s to 2008, 42 percent of the associations had contributions of 100 pesos; 11 percent,

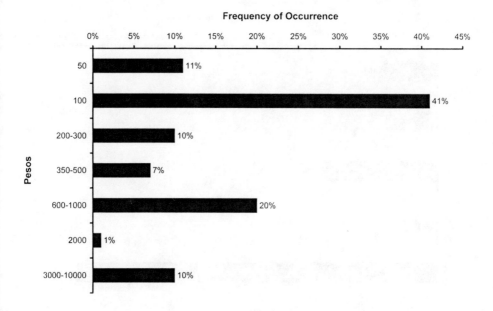

Figure 2.2 Contributions in informal and intermediate peso-denominated ROSCAs (N = 85). *Note*: Average of pre-1983 and 1983–2008 ROSCAs. *Source*: Prepared by the author.

50 pesos; 10 percent, 200–300 pesos; 20 percent, 600–1,000 pesos; 7 percent, 350–500 pesos; 1 percent, 2,000; and 10 percent, 3,000–10,000. Among professionals and market women in Mazatlan, the upper end of 100,000 pesos is not unusual (fig. 2.2).

The sums contributed in the informal dollar-denominated ROSCAs show a range of $25–$100 before 1983 and an average of $100 from 1983 to 2008. Today, with this higher amount, two people sometimes split the contribution to facilitate making the payment. The contribution is also dependent on the actual distribution cycle. Thus, ROSCAs operating on a weekly cycle would more than likely have more instances of two people sharing the same number, while ROSCAs operating on a biweekly or monthly cycle would more than likely only have one contributor per number. The modal contribution before 1983 was $100 and accounted for 62 percent of the associations, with $50 contributions being the next most frequent (20 percent of the ROSCAs); 10 percent had $25 contributions, which was the lowest amount; and 4 percent had contributions of $75. Figure 2.3 shows the frequency of contribution sizes. However,

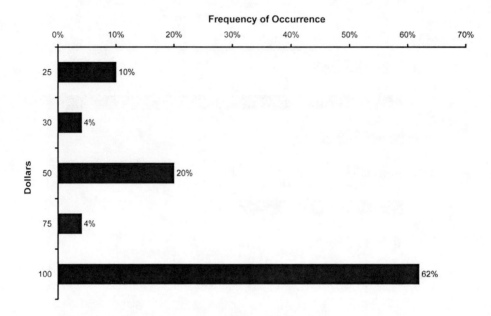

Figure 2.3 Contributions in informal and intermediate dollar-denominated ROSCAs (N = 50). *Source*: Prepared by the author.

in the post-1983 samples, the contributions averaged $100 as the lowest amount contributed in ten ROSCAs in Phoenix, Yuma, and San Luis, all in Arizona.

Before 1983, differences existed in the low and middle ranges between peso- and dollar-denominated ROSCA contributions. In comparing the dollar and peso amounts in figures 2.2 and 2.3, we find 11 percent of the total peso-denominated ROSCAs with contributions of fifty pesos or less, but only 10 percent of the dollar-denominated ROSCAs with contributions of less than $25 for that period, with a frequency of 62 percent for $100 amounts (fig. 2.3).

As a comparison of figures 2.2 and 2.3 also shows, the greater frequency of large sums in dollar-denominated ROSCAs and of small sums in peso-denominated ROSCAs reflects the fact that in border areas, where dollars are widely used in ROSCAs, family incomes are among the highest in Mexico. Incomes are appreciably higher among Mexicans in the U.S. Southwest as well. Members of the working class and the upper-middle or upper class participate in dollar-denominated ROSCAs. The $50 amounts appeared in 35 percent of the associations and are likely to come from workers in the United States who are employed in ceramic factories or in electronics assembly lines in Los Angeles or San Diego. On the other hand, in the research done from 1983 through 2008, the largest percentage of peso contributions were those of 100 pesos (42 percent; N = 55), followed by the 200–300 peso sum. The dollar amounts, like the peso sums, increased to $100 and accounted for 62 percent of the total dollar contributions, appearing even among low-paid restaurant workers in Phoenix. On the other hand, in Mexico, 30 percent of the dollar-denominated ROSCAs are more than likely those of professional upper-middle-class men and women in the border states of Baja California, Chihuahua, and Nuevo León.

Formal RCAs

In the formally organized mutualistas of Yucatán, the corporation defined the range of contributions. Table 2.2 shows five mutualistas categorized according to the number of participants, the sums contributed, and the fund share allotted.

It must be remembered that the actual amount of the contribution will vary according to each individual's luck in the lottery. The first person selected in the 150,000-peso, 393-week mutualista will always pay 320 + 190; the twenty-fifth person will pay 320 pesos for the first twenty-five turns and 320 + 190 pesos for the next twenty-five turns; and the fiftieth person will only pay 320 pesos throughout the fifty turns of the ROSCA. This scheme of contributions is followed in all the other mutualistas in table 2.2, except that the contributions vary according to the amount of the fund share and the number of participants. The formal mutualistas of Mutualista de Yucatán had minimum fund shares of 10,000 pesos in 1978 (discontinued in 1979). Shares ranged from 10,000 to 150,000 pesos, with the distribution shown as in table 2.2. Corporate officials were unwilling to divulge the frequency of each fund share.

Six other formal RCAs are discussed here: three automobile, one motorcycle, one home and property, and one a cement enterprise. Holding companies (SICREA México, Planfia, and Alfin) support the first four. According to responses to a questionnaire submitted to the company's administrative offices, the amounts actually contributed are defined in the following ways.

The amounts for the Volkswagen or Datsun (later Nissan) RCAs depended on the price of the automobile. At the time of my original

Table 2.3. Autofin México Payment Schedule (in pesos)

Payment	Balance	Fixed Monthly Payment
3	27	676
4	26	667
5	25	658
6	24	655
7	23	645
8	22	641
9	21	629
10	20	624
11	19	619
12	18	613
13	17	606

Source: Prepared by the author.

research, these cars sold for approximately 88,000 pesos, excluding interest payments. It is highly probable that no Volkswagen or Datsun (Nissan) RCA had more than 40 or 42 participants, with contributions between 2,000 and 2,200 pesos per month. By 2008, the price of the cars had doubled, as had the contribution. In 2008, Honda's RCAs formed groups of 120 participants in a forty-eight-month plan, in which automobiles were distributed by lottery or auction. Honda has a fixed amount to be paid on the particular model.

Chrysler's version of the RCA defines the amount contributed according to the model of the automobile, whereas for Nissan, the amount depends on the income of the participant. On the other hand, Mi Moto, which is an RCA for Toromex motorcycles, has a very specific funding scheme for a particular model labeled the Festival 125 cc. For the 17,230-peso bike, initial contributions include a first payment of 693 pesos, a monthly charge of 592 pesos, and three monthly payments of 1,876 pesos. Thereafter, payments are based on the ability of the person to pay. The following example provides a payment schedule according to Grupo Autofin México, the finance company (table 2.3).

The Mi Casa plan response indicated that "the scheme is similar to a 'tanda,' in that we form groups of people who, like you, want to acquire good homes and property." After an initial first month's payment and charge, the scheme revolves around 180 monthly payments to a BIC (reserve fund); the individual chooses when to withdraw accumulated funds and the amount to withdraw, depending on when that person wants to purchase a home or remodel an existing one. The person is guaranteed the purchase after a maximum of fifty-one payments during that same period of time.

The CEMEX (Cementos Mexicanos) enterprise constructs a tanda-like fund from purchased shares, in which the participant is given technical assistance, materials for construction, and access to credit to build a home at 35 percent under actual costs. Located in nineteen Mexican states and benefitting more than 95,000 families, this scheme is technically managed through CEMEX offices, which does not limit the participation of any group nor the number of participants.

Size of Fund Shares

The size of the fund shares differed significantly between peso- and dollar-denominated ROSCAs, but it was, of course, related to the sums contributed. In peso-denominated ROSCAs, 37 percent had fund shares between 500 and 2,000 pesos, with 11 percent having a range of 4,100 to 5,000 (fig. 2.4). Sizable fund shares of between 9,100 and 150,000 pesos appeared in 54 percent of the ROSCAs. Fund shares ranged from a low of 200 pesos to a high of 150,000 pesos, with the former mostly restricted to either very low–income persons, teenagers, or low-income residential areas, mostly in areas originally settled by land invasions.

Among the dollar-denominated ROSCAs, fund shares varied from $50 to $10,000 in the pre-1983 research and from $1,000 to $10,000 in the post-1983 research. In the pre-1983 research, the modal amount was between $1,000 and $1,250 and was present in 67 percent of the ROSCAs. Fifteen percent of the dollar-denominated ROSCAs had fund shares of $250. Fund shares of $50 appeared with a frequency of almost zero percent, while fund shares of $300 and $500 appeared with a frequency of 8 percent each. Fund shares of $375 appeared with a frequency of 4 percent, whereas $1,500 and $10,000 appeared with a frequency of 13 and 4 percent respectively. Figure 2.4 presents these frequencies. However, the post-1983 data clearly show that up to 2008 the most frequent fund share was $1,000, with a maximum of $10,000. The post-1983 studies found 21 percent were less than $1,000–1,250, and of these, 16 percent were less than $375 or below.

It is difficult to compare all data from all my research to Kurtz and Showman's (1978) because their data are expressed as medians rather

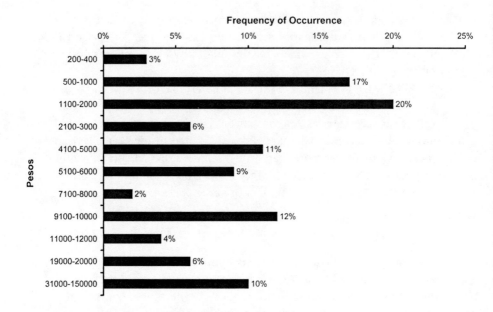

Figure 2.4 Size of fund shares in informal and intermediate peso-denominated ROSCAs (N = 85). *Source*: Prepared by the author.

than as frequency distributions, and thirty years have passed since that work was published. They do, however, mention that in the San Felipe and San Jerónimo Caleras ROSCAs, the contributions varied from 50 to 200 pesos with membership ranging from three to twenty-six people, with a relatively short cycle (670). Extracting from these data a median contribution of 125 pesos and a median of 15 (14.5) participants, then it is likely that Kurtz and Showman's fund shares rotated approximately 1,875 pesos (125 pesos × 15 participants). This is in the range of the second more frequent amount in my data: 1,100–2,000 pesos (accounting for 20 percent of the associations). But Kurtz and Showman's median is higher than my modal value of 500–1,000 pesos (accounting for 17 percent of the associations). Such comparisons are, of course, very tentative, given the differences in the way we report our data.

Not surprisingly, especially in 2008 given inflation, Kurtz's (1973) dollar-denominated ROSCAs in San Ysidro show lower fund shares than my data. Even using pre-1983 data, if a median contribution of $7.50 is assumed (based on contributions of $5–10), and a membership of ten,

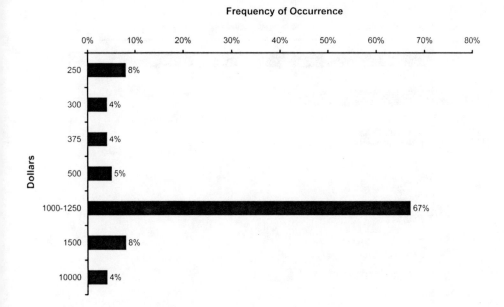

Figure 2.5 Size of fund shares in informal and intermediate dollar-denominated ROSCAs (N = 50). *Source:* Prepared by the author.

then it is likely that the median fund share for the San Ysidro ROSCAs is $75. My data show a much greater range ($50–10,000), with greatest frequency for fund shares between $1,000 and $1,250 (representing 67 percent of associations), considerably above the San Ysidro median. Inflation by itself cannot account for these differences: in the period 1972–1974, the restaurant workers in the Beverly Hills Hotel who made $150 a month had five-person fund shares of $350. The contrasts between Kurtz's data and these can only be understood in relation to class differences. However, the low end of $50 had changed to $100, with the high end at the same maximum of $10,000.

Length of Rotation Cycle

The length of the rotation cycle refers to the actual time it takes to complete all the turns in a ROSCA. As will be seen in figure 2.6, there are congruent relationships between the number of participants, the amount contributed, the size of the fund share, and the length of the rotational

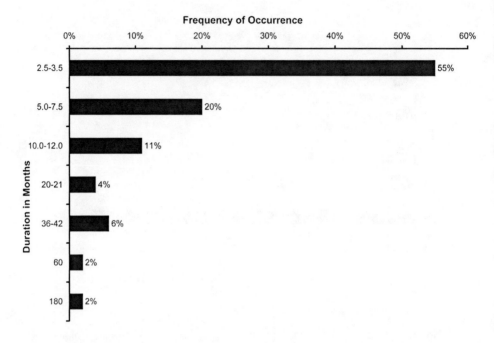

Figure 2.6 Duration of ROSCAS in months (N = 135; excludes Volkswagen, cannabis, prostitution, and formal RCAs). *Source*: Prepared by the author.

cycle. For example, a ten-person ROSCA will usually disburse its funds on ten evenly spaced occasions, whether weeks, months, or even years. The contributions will usually be in even amounts such as $10 or 100 pesos. The amounts, however, may be split up so that participants would contribute $100 monthly in four weekly payments of $25. This practice, incidentally, does not necessarily occur among participants with limited incomes, since in fact one of the most affluent ROSCAs, with $1,000 contributions, used this method of payment. Nor is it necessarily the case, as the ethnographic literature has suggested, that the poorer the membership, the longer the cycle and the more spaced-out the payments (Embree 1939; X. Fei 1939; H. Fei and Chang 1949; Geertz 1962; Kurtz 1973). The shortest ROSCA was among transient laborers in Yucatán in which five buddies (*cuates*) made contributions of $8 a week (to be used for binges). I have already mentioned the longest continuing rotational cycle, which had lasted for fifteen years when the original research was being done. Its participants were middle-management bank employees whose wives administered the process. This ROSCA was basically a hidden practice not acceptable to senior bank managers. The second longest cycle of five years was also found in a banking institution, with wives again administering the process.

These five-week and fifteen-year rotation cycles represent the extremes. Accounting for 55 percent of all cycles, the 2.5-month cycle (ten weeks) and 3.5-month cycle (fourteen weeks) were most frequently found among the informally organized ROSCAs (see fig. 2.6). Here, the most obvious factor for these time cycles is the context in which they operate, so that institutions, workplaces, and businesses are congruent with the stability of the people participating, as well as being tied to pay periods of those engaged. Those with a 5- to 7.5-month cycle were the next most frequent (throughout the duration of the research, from the mid-1970s to 2008). What is significant, however, is that before 1983, the most frequent was the 10- to 12-month cycle; since then, it has shrunk dramatically to the 2.5- or 3.5-month cycle. This speaks to the great structural changes and "shortening" of the screen of confianza, brought about by rapid demographic mobility due to the major changes in transborder political economy since 1980.

Nevertheless, frequency of the ten- to twelve-week cycle points to the congruence between it and the popular ten- to twelve-person ROSCAs (see fig. 2.1). A ten- to twelve-week rotation cycle would be less likely to be congruent with a larger membership. In addition, however, the ROSCAs with fund shares of $1,000–1,250, which account for 67 percent of those shown in figure 2.5, are also congruent with ten to twelve members in a ten- to twelve-week rotational cycle. It is likely that the rotation period of the ROSCA, the number of members involved, and the size of the fund share are congruent. Ten people contributing $100 a month for ten weeks or months make up exactly the members needed for a $1,000 ROSCA. Twelve people contributing the same amount for the same period would result in a $1,200 ROSCA. Congruence and symmetry seem to be selected for and provide ROSCA members a cultural artifact by means of which a predictive cycle of events and actions is usually kept in balance. Although the percentage distribution of the post-1983 ROSCAs varied from the pre-1983 ones, with a much higher percentage rotating larger amounts at the lower end, the rotational cycles remained the same.

A similar relationship exists for the peso-denominated ROSCAs, with 20 percent of the associations having contributions between 1,100 and 2,000 pesos and 18 percent between 500 and 1,000 pesos, and with 62 percent made up of between ten and twelve persons. Of the eighty-five peso-denominated ROSCAs analyzed, only four were of the 500-peso variety, and the rest were between 1,000 and 3,000 pesos. Other symmetrical permutations also result with contributed sums of 200–300 pesos, each of which will more than likely rotate in ten–twelve weeks with a worth of 2,000–3,000 pesos.

In the formal mutualistas of Yucatán, the rotational periods coincide exactly with the sums contributed and the number of persons participating in each mutualista (allowing for interest and fees). These relationships are carefully set down in tables that all participants follow.

Informal, intermediate, and formal ROSCAs all tend toward symmetry of operation and participation, which acts as an important counterbalance to the opposite pressures in urban living. Meaning is extracted from balancing factors even in commercialized ROSCAs. In other words, ROSCAs "make sense" as symmetrical expressions of the confianza construct, which itself is a symmetrical mechanism of balance. The tendency toward consistency and balance is also expressed in the way in which people refer to the ROSCAs, as the next section illustrates.

Commercializing ROSCAs

With the exception of my 1983 book *Bonds of Mutual Trust*, the literature on Mexican ROSCAs did not report examples of the organizer charging interest or other fees (Kurtz and Showman 1978; Lewis 1961, 1968; Lomnitz 1977). One exception was an undeveloped finding for cundinas (Kurtz 1973). It appears that the organization receives no other reward apart from getting to take the first turn. However, all of my research has found widespread commercialized practices in which the organizer takes both a first turn and a "zero turn" (also referred to as "taking the zero") in lieu of receiving a fee for organizing and administering the ROSCA. Sometimes the first turn is the zero turn, so that the organizer takes turn 1 without making any contributions. In other words, the first turn may be free without the organizer having any obligation to contribute anything to the ROSCA. It is clear from the literature (Kurtz 1973; Kurtz and Showman 1978) that the taking of fees by specialists has not been considered analytically important when attempting to define an informal ROSCA as commercialized. The opposite view prevails here. Prior to 1983, I had reported fewer than 50 percent of the organizers taking the

first turn. This mixing of a market relationship with a reciprocal relationship can be considered to have commercialized the venture.

Prior to 1983, the majority of the informal and intermediate dollar-
and peso-denominated ROSCAs did not have a free first turn or a fee. Of
135 dollar- and peso-denominated ROSCAs, including ROSCAs without
organizers, 58 percent (N = 78) lacked any fees, free first turns, or zero
turns. (Within such ROSCAs, the first number could have been given to
the organizer in recompense for his or her administrative work, and the
organizer would then continue to contribute to the ROSCA like any other
participant.) On the other hand, in 25 percent of the ROSCAs, the organizers took the free first turn, *el cero*, and 17 percent charged a 10 percent
fee or some other kind of charge, such as requiring more contributions
than what is paid out. Thus, 42 percent of the informal and intermediate
ROSCAs in this research were commercialized to some extent.

Most of the post-1983 data show that it is more than likely that "taking the first turn" is much more common in the present than in the
past. The reasons are multiple, but particularly important has been
the mobility of the Mexican population during the past twenty-five
years, especially the flows to the United States. Therefore, most informal ROSCAs let the organizer take the first turn in lieu of a fee. Exceptions are those involving relatives or very close friends, or those that are
ensconced in institutions where people have worked together for a long
time. Although reliable general statistical data does not exist to support
this, most ROSCA organizers sampled from 1983 through 2008 took the
first turn. In sixty-five post-1983 ROSCAs, 64 percent of the organizers
took the first turn. In part, this was due to the high mobility factor: taking the first turn was insurance in case someone left without paying, with
the money being used to replace that contribution. In any case, the organizer considered the first turn as remuneration for organization, maintenance, and especially, collection work. Nevertheless, in 36 percent of the
ROSCAs, the organizers did not charge any fee. However, as just noted,
these were ROSCAs that involved close friends or consanguineal relatives, long-term coworkers of the organizer, and, last but not least, ones
whose members were all women.

In Mérida, commercial associations other than the corporate mutualistas also exist. These informal mutualistas consist of forty or more
members who contribute 88 pesos weekly for forty weeks. Each member
receives 3,200 pesos, but pays 3,520 pesos. Thus, the organizer makes a
profit of 320 pesos per week, for a total of 12,800 pesos. Theoretically,

the larger the mutualista, the greater the risk of default, although default seldom occurs.

In both large and small commercial ROSCAs, there are examples of full-time specialists who dedicate themselves exclusively to organizing residential and institutional ROSCAs.

A cundina in Tijuana, for example, had ten participants who contributed $25 weekly, with the share given monthly. There were eleven monthly payments of $100 (4 × $25) by each of the ten persons, for a total of $1,000 monthly. The first turn, or el cero, of $1,000 went to the organizer, and the rest was allotted to the participants over the next ten months. When the organizer is also a participant, he or she receives a fee of $900 (not counting his or her contribution), but the organizer will also be among those rotating $900 (again excluding the organizer's contribution) during the life of the ten-member, ten-month cundina. In that particular cundina in Tijuana, the organizer was a full-time specialist who administered three ROSCAs simultaneously. Thus, analytically, fees charged by specialists structurally shift the exchange relations from generalized reciprocity to commercialized market exchange.

Some ROSCAs allow members to borrow on the not-yet-allotted share for a nominal fee. The organizer lends the money, so in the case cited above a person could borrow $500 against the share of $900, but the organizer discounts 10 percent for the advance. When that person's turn came, he or she would receive only $450: $500 × .10 = $50; $50 subtracted from $500 = $450.

Tandas Vivas and Tandas Muertas

Where the term *tanda* is used, those ROSCAs in which charges occur are called *tandas muertas* (dead ROSCAs), and those in which no money is made by an organizer are called *tandas vivas* (alive ROSCAs). The designation *tandas muertas* derives from the fact that the market relationship has replaced the normal reciprocally based relationship of the tandas vivas. As one organizer in the state of Veracruz put it, "They [tanda muertas] are nothing but business, and therefore, I do not participate in them. They are not convivial. For me, it is more important that they [the members] feel confianza because this [ROSCA] is not a business. I have a business." On the other hand, another organizer for whom the ROSCAs are a business, rationalized the organization of tandas muertas in the following manner: "Life is not a gift, so neither are my efforts."

This contrast between dead and live associations illustrates the profound social meanings attached to each. The tanda viva is alive because of the reciprocal expectations involved in a social obligation based on mutual trust (confianza), and the phrase describing the dead ROSCAs as those in which the members are not convivial reflects the opposite of the living social fabric of the live ROSCAs. The tanda muerta is dead because the social obligation based on confianza is also dead, and in its place is a material obligation for a service done by the organizer. Two modes of exchange—reciprocity and market exchange—are expressed, even though the medium of exchange, money, is the same in both.

Such differentiation is made apparent and certain for participants by the congruence between such meaning and the symmetry of the ROSCA itself. That is, a tanda viva is alive because it balances equitably all the effort, trust, relationships, emotion, sacrifice, investment, and hard-earned money that make up the individual contributions. The medium of exchange is the certain and tangible proof of all these elements that go into making up a symmetrical social universe. The tanda muerta, on the other hand, is unbalanced, asymmetrical, and, in the final analysis, indeterminate—out of the individual participant's control. Not only is the tanda controlled only by the organizer, but fellowship, which is the basis of determinacy, is also dead.

However, some informants differentiated between ahorros (savings) for the "live" types, and cundinas for those in which the organizer took the first turn. Others stated the opposite, saving the word cundina only for those in which there was no charge for participation, and ahorro for those that charged. Yet a number of informants expressed confianza, even in the semicommercialized types, when they said that it is "better for someone you know to make the money than it is for a bank, with which there is no confianza."

Uses of Funds: Saving to Save

"It is really a wonderful savings—really" (Es un ahorro bien bonito—de veras), the informant said in the middle of a marketplace in the state of Chiapas. She captured what many participants consider the primary use for the money accumulated in ROSCAs. Prior to 1983, among sixty-five informants in Mexico and the United States who responded to an open-ended question on the manner in which these funds were used, the modal response (24 percent) was that they were used as savings.

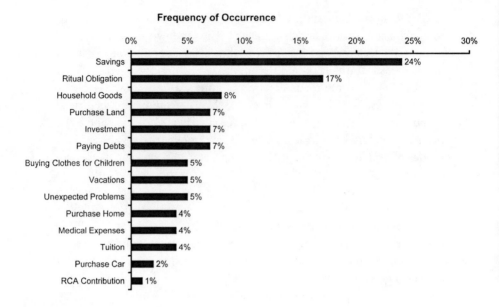

Figure 2.7 Uses of ROSCA funds. *Note*: 1983 sample only. *Source*: Prepared by the author.

The post-1983 data reinforces this same trend, with more than 76 percent of sixty-five respondents stating that saving was the primary motive for participating. As previously mentioned, once they had saved enough to feel comfortable in banks or credit cooperatives, many people placed their funds in those institutions.

In the pre-1983 sample, the second most frequent use, 17 percent of the responses, was to fulfill ritual obligations connected with Christmas, marriage, baptism, birthdays, saints' days, and anniversaries. Spending funds on household goods was the third most frequent response, at 8 percent, whereas purchasing land, investing in income-producing activities, and paying debts each made up 7 percent of the responses. Buying clothes for children, using the money for vacations, and spending on unexpected problems each constituted 5 percent of the responses (fig. 2.7). However, from 1983 to 2008, 80 percent of the respondents (fifty-two) also indicated that they would use their savings to meet short-term future obligations, such as car payments and upcoming debts, such as taxes.

As Kurtz and Showman (1978) also stated, the single most important reason for participating in ROSCAs is to save money. It is important to note, however, that savings here are not simply determined by market relations. The quality of "forced" savings is important, since many of my informants found it difficult to save at banking institutions. Consistently throughout all of this research, this quality of being forced to save with few other options was repeated in all samples, and informants participated in as many as five ROSCAs a year. As further evidence will show, in many instances, a person is obligated to save as part of a multiple-stranded relation of friendship, occupation, and kinship. Saving anchors the individual securely within the networks of relationships of which he or she is a part, for it frees people to engage in social intercourse without the disruption that would result from having to ask for the "favor" of a loan to meet other obligations. Instead of affection turning to instrumentation (Wolf 1956), savings generated by ROSCAs allow the maintenance of social relations based on other sorts of obligations. Saving avoids having the multiplicity of relations turning into a singularity of interest.

Especially for those in tandas vivas, the saving of money takes place within a dense social context, as does the spending of money for ritual obligations. In this sense, one becomes not only obligated to give and to receive but also, equally important, obligated to save. Saving thus becomes a learning process, which expands when rewarded: a person learns to save money, while the obligation to save becomes a positive reinforcing construct that contributes to the well-being of the multiplicity of dense relations that make up a symmetrical social universe.

The use of these funds, it should be remembered, has class-specific dimensions. To recapitulate, savings and ritual obligations are important in working-class and economically marginal sectors, but other sectors use their money to escape the stresses of over-indebtedness. Within middle-class sectors, ROSCA participation is one of the chief methods used to maintain an expected standard of living. On the other hand, there are networks of professionals for whom the fund share is relatively unimportant and who spend it on whatever they please. Not only do the characteristics of the ROSCAs themselves vary in relation to class sectors, but so do the uses of the funds.

Modes of productive activity can also influence the use of ROSCA funds. In Los Angeles, for example, clothing workers who had worked at piece rates frequently used accumulated cundinas to open their own sweatshops. In Ciudad Netzahualcoyótl, petty merchants used tandas to invest in merchandise, which they sold at a substantial profit. Thus,

ROSCAs can also serve as steps in vertical mobility, especially among petty entrepreneurs. However, all ROSCAs are dependent on the continued establishment, reinforcement, and successful reproduction of confianza in actual operational behaviors of which ROSCAs are but one practice among many others in the transborder Southwest North American Region.

3
Social and Cultural Dimensions and Dynamics of Their Class Contexts

Contexts and Sectors

The seriousness with which rotating savings and credit associations (ROSCAs) are regarded among many social sectors can be simply illustrated by the following ledger of payments due immediate attention. The expense ledger belonged to an individual in Chapala, a lakeside town an hour's drive from Guadalajara (the translation is mine).

Pagos (payments)
1. Pago de deuda (debt payment)
2. Tanda—200 pesos
3. Uniformes de niños (children's uniforms)
4. Compra de mercancía (purchase of merchandise)
5. Pedro (Peter—no explanation)
6. Pago de muebles (furniture payment)
7. Mercancía (merchandise)
8. Bautizo (baptism)
9. Cooperativa (cooperative)
10. Personal (personal)

There, second on his list of debts, stands this individual's ROSCA obligation. There is no need to speculate as to whether the ranking reflects the actual importance of each obligation or whether money was actually dispensed to meet these obligations. It is enough to note that for this individual the ROSCA obligation came to mind right after his debt payment and before his children's uniforms.

The popularity of the ROSCA can be appreciated by observing the myriad contexts and social sectors in which it appears. Although reference to class sectors has been made in previous sections of this work, and a variety of different types of operations have been discussed, the following analysis lists in detail most of the contexts and sectors in which ROSCAs have been found, both in this research and in that reported by others. Those already discussed will be dealt with in less detail in this section. I also categorize ROSCAs according to the contexts in which they were found, identify the class sector to which they probably belong, and discuss the importance of the social and cultural permutations that appear for each category and class sector.

However, since the original study and the very large migration of Mexican migrants to the United States, ROSCAs have also spread to almost all parts of the United States where Mexican-origin populations, as well as other Latin American–origin populations such as Salvadorans, Guatemalans, and Hondurans, live.

All the studies conducted found ROSCAs in all class sectors in Mexico except in the highest echelons of private and public executive domains, such as industrialists and members of the international academic elite. Members of their familial networks probably do participate in ROSCAs, similar to the Lomas de Chapultepec one in Mexico City organized by women (see chap. 2). One instance also exists in which relatively wealthy young men were caught engaged in what may be termed a "prostitution" *tanda* in Mexico City, but that is not normative nor does it add to this discussion.[1]

Whereas ROSCAs touch most class sectors and occupational niches in Mexico, those in the southwestern United States basically were found only in working-class and economically marginal sectors in the research done up to 1983. In the more recent research, they were uncovered in the middle class, especially proximate to the border. One was reported to exist among professionals, including the corporate officers of a Los Angeles–based southwestern food producer. I have been unable to verify its existence. On the other hand, there is no doubt whatsoever that middle-class professionals—teachers, students, middle-level administrators, bureaucrats, and other salaried employees in the middle strata of the U.S. economy—do organize, administer, and participate in ROSCAs in the United States. Some of these are specifically transborder, for example, those in San Luis Río Colorado, Sonora, and Yuma, Arizona (table 3.1), and the case of a Washington State resident who participates in her sister's *cundina* in Mazatlán, Sinaloa.

I found three categories of ROSCAs: residential ROSCAs of all class sectors, occupational ROSCAs, and, for lack of a better term, "familial" ROSCAs. The last term refers to ROSCAs made up of people who are primarily related to each other by kinship or friendship rather than by residence or occupation. None of the three categories, however, should

Table 3.1.   Cundina: Transborder Middle-Class
Informal ROSCA, San Luis Río Colorado, Sonora,
and Yuma, Arizona, 2005

Rotation Cycle

August 12, 2005	Liz Villalobos
August 26, 2005	Zaira and Mariana
September 9, 2005	José Hernández
September 23, 2005	Isabel and Gracie
October 7, 2005	Nadia Santos
October 21, 2005	Rosa Segura
November 4, 2005	Alexis González
November 18, 2005	Kathy López
December 2, 2005	Silvia Wong
December 16, 2005	Shoko Carlos

Members and Contribution

Liz Villalobos $100
Nadia Santos $100
José Hernández $100
Rosa Segura $100
Alexis González $100
Kathy López $100
Silvia Wong $100
Shoko Carlos $100
Zaira González $50
Mariana Martínez $50
Isabel Montez $50
Griselda Gómez $50

be thought of as exclusive. The three categories should be thought of as analytical constructs, because membership is relatively fluid, and residential, occupational, and familial ROSCAs each include aspects of the others. Moreover, fewer residential ROSCAs operate in the United States, which in part is explained by two factors: (1) the high urban mobility of Mexican-origin populations, and (2) a high percentage of renters within the recently arrived Mexican-origin population. Neither of these two factors select for the types of long-term density established in Mexico among neighbors even in highly urban contexts like Mexico City, Tijuana, or Ciudad Juárez. Less mobile socially but highly urban, these populations have physical home-to-work-and-return mobility, but for the most part, they purchase homes rather than rent, and they "stick" close to home, relying on neighbors and kin to meet the heavy demands of low wages and high costs in Mexican cities. On the other hand, while there are many established Mexican-origin communities in the United States, participants in tandas or cundinas are usually first-generation or generation-and-a-half residents.

As will be seen, another important factor helps explain why ROSCAs gravitate toward being established in small and large businesses and in public institutions. In contrast to highly mobile situations, a workplace is a space of greater intimacy where dense relations are created. The workplace replaces rapidly changing places and spaces, and people at work occupy these domains for large portions of their waking hours. In these domains, both men and women eventually generate relationships based on ties other than the work connection. Given the penchant for Mexican-origin populations to use the workplace as "the first step to incorporate" other relatives, especially brothers and sisters, into the labor force, it is highly probable that the workplace substitutes for the residence. Especially in urban places like Phoenix, Los Angeles, Dallas, Chicago, and New York, the likelihood of relatives living nearby is less probable, although not rare. For those highly mobile contexts in which relatives do not live close by, then the workplace becomes the most logical place for ROSCAs to operate.

Residential

Residential ROSCAs were found in Mexico in all of the sites studied. In Monterrey, for example, three residential ROSCAs represented three class sectors: one was located in an economically marginal neighborhood occupied by squatters (*paracaidistas*, literally "parachutists"), another in a large working-class area of blue- and white-collar workers, and the third in a middle-class residential area of largely professional or highly skilled industrial and government technicians. In each class sector, for the most part, women controlled the ROSCAs and were both organizers and participants. In the squatter area, for example, contributions to the tandas were siphoned from spouses' allowances for household expenses. In most squatter settlements, the usual fund share is between 400 and 500 pesos, with a contribution of 20–50 pesos weekly, depending on the number of shares in the tanda. However, tandas do exist with contributions of

10 pesos and fund shares of 20 pesos. From a woman's monthly allowance of 200 pesos, 10–25 pesos will be saved weekly for ROSCA contributions. For the most part, in Monterrey, these tandas involved relatively small contributions and fund shares. Members were people who were well known by all the residents or recommended by someone of mutual trust within the older links of the ROSCA networks.

In the working-class district, higher contributions and fund shares reflected the higher incomes. From their husbands' allowances, these women generally saved a proportionally larger amount than the economically marginal women, but they still relied on the same cultural construct of *confianza* as the stabilizing glue for the ROSCA. The middle-class residential ROSCAs were part of the women's club activities, coterminous with playing canasta, or some other card game, and the exchange of gifts. With approximately forty women in each club contributing 1,000 pesos monthly, the residential middle-class ROSCAs in Monterrey rotated substantial amounts.

This notion of a club, which was quite common in middle-class neighborhoods, was extended to upper-class sectors. I have already mentioned the women in Lomas de Chapultepec who combined gift giving with contributing large amounts for "sumptuous consumption." These women generally referred to their activities in terms of a residential club, and they even elected officers who presided over various activities. Each woman receives an allowance from her husband of 20,000 pesos monthly, so in the eyes of these women, the Monterrey women's tandas, with their 1,000-peso contributions, deal in paltry sums. In addition, in Tapachula and Tijuana, this same club phenomenon was exhibited in combination with recreational, gift giving, and, very importantly, commensal activities.

This middle- and upper-class phenomenon of integrating the ROSCA into clubs and combining it with elaborate commensal activities and with other recreational activities is in clear contrast to the pattern seen in ROSCAs in economically marginal and working-class sectors. The latter, for the most part, were ten-person ROSCAs composed of neighbors who were also friends and in many cases also kinswomen. These women did not have the time, the resources, or the inclination to meet regularly as part of their ordinary activities. The recreational aspect was taken care of for these women individually if the organizer delivered the fund share personally and on the one occasion when all the women got together and selected the numbers of the tandas in a drawing. For these women, recreational activities were organized along "natural systems"

Table 3.2   Registration Card

Name (*nombre*)	Number (*número*)	Amount and Payments (*cantidad y pagos*)				Date (*fecha*)
Sra. Concha						
	1.	120 √	120 √	120 √	120 √	March 6 (6 de marzo)
	2.	120 √	120 √	120 √	120 √	April 2 (2 de abril)
	3.	120 √	120 √	120 √	120 √	May 2 (2 de mayo)
	4.	120 √	120 √	120 √	120 √	June 8 (8 de junio)
	5.	120 √	120 √	120 √	120 √	July 9 (9 de julio)
Almendra López	6.	120 √	120 √	120 √	120 √	August 9 (10 de agosto)
Sra. Concha	7.	120	120	120	120	September 10 (10 de septiembre)
	8.	120 √	120 √	120 √	120 √	October 6 (6 de octubre)
	9.	120 √	120 √	120 √	120 √	November 6 (6 de noviembre)
	10.	120 √	120 √	120 √	120 √	December 7 (7 de diciembre)

Source: Vélez-Ibáñez 1983.

of relationships based on residence and kinship. For the middle- and upper-class women, recreational activities consisted of cultural events deliberately organized, usually on the basis of residence alone.

Regardless of whether a residential ROSCA was of the club or the natural-system type, in at least 50 percent of the cases, the organizer took the free first turn, or a fee. However, this was not done in Lomas de Chapultepec or in the upper-middle-class "clubs" in Tijuana, where taking a fee would be considered déclassé. Among working-class residents of Tijuana, on the other hand, an organizer who charged fees presented each member with a registration card on which appeared the information shown in table 3.2.

The registration card shows that this residential ROSCA had ten numbers, and Sra. Concha, whose name appears in the upper-left-hand corner, was number 7. Under the first column appear the numbers 1–10 with four check marks to the right of each number except 7. The check marks refer to the four payments made for that particular number. Next to number 6 would appear the signature of the organizer if the fund share was given. That signature indicates that the organizer gave the fund share to the member whose countersignature appears on the next line in the same column. The last column refers to the date on which the final payment was made for that number. The column under *cantidad y pagos* (amount and payments) refers to the four installments made weekly for the monthly contribution of 480 pesos. In this case, the fee for the organizer was included in each installment. Thus, for each 120-peso installment, 20 pesos went to the organizer, so that he or she received 80 pesos monthly from each person. Since the person receiving the turn does not pay for that month, the organizer receives 720 pesos per month from the nine other participants. The organizer will have earned at the end of the ROSCA a total of 7,200 pesos (720 × 10 turns), and each member will have paid 4,320 pesos and received 3,600 pesos.

Under the fee or zero-turn residential ROSCA, participants have a net loss. Nevertheless, this form of savings is still preferred by many working-class and economically marginal women, and it is not because they lack "economic" motivation or insight. For psychological reasons, these women prefer to save what they can in a ROSCA rather than earn interest from a commercial institution. They prefer to "maximize" the certainty of what they perceive to be the organizer's personal interest rather than face the uncertainty of a banking institution's impersonal interest.

In residential ROSCAs where the organizer receives no direct economic advantage, two other sorts of advantages exist. The first occurs in non-fee ROSCAs organized by petty merchants who live in the area in which they sell. In economically marginal and working-class sectors, these organizers recruit potential members from women who live in their commercial territories. In such cases, an organizer's visit could be for the purpose of collecting the contributions of the ROSCA member, delivering the fund share, or collecting money owed for merchandise. Yet because these women are under a double obligation—for the ROSCA, based on reciprocity, and for the purchased merchandise, based on the market-exchange relationship—they do not hide from the salesperson-organizer. The second advantage accrues to store owners whose customers belong to store ROSCAs. The store owner, as organizer, does not charge a fee or take the zero number, but most customers who are

ROSCA members also have a charge account with the store. This was especially true of pharmacies.

In other residential ROSCAs, these advantages did not come into play. Instead, the ROSCAs with few kinship members or occupational cohorts were organized around some other element, such as a neighborhood political-party center; a prestigious member of the residential sector, such as an older woman known for providing sound advice; or a local political leader with intense social networks made up of women.

Among some middle-class and professional sectors, different advantages accrued to the organizer. In a border region, one woman who organized separate associations among women and men from the same social milieu did not charge the women who belonged to her ROSCAs and clubs. She was a member of an intimate social network of women who participated in the same recreational and commensal activities, who visited each other's homes, and whose children attended the same private schools. Their husbands were generally in the same voluntary associations and professional sectors, if not occupations, and participated in the same set of community political activities. In the ROSCAs she organized among the husbands, she took the zero turn. Because she participated and held leadership positions in the same community political activities and voluntary associations as the husbands, she was considered to be an insider in the men's organizational activities, but not part of the old-boy networks. She was enough of an insider to establish market relations with the men and charge a fee for her ROSCA services, but not enough of one to establish reciprocal obligations and relationships. On the other hand, the confianza she enjoyed with the wives was established within the intimacy required of wives and women. She parlayed the advantages of both insider and outsider to make a substantial amount of money.

In both fee and non-fee ROSCAs with a substantial membership, rotation of commensal activities and fund shares usually occurred at each turn, except in the most economically marginal sectors. In ROSCAs with more than twenty women members, fund shares were likely to be allotted by a drawing. Each drawing would be attended by the women who had not yet received their turns. Thus, for example, during at least the first ten weeks of a weekly, thirty-five-person ROSCA, about half of the women who had not yet received their shares would show up for a drawing for the following week's share at the home of the person whose turn had been selected the previous week. By the eighteenth week, the number present at the drawings would be considerably reduced. By the thirtieth week, it was not unusual for the last five to have their names drawn at one time and have their fund share distributed together in a preselected home. At each drawing, the hostess was expected to provide some light refreshments, perhaps soft drinks and cake, so that such occasions generated information exchanges. Importantly, regardless of whether or not the organizer charges a fee, these ROSCA events generate generalized reciprocal exchange.

In the Southwest North American Region where Mexican-origin populations reside, the only significant difference in residential ROSCAs is their absence in upper-middle-class residential areas. There are, however, few upper-middle-class areas in the United States predominantly inhabited by Mexicans. Except in working-class or economically marginal Mexican barrios (neighborhoods)—such as those in East Los Angeles; portions of San Pedro, Monterey Park, and Wilmington; and in some parts of Phoenix and Dallas—residential ROSCAs are not as common as in Mexico. In most of those analyzed, the organizer had established long-standing confianza relationships with the members through occupation, kinship, or residence. These were not purely residential ROSCAs, in fact, and unlike most ROSCAs in Mexico, both men and women participated, but the women tended to predominate.

Even with confianza, some residential fixity, and kinship affiliation, many of these ROSCAs, unlike most of those in Mexico, collected their weekly contributions and delivered the fund share at the same time. The residential mobility among wage earners makes residential fixity difficult to maintain for extended periods, especially in the Los Angeles area. The shift to zero-turn or free-first-turn ROSCAs is congruent with this mobility, and one may speculate that commercialized practices appeared originally because organizers cannot establish confianza in a mobile population, rather than because they have "learned" profit motives. The latter is not excluded from consideration, but an organizer's switch from a non-fee to a fee ROSCA may have its genesis in disrupted social relations rather than in economic motives. This may also be the case in Mexico, especially in areas experiencing rapid population shifts, such as border cities and cities in central Mexico.

For example, this mobility was visible in the origins of the members of one originally noncommercialized residential cundina in Hollywood. The organizer was from the Mexican state of Sinaloa, whereas her husband, who also participated in the ROSCA, was from the state of Durango. Two other male members were brothers-in-law from the city of Guadalajara. One woman came from Guatemala, two sisters had just arrived from Mazatlán in Sinaloa, and another woman was from the state of Michoacán. Importantly, all rented apartments or modest homes, remaining in them for an average of 2.3 years. All had been in the United States for 10 to 20 years, including visits to Mexico of less than 1 year's duration. For these individuals, inflationary rent increases, wage-sector changes, and voluntary and involuntary returns to their country of origin had caused frequent residential shifts. For a ROSCA organizer, those conditions and pressures create uncertainty and force them to take out the "insurance" of a free first turn or zero turn.

The residential diversity apparent in the informal ROSCA can be represented by categorizing residential areas according to the approximate occupational level of their inhabitants. "High-white-collar" includes professional occupations and proprietors; "low-white-collar," semiprofessional and service-oriented occupations and small business proprietors; "high-blue-collar," skilled industrial and crafts jobs; "low-blue-collar," semi-skilled and unskilled occupations; and "other," including students, welfare recipients, retirees, prisoners, and unemployed workers. Table 3.3 shows the social diversity of residential areas in 130 informal ROSCAs in Mexico and the United States (intermediate and formal ones are excluded). Also included are areas reported by Cope and Kurtz (1980), Kurtz (1973), Kurtz and Showman (1978), Lewis (1959, 1961, 1968), and Lomnitz (1977), as well as a few uncovered in my research between 1984 and 2008.

The various residential areas and class sectors are not representative in a statistical sense of these sectors' distribution across the 130 informal ROSCAs studied. However, the sectors and areas in which the associations are found are representative of the social structure of Mexico and of the ethnic and social structure of Mexican-origin populations living in the Southwest North American Region. Importantly, however, both in Mexico and the United States, ROSCAs in residential areas have declined since 1983, whereas those in workplaces have increased.

In Mexico, all social sectors are represented (table 3.3), but further empirical study is needed to verify whether rotating associations are present in high-white-collar residential areas in Ciudad Juárez, Chihuahua, Culiacán, Guanajuato, Puebla, and Oaxaca. It is unlikely that any high-white-collar residential ROSCAs will be found in the southwestern United States since, as I have pointed out, most Mexicans in high-white-collar occupations are dispersed in non-ethnic residential areas.

Table 3.3. Social Diversity by Occupational Structure in Informal ROSCAs (N = 130)

Area	City (State)	Occupational Structure				
		HWC	LWC	HBC	LBC	Other
Northern and Northwestern Mexico	Monterrey (Nuevo León)	+	+	+	+	+
	Ensenada, Mexicali, and Tijuana,[1] (Baja California)	+	+	+	+	+
	Chihuahua and Ciudad Juárez (Chihuahua)	–	+	+	+	+
	Colima (Colima)	+	+	+	+	+
	Concordia and Mazatlán (Sinaloa)	–	+	+	+	+
	Culiacán and Esquinapa (Sinaloa)	+	+	+	+	+
	El Cerro (Sinaloa)	–	–	–	+	+
	Nogales and San Luis Río Colorado (Sonora)	+	+	+	+	+
Central Mexico	Ciudad Netzahualcoyótl and Mexico City,[2] Federal District (Mexico)	+	+	+	+	+
	Guanajuato (Guanajuato)	–	+	+	+	+
	Hidalgo	–	+	+	+	+
	Puebla,[3] San Felipe, and San Jerónimo Caleras (Puebla)	–	+	+	+	+
	Zacatecas (Zacatecas)	–	+	+	+	+
South-Central Mexico	Guerrero (Guerrero)	+	+	+	+	+
	Chapala, Guadalajara, and Tonalá (Jalisco)	+	+	+	+	+
Southern Mexico (Gulf of Mexico Side)	Mérida (Yucatán)	+	+	+	+	+
	Poza Rica, Papantla, and Xalapa (Veracruz)	+	+	+	+	+
Southern Mexico (Guatemala Side)	San Cristóbal de las Casas, Tapachula, and Tuxtla Gutiérrez (Chiapas)	+	+	+	+	+
	Oaxaca (Oaxaca)	–	+	+	+	+

(Continued)

Table 3.3. (*Continued*)

Area	City (State)	Occupational Structure				
		HWC	LWC	HBC	LBC	Other
Southwestern United States	Casa Grande, Coolidge, Gilbert, Mesa, Nogales, Phoenix, Tucson, San Luis, Yuma (Arizona)	–	+	+	+	+
	Las Vegas (Nevada)	–	+	+	+	+
	Hatch, El Milagro, Las Cruces, Mesilla, Placitas, Rincon, Rodey, Salem, and 27 other colonias[4] (New Mexico)	–	+	+	+	+
	El Paso, and 1,500 colonias[5] (Texas)	–	+	+	+	+
	Chula Vista, National City, San Diego, and San Ysidro (California)	–	+	+	+	+
	Los Angeles[6] (California)	+	+	+	+	+
	Beverly Hills, Hollywood, San Pedro, and Wilmington, (California)	–	+	+	+	+
	Unincorporated East Los Angeles (California)	–	+	+	+	+
Midwest	Illinois, Indiana, Michigan	–	–	+	+	+
South and East	Florida, Mississippi, and North and South Carolina New Jersey and New York	–	–	+	+	+

Source: Vélez-Ibáñez 1982 and post-1980 fieldwork.

Note: HWC = high-white-collar occupation; LWC = low-white-collar occupation; HBC = high-blue-collar occupation; LBC = low-blue-collar occupation; Other = students, welfare recipients, retired persons, prisoners, and unemployed workers.

[1] Reported by Kurtz (1973) and verified by this research.

[2] Reported by Lewis (1959, 1961, 1968) and Lomnitz (1977) and verified by this research.

[3] Reported by Kurtz and Showman (1978) and Cope and Kurtz (1980).

[4] Galan 2000a.

[5] Vélez-Ibáñez 2004b.

[6] Reported by Kurtz (1973) and verified by this research.

Occupational

Probably the best source of contextual data in both Mexico, and especially in the southwestern United States, is occupational sectors. The usual occupational ROSCAs are of two types: those in which the employees of a firm are both participants and organizers, and those composed of employees but organized by nonemployees. The former are the least commercial of the informal ROSCAs after the familial ROSCAs.

Mexican film theater chains in Los Angeles have both types of occupational ROSCAs. An in-depth consideration lets us appreciate both their differences and their similarities and provides insights into the structural contexts in which membership in these associations occurs.

Within employee-organized ROSCAs in Mexican film theater chains in Los Angeles, two subtypes appear that are also found in other businesses: those in which the manager is the organizer, and those in which employees who are at the same level do the organizing. In the former, the ROSCA participants may ask the manager to be an impartial money keeper using the local theater's accounting system, or the manager may initiate a ROSCA in order to make a profit from a free first turn or zero turn. In an employee-initiated ROSCA, where the manager does not participate and is only the money keeper, it tends to shift to a more intermediate sort of association. In either case, the manager usually hides the ROSCA from the chain's general management. Since the organizer is always a member of the same cultural group as the participants, ROSCAs in theaters having non-Hispanic managers do not shift to intermediate ROSCAs because only the employees are involved in organizing and running the association.[2] Those managers who have been money keepers or accountants tend to be perceived as organizers in later ROSCAs, and in time, the practice becomes integrated into the normal operating activities of the theater. Such a process, however, can be interrupted if a new manager is hired.

A ROSCA initiated by a manager begins with intermediate practices involving bookkeeping. More than half of a single theater's employees are likely to participate. In employee-initiated ROSCAs, fewer employees within any one theater participate, but the membership includes employees from other theaters.

In ROSCAs in which same-level employees are organizers and participants, the cashiers, all of whom are women, organize the associations, rather than the ticket takers, candy and refreshment vendors, ushers, or janitorial employees.[3] The reason may be the cashier's obvious facility with numbers, which provides her with some legitimacy. These women have ready access to informational networks encompassing all the theaters within the various chains. Since they are literally out front, they are highly visible as representatives of the particular theater, and therefore, they have public reputations of trust. Their reputations are even nurtured through the telephone. In every cashier's booth is a telephone that she uses to answer questions about performance schedules and the like. The cashiers, however, also use the telephone to organize employee-directed ROSCAs and keep each other informed about who is ill on the days contributions are collected, whose turn has been reached, who has informed them of late payments, and who is likely to leave his or her job. This is extremely important, since those who leave are less likely to contribute to the fund.

While the ROSCAs indigenous to the theaters have a reciprocal quality that is reflected in the seriousness with which employees invest money, energy, and trust in the association, the same cannot be said of the more commercialized ROSCAs organized by outsiders. In these, more conflict over payments and local-level political competition exist. Both organizers and participants agreed that "everyone faithfully receives the fund share but is very hesitant to pay the contribution." On the other hand, both also agreed that "like all Mexicans, we are honorable." This aspect of receiving and then hesitating to fulfill an obligation, but carrying out that obligation because of honor, marks the basic relationship between theater employees and outside organizers. This is because these organizers are not part of the natural systems of close interpersonal networks maintained by the theater employees. The employees are obliged to interact socially with the outside organizer, as if they were members of a noncommercialized employee ROSCA. Yet participants resent the instrumental interest of the organizer, and ambivalent relationships between them ensue.

This ambivalence is expressed, for example, when the *cundinero* (someone who collects money commercially) seeks out the employees to get their contributions. Collections are made during rest and eating periods, and for the most part, participants greet the cundinero with derisive remarks and hooting. As the organizer approaches a group of employees, it is not uncommon to hear barely audible remarks like "Tiene cara de ladrón" (He has the face of a thief) or "No más quiere para pagar sus borracheras" (He only wants money for his drunken binges). Worse, however, among Mexican men is the overheard remark, "No más quiere para su mujer y así nos obliga" (He only wants money for his woman, and that is why he obligates us). The underlying meaning is that the organizer is supposedly under the control of a woman, and he indirectly obligates the members of the ROSCA to also be under her control because they contribute to her support through the organizer's ROSCA.

Other *flechazos* (barbs) said to the organizer's face upon his arrival included "Ya le cayó vidrio al agua" (Glass has fallen on still waters, or Still waters have turned to glass which breaks). Equally direct was the sentence "Ya tan bien que estábamos y ya veniste a fregar" (We were so comfortable, and now you have come to bug us). More direct, as he was sitting down with the employees, were personal labels such as *cabrón* (cuckold), *ratero* (racketeer), and *estafador* (cheater). Yet none of these overheard remarks, direct barbs, or personal labels could be uttered if in fact confianza had not been established. In working-class sectors, personal insult is not taken lightly, and both verbal and physical responses should be expected. Therefore, even though the organizer is considered an enemy, he is also a friend, and thus the joking expresses the inherent contradictions between the instrumentality and affectivity of these roles.

Problems, however, do arise with manager-controlled intermediate ROSCAs in some of the other business contexts. There have been reports that in some restaurant ROSCAs in which the owners are also the organizers, the owner procrastinates about turning over the employees' fund shares and threatens to dismiss anyone who voices complaints. In one chain of Mexican restaurants in central Los Angeles, the father and daughter owners consistently withhold pay from their employees for their cundinas and take the free first turn, but they then rotate the cundina share weeks late. They are able to do this because most of their employees are "undocumented workers" and have little legal recourse. In some cases where confianza is violated, employees quit.

Nevertheless, for the most part, cheating by organizers is rare. There was no cheating among the employee-organized cundinas in the theaters, in ceramic factories in West Los Angeles, and among garment workers in central Los Angeles, Chula Vista, and San Diego. In those contexts, the process of cultural and behavioral exclusion is quite marked, so that only those with proven confianza are invited to join. As is discussed in the next section, behavioral nuances are carefully noted, and people not meeting quite explicit standards are bluntly excluded from participation despite employment seniority and stable salaries.

In Mexico, a broader representation of occupational sectors was involved in the ROSCAs. In the professions, there were many ROSCAs among medical practitioners, especially in large clinics. Specific medical areas had their own status-specific ROSCAs. For example, in one medical clinic in Monterrey, there were four ROSCAs: the doctors had one of 20,000 pesos; the pharmacy employees had one of 15,000 pesos; the medical assistants had one of 5,000 pesos; and the records and administrative personnel had one of 1,500 pesos. Occasionally, one of the pharmacy employees might participate in the doctors' ROSCA, but he would deal only with the interns and not with the staff physicians. Nurses had their own ROSCA, but female nurses were able to participate in all the other ROSCAs, except those of staff doctors. It would seem that female nurses, simply because they are women, are exempted from the usual status restrictions.

The Mexican Social Security Institute (Instituto Mexicano del Seguro Social) and city, state, and federal agencies had well-developed ROSCAs in most administrative and non-administrative sectors. In the National Anthropology Museum in Mexico City, ROSCAs crosscut departmental divisions among working-class employees. Each department head (*maestro*) was in charge of a ROSCA in which employees from several departments participated. The museum is divided administratively into various sections, each responsible for maintaining artifacts of a particular material, such as plastics, leather, metal, wood, and cloth and thread. In addition, the clerical and administrative assistants participated in separate ROSCAs from those of the skilled technicians. At the time of my original research, no upper-level administrators or professional anthropological staff participated. Indeed, few of the professional staff were even aware of the existence of the ROSCAs operating in the museum.

In most private and public bureaucracies, one finds ROSCAs. They are well rooted among the administrative staff of PEMEX (Petróleos Mexicanos) in Veracruz, the librarians of Mérida, the maintenance crews of the transit departments and their administrative heads in Monterrey, the tourist departments of Tijuana, the middle administrative level of the Bank of Mexico in Mexico City, the police department of Tapachula, the officers and directors of the International Brotherhood of Voluntary Associations (a pseudonym) of Mexicali, and the maintenance workers at the University of Southern California and their cohorts at the National Autonomous University of Mexico (UNAM) in Mexico City.

Similarly, one ROSCA involving teachers and administrators in San Luis Río Colorado, Sonora, and Yuma, Arizona, folded after the organizer moved away. However, her sister restarted it at another school by sending out e-mails to original members and to her coworkers at the new school. She kept a list of members and collected $100 on each payday, with most participants giving her cash by the deadline of 3 p.m. so that she could deliver the entire amount to the corresponding party before they left at 4 p.m. Checks are necessarily more cumbersome, since she has to go to the bank to cash them before paying out the fund share. Some non-professionals had participated in the previous cundina, but this version was closed to them because it had been a "hassle" to collect from those particular individuals. Particularly noteworthy about this ROSCA is that non-Mexican-origin members participated, and, as one Mexican-origin participant said of a fellow teacher, "Era gringa simpática"—She is a pleasant American.

All the participants in this particular cundina agreed that the organizer took extraordinarily good care in maintaining records (see the list she developed, illustrated in table 3.1). On the list, she would highlight in yellow the name of the person whose turn it was, and as people paid her, she would highlight his/her name in a different color and put a check by his/her name. She then made ten copies, one for each participant, and noted any special requests, such as paying on another day or after work hours, and she would staple the note to the payer's sheet. When the cundina ended, she shredded the note.

Table 3.4 shows the occupations found within the 130 rotating savings and credit associations examined in this study. Because of the many ambiguities and difficulties involved in classifying occupations, the participants' actual occupations are listed next to the general occupational categories.

As can be seen, the occupations represented in this study cover a wider range than those previously mentioned in the literature. Cope and Kurtz (1980) reported that participants in the Puebla area were associated with industry, with the largest number in the category of workers. Cope and Kurtz's occupational classification differs from the one used here, but their data do not seem to show any high-white-collar participants. My sample is not technically a random one, so it is not possible to claim that my categories are representative in a statistical sense of the actual distribution of occupations among ROSCA members. What can be said with certainty, however, is that the occupations reported here do represent broad parts of the occupational structure of Mexican-origin populations in the transborder region and beyond.

Table 3.4.   Occupational Structure of Participants in ROSCAs
(N = 130)

Category	Occupation
High-white-collar Professionals Proprietors	Executive managers, lawyers, physicians, businesspeople, architects, academics, bankers, upper-level bureaucrats, researchers, accountants, economists, psychiatrists

Low-white-collar
Semiprofessional and
  service-oriented
  occupations
Small business
  proprietors
	Tellers, typists, stenographers, office workers, librarians, teachers, bartenders, traveling salespeople, pharmacists, bookkeepers, cashiers, clerks, theater employees, produce-market proprietors, nurses, social workers, tourist guides, food vendors, reporters, police officers

High-blue-collar Skilled (industrial and crafts)	Oil-field workers, technicians, electricians, welders, telephone employees, ceramicists, factory workers, projectionists, museum craftsmen, fishermen
Low-blue-collar Semiskilled Unskilled	Waiters and waitresses, busboys, assemblers, seamstresses, pottery shapers, janitors, maintenance workers, laborers, day laborers, street hawkers, domestics, guards, night watchmen, gardeners, taxi drivers
Other	Students, welfare recipients, retirees, prisoners, unemployed workers

Familial

Familial ROSCAs occur within economically marginal, working-class, and petty-bourgeois sectors. Kinship relationships are the embedded networks used as the foundation for these ROSCAs. In addition, intimate friends of the family who have no recognized familial ties other than intimacy also participate. The relationships between participants are dense and multiple and generate reciprocity without the intervening market relations that mark the more commercialized ROSCAs. However, the only caveat is that although ROSCAs were embedded in familial networks in the United States, many times these were also embedded in family members' workplaces. Thus, a kind of double-density insurance manifested—by both kinship and institutional context.

By density, I mean "the extent to which links which could possibly exist among persons do in fact exist" (Mitchell 1969, 18). These links are potentially available to stimulate some kind of exchange, which can involve emotions, resources, support, and also disapproval. These potential exchanges are, in turn, closely related to the social relations that have been established in recreational, residential, employment, kinship, religious, political, and any other human domains. When the same people are engaged in a number of the same domains, it generates multiple (multiplex) relations among them. For example, in the tanda illustrated in figures 3.1–3.6, the organizer's best friend was an important member of the tanda. He and the organizer had the same surname, were from the same town, engaged in the same business, lived in the same area, and had participated in the same political activities. They frequented the same bars and dance halls, visited each other's homes, and celebrated holidays together. Both returned to their hometown to celebrate the fiestas for that locality's patron saint and maintained and replicated equivalent sorts of relationships there. At the fiestas, they sold merchandise that they had purchased jointly to increase their volume discount.

Figure 3.1 illustrates these multiple relations between the organizer, Armando López, and his intimate friend, Felipe López (both names are pseudonyms). It must be pointed out that the relations represented

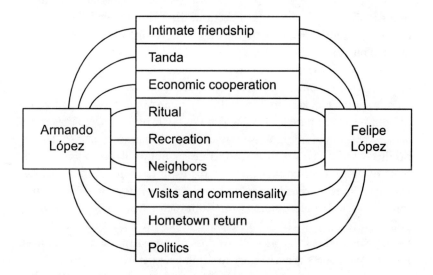

Figure 3.1 Armando—Felipe. *Source*: Vélez-Ibáñez 1980.

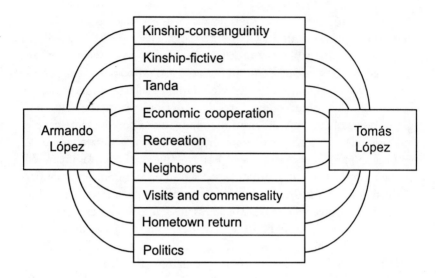

Figure 3.2 Armando—Tomás. *Source*: Prepared by the author.

are partial and do not include those between Felipe and the rest of the tanda membership or those among the other members. This figure, illustrating the density and multiplicity of relationships, is only an example of the ego-centered networks of the organizer with those of his tanda network. In a later section, the entire network of another tanda is presented, showing in detail the interesting balance existing in familial tandas.

Figure 3.2 illustrates the relations between Armando and his younger brother, Tomás López, a third member of the tanda. Tomás has a small tailor's shop a block from Armando's home. Armando is the godfather of Tomás's eldest female child, which ties the brothers together as *compadres* (co-godparents), as well as making Armando *compadre* to his brother's wife. The brothers cooperate economically. Armando buys bolts of cloth at discounts through his business, and Tomás and his wife make inexpensive dresses for Armando to sell door-to-door to customers in Ciudad Netzahualcoyótl. Both men participated in the same political protests, and both participated in the ritual celebration of their hometown's saint's day as well. Almost nightly, Armando and Tomás meet in Armando's grocery store to drink beer before going home.

The fourth tanda member is Guadalupe Luna, Tomás's mother-in-law. She lives in a different neighborhood of the same city, but engages

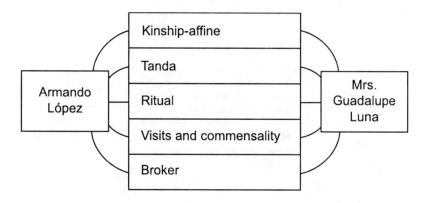

Figure 3.3 Armando—Mrs. Luna. *Source*: Prepared by the author.

in the same ritual and commensal activities as Armando does for such important events as birthdays, saints' days, national holidays, and religious observances. She also visits Armando's household with some frequency. The relationship is complicated by Tomás's heavy drinking. He overspends his limited income and borrows money from Mrs. Luna for household expenses. In turn, Mrs. Luna must call upon Armando to serve as a domestic broker between Tomás and her daughter when quarrels erupt over his drinking, and to collect money when Tomás does not pay back what he owes her. Armando, on occasion, has made Mrs. Luna's contribution to the tanda to pay debts incurred by his brother. On other occasions, out of his own pocket, Armando has paid Mrs. Luna money owed her by Tomás. Figure 3.3 shows the levels of multiplicity in this relationship within the tanda.

Graciela López, Armando and Tomás's oldest sister, is the fifth member of the tanda. She resides in Armando's household, keeps house for him, assists in his business, participates in the same ritual and commensal activities as he does, and goes with him to their hometown. Consequently, the relations between the brother and sister are quite dense. Significantly, Armando is Graciela's main source of support and the authority figure for her and her ten-year-old son, and all three reside in a kind of primary group replication in the household (fig. 3.4).

The sixth and final member of the tanda is Mrs. María Cicote, the next-door neighbor and a relative by marriage, since her son is wed to Armando's younger sister, Virginia. Mrs. Cicote also has a small sewing business and purchases cloth from Armando, and he, in turn, sells the

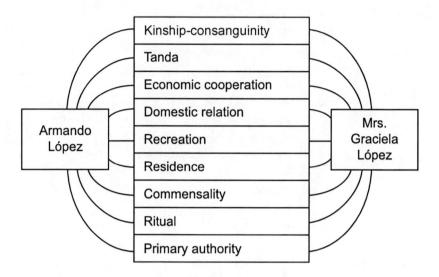

Figure 3.4 Armando—Graciela. *Source*: Prepared by the author.

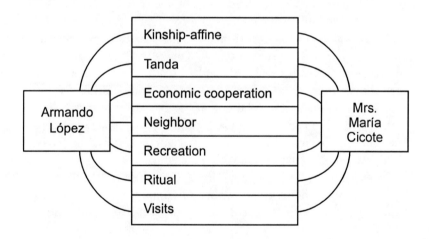

Figure 3.5 Armando—Mrs. Cicote. *Source*: Prepared by the author.

clothing she makes on consignment. There is no competition between Tomás and Mrs. Cicote since the articles they sew are intended for entirely different functions. Mrs. Cicote and Armando share ritual and some commensal and recreational activities, and they visit daily to talk over business or family matters (fig. 3.5).

As the diagrams illustrate, the organizer has built his tanda operation on a variety of intimate familial relations. The diagrams do not, however, indicate the quality of those relationships, only the potential density and multiplicity of ties. Boissevain (1974) and Kapferer (1969) have tried to measure "transactional content," or the quality of multiple relations, by measuring the elements exchanged in each relation. Although these attempts are laudatory and meaningful in social arenas beyond primary group activities, within the intimate networks described here that sort of analysis is not a fruitful exercise.

The values a culture places on nonmaterial and material exchange are relative and vary with the particular cultural system. Although it is certainly methodologically possible to ascertain some hierarchy of value or values, it would be very difficult to compare the before-and-after states when individuals' contexts and fortunes are shifting. For Mexicans, *compadrazgo* (co-godparenthood) is a highly valued personal relationship, especially between *cuates* (pals) like Armando and Felipe. But the relationship between brother and sister is also extremely intimate. Within such intimate familial networks of confianza, the qualitative dimensions of exchange must be described culturally, not in terms of a numerically operationalized standard.

To understand the cultural dimension, it is necessary to rely on the anthropologist's observational material and the best scaling techniques of cultural extraction available. Assuming this statement is correct, Armando's tanda can be understood best as one embedded in the most intimate of culturally valued networks, and it is contextually expressed by the constant reliance on reciprocal exchanges of symbols, artifacts, affect, assistance, favors, intimacies, commensality, ritual cooperation, and even money. The quality of these relations does not stem from the number of exchanges, but rather from the reciprocal exchange of culturally valued material and nonmaterial artifacts. It is probable that in such intimate contexts more will be exchanged, but quantity does not affect the quality of the exchange. More may be exchanged, but if what is exchanged is not culturally valued and swapped in a reciprocal mode, then the quality and density of the multiple relations will be questionable.

Each context and sector analyzed here—residence, occupation, and family—has distributed within it various culturally constituted values that vary according to the quality of the relationships. However, the greater the congruence between the reciprocal exchange mode and those relationships, the more likely the occurrence of intensity and intimacy.

Their presence can only be determined through observation and intimate knowledge of the cultural system of each context.

Underlying all the contexts discussed here is the cultural quality of fixity. Each context is culturally constituted, fixing persons in categories and relationships, which are used as physical, emotional, and social references. Yet each context, be it residential, occupational, or familial, is mutable and cannot supply permanent references or the means to fix persons permanently. Such is the paradox that unfolds from our data, but in this paradox lies the key to understanding the importance of the practice of the rotating savings and credit association.

Risks and Safeguards

In his excellent discussion of the ethnic rotating credit associations in the United States,[4] Light (1972, 59) has stated that risk is an innate property of lending and that risks exist even for those engaged in informally based ROSCAs like the familial ones described here. Light notes, however, that for members of Japanese and Chinese ROSCAs in the United States, risk is appreciably reduced because these ROSCAs are embedded in ascriptively defined regional and corporate kinship groups. Nonmembers of the ROSCAs who were corporately related were "morally and 'legally' obligated to make good the debts of a member. Should a member [of a ROSCA] default, die, or prove unable to repay his debts, his kin were expected to make good the obligation. Hence, the credit of every participant in the rotating credit association was guaranteed by his family" (59–60). Default, fraud, or theft was the exception. This was also true in Chinese *hui* in New Guinea (Wu 1974, 573).

On the other hand, Kurtz (1973, 53) has reported frequent cases of default in cundinas in San Ysidro, and police in Tijuana have reported cases of organizers absconding with the fund share. In fact, Cope and Kurtz (1980) have developed the thesis that organizers and participants in ROSCAs take special care to include only certain trusted people in tandas because of the "concern with reducing the risk of default to a more acceptable level" (228). They do not, however, present any data on potential or actual default. Kurtz and Showman (1978) have stated that default was the most common problem in the tanda, but they do not present its frequency of occurrence. Although they report that the risk of default was not a serious consideration among tanda members, they also state that nonparticipants seemed to believe that tandas were poor investments because of the risks involved (69).

On the other hand, for most of the 130 ROSCAs studied (including those studied prior to 1983 and those studied from then through 2008), informants frequently raised the issue of risk, although few had actually suffered from someone defaulting or the organizer absconding with the fund. However, with the increased transborder and urban mobility since 1983, risk increases as a probabilistic dynamic. In the pre-1983 research, I found four people who had experienced default. In the post-1983 research, I found three who had experienced default, and two others in the United States recounted that the organizer had left with the pool of money. One recounted the story of how his sister-in-law, whom he called a *mujer sin moral* (a woman without morals), collected the first turn of $5,000 from ten others and then fled back to Guadalajara. He also stated that she would cheat anyone with whom she came into contact. In one instance, a woman asked the sister-in-law to sell furniture for her, and the cheat kept the money from the sale. He was profoundly suspicious of her, and she was not allowed in his home, especially after she tried to borrow money to set up a business selling furniture. His own relationship with his brother suffered as a consequence, and they only saw each other in the local bar or at soccer games.

However, on occasion, individuals defaulted on their payments, but for the most part, they would inform the organizer, sell their numbers to someone else, or find a replacement willing to make the contribution for them. Although two participants knew of cases in which an organizer founded a ROSCA, took the first number, and fled, there are few verified instances of default without restitution and fewer cases of fraud. The frequency of dishonesty among participants or organizers is extremely low. The notoriety of the occasional case of fraud or default results from the attention lavished on such cases by scandal magazines like *El Nuevo Alarma!* (the Mexican equivalent of the *National Enquirer* in the United States). Although all informants admitted the possibility of fraud or default, most discounted the likelihood of it occurring. Widespread social and cultural parameters select against dishonesty. Thus, out of 130 ROSCAs, with a total of 1,300 members (assuming 10 persons, which is the normative size in cundinas), the four defaults prior to 1983 and the five defaults after 1983 result in a default rate of slightly more than 0.005 percent.

Yet informants in institutions have noted that dishonesty could bleed into the workplace or create institutional conflict within the workforce itself. Amy Silverman, a reporter for the *Phoenix New Times*, reported that a supervisor and a co-worker had defrauded a file clerk who worked in the Arizona Department of Economic Security. However, the reporter simply did not understand how cundinas function, and in fact, no fraud had occurred. Instead, the clerk had resigned from the agency, but she expected to be paid the full amount when her turn came up, even though she had not contributed that much.[5] However, the case does illustrate that a government agency may not be the best context in which to organize ROSCAs. The municipality of Esquinapa in the state of Sinaloa has forbidden the creation of ROSCAs in government offices without governmental permission, as seen in this regulation (I have eliminated sections that are not pertinent to this work):

Anexo
Bando de Politicía y Bueno Gobierno
Para el Municipio de Escuinapa, Sinaloa

Artículo 10. Son faltas relativas a la prevención de delito:

I. Vender boletos para espectáculos y diversiones públicas fuera de la taquilla;

II. Realizar cundinas, quinielas y todo tipo de rifas sin permiso de la autoridad municipal;

Appendix
Police and Good Government Relations
For the Municipality of Escuinapa, Sinaloa

Article 10. These are misdemeanors relative to the prevention of illegal acts:

I. To sell tickets to public events and spectacles outside of the ticket office (scalping);

II. To form cundinas, quinielas, or raffles of any type without the permission of the municipal authority.

By presenting testimonials from people who have been cheated, one author in the United States has also admonished potential depositors against joining tandas.[6] Newspaper articles have also provided testimonials both for and against participation, but the consensus of opinion in these articles was that they were well worth the effort if careful selection of other participants was practiced. According to one person in a recent article (Loera 2002), "Para Susana Ibarra, las tandas son más que una forma de ahorro, una manera de afianzar la amistad y solidaridad entre sus compañeras de trabajo, las que 'son muy legales en sus pagos y nunca me han transado.'"[7] (For Susana Ibarra, tandas, more than a form of savings, are a way to hone friendships and solidarity among her fellow workers, "who are very faithful in their payments and who have never cheated me.")

Fixity and Density of Confianza

The rarity of actual fraud or default results from social and cultural dimensions that are as important as the individual evaluation of a person's reputation. Any individual's reputation is based on specific sets of relations and behavioral indicators of cultural legitimacy, which attach members to statuses and contexts. This attachment to statuses and contexts generates the density of confianza, while lessening the uncertainty inherent in participating in risky economic relationships. Although most Mexican communities north and south of the Río Bravo do not have the sort of traditional regional and corporate kinship groups that the Japanese or Chinese have to protect them from default or fraud, Mexican residential, occupational, and familial networks and contexts attach people to statuses and generate binding reciprocal obligations that *function equivalently to corporate group obligations*. It is not fear of default (Cope and Kurtz 1980) that selects for fixity. Instead, for most *tandas vivas*, it is social demands that are initiated by the nature of reciprocal exchange and the underlying cultural construct of confianza.

People are attached to statuses by the internal density of the ROSCA and by the density of relationships outside the ROSCA, which are brought into the ROSCA and define the total density of the ROSCA itself. What must be recalled is that the most frequent number of participants in the ROSCAs is ten, and this number selects for greater density as expressed in the natural systems of the residential, occupational, and familial ROSCAs discussed. In other words, the ROSCA as an association becomes a "social fact" and operates not only according to the norms of the ROSCA but also according to the terms of all the relationships the members bring into the association from a variety of other contexts.

When, for example, an organizer is a member's aunt, the fixed relation of aunt and nephew makes the operation of the ROSCA much more certain. The density of relations among members, not just the relation between the members and the organizer, also solidifies the operation of the ROSCA. These two aspects of density, then, that were created by the operation of the ROSCA as a social fact, with its constituent activities (drawings, shared meals, gift giving, visits, and exchanges of information), and that were created by the multiplicity of relationships brought into the ROSCA, together with their probable density, fix members within the ROSCA and also reinforce relations established and operating in other contexts.

The probable density and the multiplicity of relations in a working-class residential rotating savings and credit association in San Pedro, California, are illustrated in figure 3.6. The diagram illustrates how people are not only attached within the association to the organizer but also,

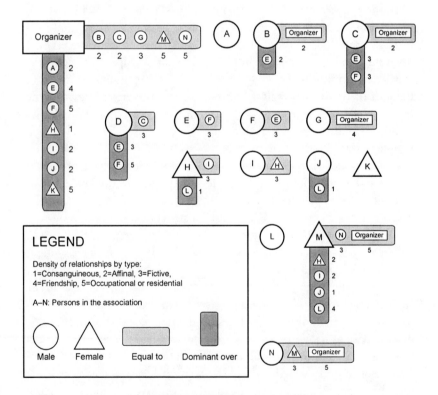

Figure 3.6 Density of a working-class urban *cundina* in San Pedro, California. *Source*: Vélez-Ibáñez 1980.

from a variety of contexts, to each other. The diagram shows two kinds of density. The first refers to the type of relationship that exists between each member and the organizer and between each member and the other members. These are five in kind: affinal, consanguineous, fictive, friend-ship, and occupational or residential. The first refers to the type of rela-tionship in which there can be a differentiation of authority or prestige because of age. These relationships are of two sorts, dominant and equal. Not shown in the diagram is the relationship between any member and the organizer in regard to the operation of the ROSCA itself. These are of two sorts: "direct" transactions in which the organizer and a member have direct access to each other with regard to the collection or disburse-ment of funds, and "indirect" in which another member "plays" (*jugar*) for someone who is prevented by distance from participating. Indirect transactions are not common, but they can occur when the organizer and the surrogate member have established confianza. The type of den-sity is indicated by numbers and by solid lines.

As can be seen from this ROSCA, the totality of the relations that can be brought to bear to lower the probability of default is impressive for most members. All participants are "fixed" within the association by something other than the financial transaction. Person D, who is an "indirect" member, with other people playing the number for her, has no fixed status with the organizer. Instead, she is fixed with three oth-ers within the association: C, E, and F. These three, in turn, are fixed affinally or by friendship in status relations with the organizer. As the organizer remarked in commenting about the lack of direct connection with D, "The rest lend her mutual trust." The only other person without a direct fixed status with the organizer is L, but, like D, she is lent con-fianza by H, J, and M.

Safeguards

Other safeguards against default exist. I have already mentioned that many organizers will have access to the first turn if no fee is involved, which serves as a reserve in case members have difficulty with their contributions. Membership seniority is considered another safeguard because if no lottery is used, those joining last usually receive the fund share last, and thus pay in their full share before receiving any money. In addition, in some institutional contexts, two ROSCA members can witness delivery of the fund share to a third member, which safeguards against an organizer claiming falsely to have delivered it. These are among the obvious, explicit sorts of safeguards against uncertainty and the normal risk described by Light (1972). Certainly, the cultural construct of confianza is congruent with the density and multiplicity of relations involved in ROSCAs and is insurance against indeterminate social relationships.

Additionally, on both sides of the Río Bravo, cultural boundaries and behavioral expectations are used as means to secure determinacy and fixity against the uncertainty of these economic relationships. For example, north of the Río Bravo, non-Mexicans (except for other Spanish-speaking populations or those considered equivalent to Mexicans) are generally excluded from participating in most ROSCAs.

However, three Anglo-American women in a Texas clothing factory, who belonged to the same task section as the Mexican women, had sufficient status to be asked to join. The transborder ROSCA in San Luis Río Colorado also boasted of an Anglo male participant. In another exception, Filipino workers in Chula Vista were invited to participate in Mexican cundinas. The rationale given by the Mexican workers was that Filipinos *saborean de lo nuestro* (they have our flavor). In this case, the Filipinos were regarded not as Mexicans but as culturally equivalent. Furthermore, Filipinos could participate with Mexicans in enjoying (*saborear* also can mean relish in the context in which this was stated) the conviviality of the ROSCA.

Cultural boundaries are not, however, generally relaxed for non-Hispanic national groups. Informants pejoratively referred to Anglo-Americans as "gringos" when the question arose as to their acceptability as members. African Americans, unless they are Latin American, are regarded as *duros* (hard to get to know), and therefore, they are not in the universe of probable candidates. Black Puerto Ricans, Panamanians, and other Central Americans are not only participants but also organizers. These perspectives are reinforced by the structural conditions under which most Mexican residential, occupational, or familial ROSCAs operate in the United States. Although occupations may have a cross-section of other nationalities and national minorities, ROSCAs usually replicate cultural boundaries, especially in working-class or service-worker contexts. Residential and familial ROSCAs are equally closed, owing to the social endogamy of both contexts.

On the other hand, there are class-specific behavioral expectations and clues within Mexican universes that operate as exclusive and inclusive boundaries. For example, among working-class women in Chula Vista, *pretenciosas* (pretentious women) are excluded because it is believed that they will probably not pay their contributions on time. The rationale for this belief is that those who boast of their material belongings are likely to claim that they work for pleasure and not out of necessity. Such claims are deemed to be false and are thought to be a cover hiding economic problems and the lack of resources to meet social and economic obligations, including obligations to members of the cundinas. Even when such pretentiousness is not expressed, an individual's style of language may exclude him or her from consideration for confianza. University students, for example, who work during summer vacations, may not be asked to join, not because they are temporary workers, but because they are generally regarded as interested in only intellectual topics that are outside of the discussion ranges of blue-collar workers. An organizer can also fear that a student might reject an offer to participate because of perceived class differences.

The qualities expected of a potential member in working-class sectors may include expertise in verbal dueling. *El coterreo* or *la cábula* (literally, "chatter," but analogous to "rapping" among African Americans) is the main signaling device used to designate acceptance or nonacceptance, although general speech patterns and proxemic signals are also important. For example, a *coterreo* about a sister is quite common, a sort of verbal gauntlet used by men in which one person will say "¿Cómo está tu hermana?" (How is your sister?), the other will ask, "¿Cuál hermana?" (Which sister?), and the first will respond with "La que se acuesta en mi cama" (The one who sleeps in my bed). Here the ending words rhyme in Spanish so that the challenge and responses are quite melodious. In addition, if a person is not given an individual nickname marking his personal appearance or some mannerism, he will usually be excluded. A new ceramic factory worker in Los Angeles was given the nickname of Cebolla (green onion). The rationale was that he had white hair on top of his head, but green roots in the lower extremities, as evidenced by his numerous amorous activities. Soon after he received his nickname, he was invited to participate in one of the cundinas.

Among women, joking patterns or nicknaming are also used to designate acceptance into confianza circles, especially in the working-class occupational ROSCAs. One woman member of a ROSCA in a San Diego electronics factory was known as Teflón because "she was so dumb that nothing stuck to her." For both women and men, nicknames of a personal sort based on appearance, an infamous event, or a speech mannerism (one stutterer was known as Lenguas, "tongues") indicate acceptance. Each marks the individual not pejoratively but rather in recognition of her or his individuality within the fellowship of the collective group.

In petty-bourgeois sectors, with the previously mentioned clubs, people observe numerous behavioral clues before extending an invitation. Speech mannerisms that mark women as having rural or working-class origins eliminate candidates from clubs, even when they meet residential requirements. Class-specific dress, hairdos, access to automobiles, knowledge about certain types of entertainment, and assurance in certain behavioral patterns, such as controlled laughter and emotion, are all used as class indicators in petty-bourgeois sectors. In middle-class club ROSCAs in Monterrey, however, working-class relatives of members participate secretly, by sending a messenger, often a young daughter, with the contribution to the bourgeois relative in her bourgeois neighborhood. This was done to avoid offending middle-class sensibilities because a young girl entering the front door of a middle-class home is not as conspicuous as a working-class adult. Of course, the middle-class resident will not reveal to members of the club that she is, in fact, playing a lower-class relative's turn.

In some tandas, far subtler clues than those so far described may be observed. In the theater chains in Los Angeles, if a person too readily agreed to participate, without questioning the operation, duration, and cycle and distribution of payments, he or she was generally perceived as not serious and therefore not a good candidate. Someone who accepted initial total confianza in the ROSCA without any analytical questioning could not be trusted to think on his or her own or to behave convivially with others. As one informant put it, "One can be very certain, but not too certain, initially."

These boundaries, safeguards, behavioral clues, and other cultural requirements are not present nor are they needed in the well-established intermediate ROSCA and the formally organized *mutualista*. Since the former are integrated into a company's accounting system, it is difficult for employees to default on their contributions. There is always a possibility of accountant-organizers manipulating contributions, as has been indicated, but the risks involved are great, and dishonesty is rare. In the formal mutualistas, legal sanctions protect both the members and the organizers from either default or fraud. However, given the reticence of the corporate officers to supply data for this research, there may be dimensions of the operation that were not made public. (These remarks are in no way intended to suggest any wrongdoing on the part of the corporation.)

Nevertheless, there are other uncertainties against which safeguards, fixed relations, and cultural boundaries are useless. Unexpected acts of men, women, and the gods occur frequently enough to shatter confidence in the most well-developed systems. The Mexican ROSCA is no exception. Regardless of intentions, trust, fellowship, historical associations, ritual practices, density, multiplicity, protection, promises, cooperation, and cultural constructs, the sudden and unexpected appearance of inflation, the death of a relative, a lost or misplaced wallet, a sudden illness, an immigration raid, or unemployment—all mock the best of intentions, and the safeguards against uncertainty melt away. An unjust arrest, broken spousal promises, or a sudden Border Patrol raid can all lead to the disruption of the platforms upon which ROSCAs operate. In these circumstances, confianza may fail, and old and treasured relationships may shatter. Unexpected events confirm personal uncertainty. What has been determined by definition and practice becomes indeterminate by actions and accidents. In these times, tragedy fills the cultural and social spaces of living, but many also arise from the ashes of failure and despair.

The Southwest North American Region, particularly, is in the midst of great economic, social, political, and cultural change. This presents an enormous challenge to the populations seeking a better life for themselves and their families. These challenges increase the uncertainty and indeterminacy of predictive social relationships in spite of the best application of confianza, social exchange, and the willingness to take risks to improve life's chances. As the next chapter illustrates, the Southwest North American Region is a cauldron of change, and individuals using the best of their abilities—including organizing ROSCAs and many other tactics—may end up much changed, much chagrined, and much bruised, but almost certainly, not defeated.

4
Living at a Slant in the Midst of Megascripts in the Transborder Southwest North American Region
Dos mujeres sin fin

There can be no doubt that the spread of rotating savings and credit associations (ROSCAs) are the local and transborder expression of much larger economic, demographic, social, material, and political processes in the transborder region and the Southwest North American Region, as I postulated in chapter 1. However, a number of important dynamic economic and demographic processes support this even more, including:

- In 2009, there were an average of of 722,000 (24 million per month) passenger crossings per day at the 35 points of entry on the 1,952-mile border between the United States and Mexico, and the United States issued 906,622 nonimmigrant visas for Mexicans in fiscal year (FY) 2005. In addition, 732,566 laser visas (which replaced the old border crossing cards for those who live on the Mexican side of the border but work in the United States) were issued in FY 2005, down from 1,990,402 in FY 2001.[1] As of 2009, the estimated unauthorized population in the United States was 11.9 million, of which 4.5 to 6 million entered legally with inspection and 6 to 7 million entered illegally without inspection.[2] Of the total 11.9 million, 59 percent were of Mexican origin.[3]
- Approximately 60 percent of the 500 million visitors admitted into the United States enter across the U.S.–Mexico border, as do 90 million cars and 4.3 million trucks annually, all contributing to the $638 million in trade conducted at the border with Mexico every single day.[4]
- There is a massive regional economic movement from the central and southern parts of Mexico to the northern border areas (fig. 4.1), which has led to an economic and demographic explosion in the U.S. border states.[5]
- The Mexicanization of former Anglo towns, and the creation of Mexican rural population settlements in vacant lands in the United States, termed "colonias," are now home to hundreds of thousands of people, 97 percent of whom are of Mexican origin (see fig. 4.2).[6]

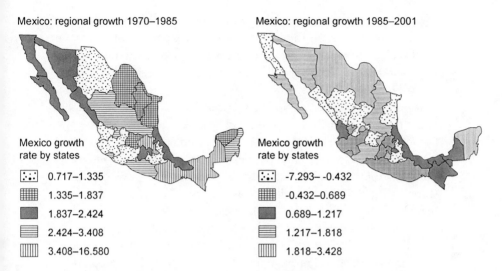

Figure 4.1 Mexican regional growth, 1970–2001. *Source*: Gilmer 2006.

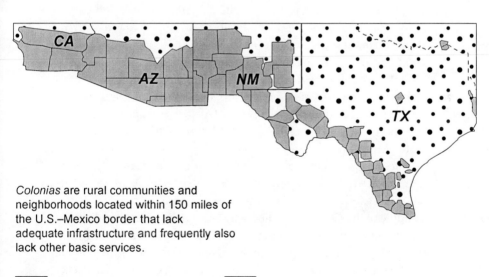

Colonias are rural communities and neighborhoods located within 150 miles of the U.S.–Mexico border that lack adequate infrastructure and frequently also lack other basic services.

Counties that contain *colonias*   Non-*colonias* counties

Figure 4.2 Location of *colonias* along the U.S.–Mexico border. *Source*: Galan 2000b.

When these figures are coupled with almost $200 billion in imports into the United States and almost $137 billion in exports to Mexico, then the old adage of "follow the money" easily explains how transborder labor markets can be created along with a type of regional centrality, especially for Mexico.[7]

Regarding the Southwest North American Region, I would suggest that we can no longer consider the border to be a place to cross, or merely a "border." Rather, the U.S.–Mexico border region has become the central axis and node for trade, commerce, population crossing and re-crossing, linguistic experimentation, institutional development, academic interest, population settlement, class creations and divisions, and cultural emergence and conflict. In this lie the great contradictions of citizenship, unitary cultural identity, and "one-nation and one-culture" premises. In a peculiar sense, the "border" has become the center from which populations and material travel throughout both nations to peripheral locations in the Southwest North American Region, the East Coast, the Deep South, and the Midwest. This is, however, a subject for another book, but suffice it to say that the regional importance of the Southwest North American Region as a center will continue in spite of 9/11. Economic and cultural practices like ROSCAs are emblematic of the "diaspora" of economy and polity throughout the Southwest North American Region and its creation as an important center of influence and expansion that radiates out.

The border region center is a persistent and dynamic presence that is characterized as a "transnational," transgenerational, and transcultural phenomenon that permeates the region's historical shape and memory. Its creation and continuance is part and parcel of its institutionalism since the Mexican-American War and the Treaty of Mesilla, and it is not just imaginary or a "cultural artifact." Instead, it entails lived, experientially supported, empirical realities. The border center is carried within, whether by a third-generation schoolteacher in Mecca, California, in the middle of the Coachella Valley; a fifth-generation anthropologist; or a recently graduated undocumented computer specialist from Mexico City working as a painter in Phoenix, Arizona. Because of the constant reminders in and around us—all of this center's existence, persistence, and often-masked actuality—it becomes an unthought-of presence.

The following discussion broadly describes some of the major megascripts that guide human behavior in the region, using ROSCAs embedded in people's daily lives as a lens for the study. Yet, as will be seen, these megascripts themselves are like all human inventions: problematic and contradictory for the people who follow them. The region offers an opportunity to fundamentally understand how gender and race are often primary for the playing out of megascripts, as will be shown in the case studies of *dos mujeres sin fin* (two women who never quit).

The Transborder Region and Its Megascripts: Success, Material Gain, and the Double Helices of Race and Gender

The transborder region's underlying megascript[8] is the quest for individual and familial success and material gain, with their accompanying social, political, and cultural perks, with rationalizations utilizing the presence of melanin sometimes thrown in as justifications. The notion of megascripts refers to ideologically driven, naturalized rationalizations of power, dominance, and exploitation buttressed by local and regional scripts. These may be constituted and expressed as "values," beliefs, rituals, symbols, and accepted "civil" discourses of many sorts. The "successes" of nations, regions, and global markets—formed and rationalized by centuries of colonial economics, nineteenth-century industrial national and transborder capitalism, and now global and transnational chains of production and labor—are linked through institutions to households and individuals by both material reality and agreed-to megascripts that filter down to local fields and arenas. At local levels, people who want the best for their children rarely question the script. With that implicit agreement, scripts of various sorts become legitimate rather than coercive. Individuals believe that following these scripts is in their best interests, with observation providing the empirical support for that assertion.

The prevailing educational system, messages and information directly championed by national and international groups and institutions, and expected behaviors associated with those systems and institutions manage and transmit these megascripts. Thus, "consumerism" is a megascript in the United States that drives much of its economic system through elaborated debt structures. Individuals, groups, networks, and corporative bodies must function within these structures, so that "consumer spending" becomes the hallmark of economic success and a measure of the health of the U.S. economy. Yet the efficacy of that spending in times of economic uncertainty goes unquestioned. Being a consumer rather than a producer becomes a legitimate activity and an aspiration shared with others.

Unappreciated but certainly undergirding this script is a U.S. version of "success," so that the allegedly central premise of the consumer-driven economy is a successful one for all participants. The "success" mega-script is the driving premise for migration, maquiladoras, use of low-paid labor by businesses, and many of the political scripts that spin off it that are both in opposition to and in support of the larger script. Thus, at one level, transborder cooperation between Mexican and U.S. health authorities seeks a "safer" means of ensuring healthy cross-border traf-fic and simultaneously labels the Mexican side as a source of undesirable diseases to be "kept out." There are double messages in this last example: The United States wants only the healthiest of labor migrants, which may lead to their own "success" even as they contribute to their employ-ers' "success." At the same time, it maintains a medicalized negative per-ception of those "others" across the border, as people who are unhealthy might become a public health hazard and, from this perspective, in real-ity, are a potential liability to continued U.S. economic health.

The Double Helices of Race and Gender

Given this penetrating and agreed-to megascript, success-driven actions easily convince populations these scripts are "normative" and "natural." Thus, at the level of action, people also agree to the scraping of labor and energy value from things and people, including oneself, to achieve suc-cess. Institutions of many sorts support these scripts, and it is the case that judicial authorities of various sorts, including police and judicial agencies, protect the privilege of individual achievement and success. "Illegal" border crossers certainly are chastised for their attempts to fol-low the megascript of individual success because it is restricted to those of us who are "citizens"—a privileged status often associated with the absence of melanin and/or cultural concerns, especially in relation to language, familial dynamics, body shapes and sizes, and simple things such as dress, proxemics, and sundry other cultural expressions. There may be something to the notion that if one has a greater amount of melanin and is elderly, a woman, Mexican, short, poor, and left-handed then there is less probability of being or becoming successful.

Transborder living gives us an unusually twisted manner in which to consider another dimension of this individualistic megascript. For many in the Southwest North American Region, transborder populations carry double helices from both sides of the border. I am using this of course as a metaphor to indicate tightly coiled but also flexible and racialized historical scripts and strands about gender and melanin that people use to rationalize the previous statement about the most negative of social characteristics. The first strand of the helix—often promulgated by machista ideologies of women as secondary partners or, worse, as only valuable for their bodies—passes through the Spanish colonial and Mexican Republic periods. Too many Mexican households in the present and even women themselves reproduce these patri-centered ideologies. Males especially see themselves as privileged to acquire all the trappings of success in comparison to women, who must be secondary partners deriving their own success from their husbands. This version of sexism then moves north to join with that which Americans and Mexicans before the Mexican-American War and during the Spanish colonial period had already established long ago.

A second, melanin-defined strand harkens back to the racialized Spanish caste system. Mexican familial practices and ideologies of darkness and lightness (with the latter a positive attribute despite tremendous nationalistic and public attention to the great pre-Hispanic indigenous past, especially after the Mexican Revolution) informally reinforce it. Class divisions in Mexico are often articulated along melanin-measured dimensions. Certainly, regardless of the public expressions about the wonder of Mesoamerican civilizations, elites and bleached-blond, upper-class women express a preference for "whiteness," with the males expressing a preference toward dark-skinned consorts and light-skinned wives and children. Mexican class-related whiteness is accentuated in most media of expression. When a new baby comes along, grandmothers often ask first, "¿Cómo es?" ("What color?"), rather than asking if the infant is healthy. There is a tacit agreement that an answer of "light" will privilege the child with an easier lot in life because less melanin is positively valued.[9] However, because upward mobility is hindered by class privilege in Mexico—the domain of the elite and the ever-growing wealthy—the professional class increasingly works two or three jobs or migrates to Europe and, especially, to Canada and the United States. Both countries have benefited enormously, especially in the sciences and mathematics. Nevertheless, the racialized strand also moves north with all classes, as it always has since the Spanish colonial period. Thus, racialization is part of the Mexican cultural repertoire, just as sexism is.

Combining the two creates the "other" within the first half of the same, and just as twisted, double helix.

However, there is another strand of the second half of the double helix for Mexicans who have had the border cross them and those who cross the border. That is, the third strand consists of Mexicans being regarded as only "cheap labor," creating a strand of an identity as a basic "commodity." "Mexican" and cheap labor become one and the same, and achievement is not included as part of the formula. There is a long history to how this occurred, but without too much embellishment, Mexican-origin populations in border regions try like mad to rid themselves of the degrading term "Mexican." In that effort, many attempt to take on respectability by labeling themselves with more-accepted terms such as "Hispanic" or "Latino" or other versions. In a previous work (Vélez-Ibáñez 2004a), I traced the human rights dimensions of a commodity-based identity that, coupled with melanin preferences in the United States that privilege "whiteness," racializes Mexican-origin populations' low status. Even when contradicted by individual achievements and historical reality, such racialized strands of the double helix remain in place, and they are accentuated institutionally, as the case study in this chapter illustrates. Thus, Mexican-origin populations carry the burden of contradicting the homebred Mexican racialism generated from entirely different histories and the American commodity-based racialism encountered since the nineteenth century from the outstretched imaginings of Manifest Destiny and the need for "cheap labor."

The fourth strand is a complicated twist of commoditization, sexism, and racialized identity. For many foreign-born and first-generation Mexican women, especially, their commodity identity is gendered and associated with housework, caretaking of Anglo children and Anglo elderly, and service employment. The shadow cast on Mexican women and often replayed in the public sector by movies, television, and newspapers is too obvious to repeat here, but suffice it to say that such repeated associations with gender and commodity concretize a strand that is glued as the completing link to the double, twisted helix of racialized and commoditized identity for men and a gendered one, as well, for women.

Thus, in this transborder region, people must address these double helices on a daily basis, and as individuals, they have to deal with running smack into the prevailing megascripts that call for success, achievement, and individual mobility. This can make people a bit stressed.

Transborder Living and Gender

Coupled to this reality is the fact that transborder living also involves a way of emotionally, cognitively, socially, economically, and, most importantly, culturally deciphering and living out the multitude of cultural scripts that transect daily existence because of border influences. Transborder living and remembrances touch all in the region and beyond it. Whether expressed in the latest anti-immigration T-shirt, intemperate ethnocentric remarks uttered by the ignorant in a clothing store, the daily life of people crossing our paths wearing Brooks Brothers suits with brown faces and Aztec noses, workers waiting patiently on the corner in 110 degree weather for a hopeful ride to a low-paying, backbreaking job, or the domestic worker making our bourgeois beds and caring for and loving our children, the presence of the border and the necessity of transborder existences touch everyone within eyesight or earshot through the media, on the street, in our work places and schools, and in the multitudes of daily settings.[10] In a most contradictory manner, many transborder Mexicans have to live their lives constantly changing and shifting identities, outlooks, positions, and selves to cope with the double helix and the quest for achievement in a transborder reality.

Many women, especially, carry transborder adjustments, adaptations, and innovations to great lengths. The reason is fairly simple: they carry most of the weight of raising children, keeping hearth and home, and ensuring that relationships are maintained and that social capital is guarded and spent. They have to be sure that their families remain healthy, physically and emotionally, and above all, that the delicate "economic calculus" that transborder people manage and create is balanced and functional. They have to be sure that their "social calculus" operates to keep them just out of the reach of eviction from the apartment, or that it contributes to their being able to fix the aging means of transportation, or that it allows for a balance between eating well, eating poorly, or eating very little at all. These are terrible responsibilities, and because of the border, they become greatly problematic for many women in many different ways. These struggles are kept in the hidden folds of what seem to be daily "normal" experiences—things not spoken about nor much heeded. They seem to be normal, standard, stereotypically acceptable, and beyond analysis. But they are also double helical in that whatever sacrifices these women make for their children, it will be most likely in the name of a "better life," added opportunity, more education, and, finally, making sure that children get what the adult never had or could have. Thus, the quest for achievement and success permeates many households. And the women guiding the unfolding of that quest are often caught between multiple transborder pressures to stay whole, in a nonindividualistic manner and crazy-making way, as they seek to ensure that the next generation does not suffer what they suffer now, and as they sacrifice themselves, and even their children, in order for those children to eventually become successful.

Slanting

Often the only way for many women to take hold of self and space in these circumstances is by creating, developing, adjusting, inventing, and simply innovating "best practices" for excellence and survival that coincide with broader megascripts. They, in fact, act in a "slantwise" manner.[11] That is, they slide into the edges of interstitial spaces and places that Wolf (1956) long ago suggested were anthropologists' province of study, because here, in between great structures of economy and polity, exist the connectivities and spaces that can be negotiated, manipulated, and traversed. At the same time, those having direct access to domains of influence and power often do not recognize these spaces.[12]

Howard Campbell and Josiah Heyman (2007), who coined the term "slantwise," concentrate less on its economic than on its political meaning and usage. They are critical of the bipolar model used in many discussions concerning the agency versus domination opposites along an axis. They emphasize acts that frustrate "the normal play of a given power relation by acting in ways that make sense in their own frameworks but are disconnected or oblivious to that power relationship's construction or assumptions" (2). However, I add to this idea with the notion that slantwise behaviors and strategies have much to do with borderlands populations "going around," underneath, sideways, or slipping by the structures of economy and power in order to access or to acquire needed resources and legitimacy in a context of alienation or marginalization. Just as importantly, they maneuver in between the spirals of the double helices of transborder racialism and gendered existence.

I suggest that ROSCAs function in a "slantwise" manner in that they "take on" all normalized spheres of borrowing, lending, investing, and saving by creating their own spheres of slantwise action. The irony, however, as will be discussed in later chapters, is that the formal economic sector has recognized the efficacy of these spheres, and it has appropriated their forms and functions.

In my estimation, transborder people are situated on the most advantageous and, simultaneously, on the most precarious social perches within those undefined interstitial spaces. They conduct and induce slantwise behaviors in order to excel, survive, support, and manage their own and others' lives and in order to deal with the inherent contradictions that arise from following the megascript of success while simultaneously maneuvering between the vortices of the double helices of racialism and gender.

Dos Mujeres Sin Fin: Lo que les pasó a Paloma y Valentina[13]

Two women illustrate to great degrees the "slantwise" approach of working in the interstitial, unoccupied spaces that the state or institutions only partially define or control. They create opportunities, squirm into the in-between, devise strategies, and invent methods and techniques that increase their likelihood of successfully managing their transborder lives and the attempted vertical climb to "whiteness." Paloma and Valentina are women who operationalize a type of economic calculus, in which they balance imperfect income, debt, savings, investments, and expenditures. They participate in ROSCAs; favors and exchanges with relatives and friends; flea markets, selling high and buying low; creating small businesses; working three jobs; investing in houses for rentals; and myriad other activities. All of this is centered around an economic calculus of survival, excellence, achievement, and slanting their efforts and achievements just under the radar screen of the legal and institutional authorities.

Both have been, and one still is, an unauthorized immigrant. Both had men playing central roles in their lives. Both have seemingly great control over the processes in which they are engaged until unpredictable events smash their dreams and efforts. But being who they are, they rise up again from the pummelings that attempt to grind them down, and using all their energy, efforts, and just plain smarts, they outwit the authorities, slide by immigration officials, duck the impossible odds, and simply create their own spaces and places in their transborder slantwise worlds.

Paloma

I met Paloma for the first time in a federal prison. I entered the colorless visiting room one cold, wet morning. Her attorney, Shelly Newman, and I had been ushered through security checkpoints by very efficient federal officers as we showed our "get in and out of jail" cards, which Shelly had previously obtained. Passing through two locked, inner rooms, we were led by an attending officer into a space that looked like a cheap "ball-room." Arrayed around it were a few glass-enclosed inner offices. Each served as the interview space for clients, lawyers, and their consultants.

I served as the latter. Shelly had asked me to serve as a consultant for Paloma's defense. She was charged with a number of federal criminal activities, not the least of which was money laundering, and given her less-than-privileged position as a socially defined "non-white" person, it was unbelievable that she was not engaged in illegal money deals given the level of wealth she had accumulated. Shelly had mentioned that Paloma had repeatedly told her that the money she earned was partially from organizing and participating in "tandas." So, Shelly decided to look into them, which led her to my 1983 book, *Bonds of Mutual Trust*. She contacted me and asked for my help in understanding how tandas, or ROSCAs, could have contributed to the wealth Paloma had created and earned.

As I explained to Shelly in our initial conversation, in urban and rural Mexico and the United States, *tandas* (as ROSCAs are known in central and southern Mexico) and *cundinas* (as they are called in northern Mexico) are of central utility for many people. ROSCAs cross class lines so that low-, modest-, and middle-income people participate in them in multiple sites. I added that they basically work on the principle of mutual trust (*confianza*) because a number of individuals contribute a set amount, weekly or monthly, to a pool. Each receives the amount in the pool once, based on a lottery or random-number selection. Essentially, the ROSCAs are still "slantwise" practices, in that they are not part of most institutional frameworks (except for some now-notable exceptions, as this work illustrates in other chapters).

The government based its case on the assumption that Paloma's modest income from working in a packing plant and as a fry cook and waitress, as well as from working in the fields on weekends, was insufficient to generate the amount of monies necessary to buy properties. There had to be an extra-legal source for that money. Her properties included three houses and a duplex bought over a period of ten years. She also participated in the purchase of two cherry orchards in Oregon, where she and her family migrated to from California during the picking seasons. At different times, she had owned a secondhand 2000 Mercedes-Benz sedan, a Cadillac Escalade, and a 2000 Lincoln Navigator. At the time of her arrest, she was wearing a 24k gold necklace and chain matched by two heavy gold bracelets, and almost $5,000 was in her purse. All of it was confiscated. A federal grand jury indicted her as a co-defendant with four others on a variety of drug charges. After a series of motions made by the defense attorney, she was separated from the others and charged solely with conspiracy to launder money, allegedly through land transactions with one of the four defendants, Mario García. Essentially, this indictment emerged from her agreeing to partner with García in the purchase of Oregon cherry orchards, allegedly using drug money, and, according to the charge, for the purpose of growing marijuana.

These were the allegations in the case at the time I entered the "ballroom." It had numerous folding chairs, arranged in many different ways, and was filled with federal prisoners of all ilks, including young men and women in light green smocks, making the best of the time spent with their loved ones during visiting hours. A tattooed mother, tall and blond, held her squirming, pink-dressed child. Tears streamed down Mom's cheeks, while her own mother sitting nearby wept in tandem. Some fathers walked their two- and three-year-olds around the room. They seemed to be expressing glorious feelings for their kids simultaneous to their quick furtive looks of anxiety towards the two unsmiling guards, sitting on an upraised governmental gray desk along one wall, but prominently situated. The guards had microphones sitting nearby, by which they checked and then called the prisoner who was next to be visited.

What impressed me most strongly was that most of the prison population in that "ballroom" was Latino, African American, or Asian. Of the forty-eight or so individuals, only about eight were seemingly "Anglo." My estimate was that at least twenty were Latinas/os, ten were African Americans, and ten or so were "Asians" of various origins, including Filipino, Chinese, and Vietnamese. I did not observe any East Indians. We will return to this later.

As we waited in the inner office, a dull, restrained, but powerful command was heard for Paloma to enter from a barred enclosure. A burly guard escorted her to an open bench next to our room. Shelly then was able to call her in, and it was there that I would come to know Paloma over the next few months.

Shelly introduced me to a fragile, thin, and slightly hunched-over thirty-something Mexican woman, with large doe eyes, an angular face with no makeup, and hair combed into a tight bun. She was dressed in the same kind of smocks all the other prisoners wore, except this one hung like a badly fitting, oversized prison sheet. She looked almost emaciated, with the clavicles of her shoulders pushing up to form two cloth pyramids, while the rest of the smock hung loosely, hiding any sense of her physical form. She sat down, and Shelly and I explained my role in the case. We told her that I would be trying to understand how she came to accumulate her wealth, especially that earned through the ROSCAs. Months of intensive interviews followed during winter 2005. The story, however, was more complex than just "calculating" how she got to this point in time. Instead, it was necessary to contextualize her abilities to establish hearth, home, and wealth—all in a matter of ten years—as part of her role in the local version of the megascript for whiteness.

The Process of Becoming Successful. From a materialist point of view, Paloma always sought to be successful, whether in Mexico or in the United States. But things are not what they might seem.

Paloma was born in 1967, in what she referred to as a "wretched" rural town in Michoacán. She was one of fifteen siblings. Her father—a brutish, poor farmer who abused Paloma's mother throughout most of their marriage—moved the entire family to the State of Mexico, following in the footsteps of one of his older children. There, they lived in one of the commuter cities that surround Mexico City itself. The State of Mexico serves as a long-standing migratory space from rural areas, especially from the states of Michoacán and Oaxaca and from other communities in the State of Mexico itself. In fact, the commuter city where she lived is almost indistinguishable from the rest of the urbanizing areas that surround Mexico City, even when they are located in different state entities, not unlike the cities and towns in Virginia or Maryland in relation to Washington, D.C.

Although she attended middle school, she did not complete it, and she got a job in the same bakery where her violent and abusive father worked as a guard. What is salient about Paloma's economic and social behavior is that during her time in the bakery she held down two shifts: from 6 a.m. to 2:30 p.m. and from 4 p.m. to 10 p.m.

She also participated in multiple tandas. In 1986, she was a member of two 200-peso tandas. Both ran for three months, with eleven numbers. She held one number in each tanda, and when she was low on cash, her brother would lend her the weekly contributions. Thus, while paying 200 pesos each turn, she was able to accumulate 4,400 pesos in three months. In 1987, she again participated in a tanda, and coupled with the money she already had, she was able to put a down payment of 5,000 pesos on a 25,000-peso house that she would share with her mother and siblings. Finally, her mother was able to escape the violence of her husband.

Thus, Paloma's early version of whiteness had much to do with altruism, not individual achievement. Moving her five siblings into this home set a pattern for home purchases—the sharing of her hearth with her brothers, sisters, and mother—as well as her participation in tandas, which was to become an important source of savings, investment, and purchase later in the United States.

Here it is important to signal how Mexican families of modest income initiate "slantwise" strategies to slice against their circumstances. They do so by pooling their resources in order to purchase major items like a home, car, land, or appliances. They also frequently purchase these goods from people they know, thereby getting reduced prices. In this case, Paloma bought the home from the sister of her brother-in-law (her sister's husband) for the price mentioned, even though it had a higher value.

This transaction also illustrates how Mexicans utilize kinship relations to conduct economic activities. People leverage their dense social relations. The glue for those relations is confianza or mutual trust, which is the highest value held among Mexicans and Mexican-origin populations in the United States, persisting with the latter at least through the third generation, until they become totally "white." In all of her transactions, Paloma relied on confianza to participate in the tandas. When she was not in a relationship of confianza with the organizer, then one of the participants would "lend" her the needed mutual trust. In other words, a trusted person may vouch for someone who is not known personally to the organizer (for example, an organizer of another ROSCA or a person involved in a transaction of another sort such as exchanging labor).

During 1987, while still working two shifts in the bakery, Paloma continued to participate in tandas. These now had thirty people each, with eleven numbers over three months. She participated in four altogether, generating 8,000 pesos, which she used to make her house payments, purchase furniture, and help support the eleven people now living in the house. In 1988 and 1989, she repeated the same pattern. By 1989, she had finished paying for the house, while continuing to help her mother as well. In 1989, she gave the house to her mother, and shortly thereafter, in 1990, she managed to go to the United States. She and two of her brothers moved in with another brother, who had established residence in Brawley, California, in 1982.

Her brother was a foreman in the agricultural fields, so in 1990, Paloma began working at $4.25 per hour for ten hours per day, from 6 a.m. to 3:30 p.m. She picked nectarines, peaches, and other fruits, as well as working by contracted amounts of table grapes. During that first year, a fellow worker, who saw her struggling with baskets of fruit while she ascended a ladder, suggested that she work in something more suited to her size and strength and referred her to Acosta Foods, a processing plant, where she began to work as well.

In Brawley, she continued her former pattern of holding down two jobs and working seven days a week. She also continued her pattern of participating in tandas. Her brother, the foreman, managed a tanda for the agricultural workers of $150 dollars with eleven numbers for a total of $1,500. With these funds, she was able to send $300 to $500 a month to her mother, and she also helped her brothers defray household expenses. As she explains, "I loved to work with my friends and my brothers in Acosta and in the fields because it was more like a party, of people working together so you forgot the inconveniences of the heat, the bugs, and dirt of the fields, and the long hours in Acosta Foods."

Gold, Citizenship, and Success. In 1990, Esmeralda, one of her friends at Acosta Foods, began to sell gold bracelets. This piqued Paloma's interest, and slowly her friend introduced Paloma into the business. That year, she joined a tanda that finished in January 1991. It was for $100 dollars per week with eleven participants. She used the money for her wedding to Manny, a Chicano from Brawley, and a year later, she gave birth to their first child. Manny was an avenue toward her legal residency, and her U.S.-born child reinforced Paloma's claim to residency as well. However, she pointed out that Manny "was lazy and didn't have the balls to be successful even though he was a kind and responsible man." She said, "I had to do and think about everything. He just worked, came home, played with our child, was kind to me and his mother, but he didn't do anything."

At this point, she moved out of her brother's house, to a $300-a-month two-bedroom rental house. During the year, she again participated in four tandas with her husband's brother. They both contributed $100 each to an eleven-member tanda, and each received $1,000. With the accumulated savings of $4,000, she bought her first car—a 1977 Chevy van. In addition, Paloma saved between $2,000 and $3,000. She stated that she had not thought about putting it in the bank because she "simply was not aware of it" (that is, the institution of banking), which basically meant that it was not part of her experience. At this time, she was already thinking of buying a home, and from her paycheck, she also was sending $300 to $500 dollars to her mother, paying for her own *lonche* (lunch), and keeping the rest.

At this time, she scrimped on food, only cooking *albondigas de pollo* (chicken meatballs) and taquitos with lots of nonmeat fillings, as well as buying very little meat or chicken for the meals she served her husband. Between 1991 and 1993, by scrimping on food, saving part of her paychecks, and acquiring money from the tandas, she was able to accumulate enough to make a down payment of $4,000 on a five-bedroom home on Calle Hanson in Brawley. One brother and one cousin moved in as well. Each paid her $80 per month, while she paid the balance of her $583-a-month mortgage from her wages, her husband's wages, and from tanda earnings when she was short. In 1993, she participated in four tandas for a total of $9,600 over twelve months, and for the first time, she opened a bank account (at a Bank of America branch), bought furniture for the bedrooms and living room as well as appliances, and opened her first Sears credit card account. She was well on her way to "whiteness." Yet she also sent money to her sister, Lola, so that she could hire a *coyote* to cross her into Brawley from Mexico. She also simultaneously continued sending money to her mother.

Thus, by 1993, three years after arriving in the United States, Paloma had combined monies from tandas, her salary, and the modest rents paid to her by the relatives. This served as the basis for her integration into the U.S. economy and her induction into the use of credit. However, none of these efforts probably would have come to fruition if it were not for the presence, use, and articulation of the dense social relations surrounding her. These are essential parts of slantwise living, for they facilitate, support, and make possible "sideways" penetration of capital and labor. These are not "white" practices, but rather the basis of local exchange and of values, but not values of individual achievement and success nor of vertical mobility. I will return to the chronology of events shortly.

Density, Reciprocity, Exchange, and Confianza: Mediums of Slantwise Living

Mexicans and Mexican-origin populations in the United States, especially immigrant and first-generation individuals, participate in multiple dense relations with many people. Put differently, not only is a person a sister, friend, confidant, and blood kin, but in many cases, ritual and participation in many joint activities multiply these relations. Thus, Paloma's brother, Saul, is Paloma's *compadre* because she was the godmother at the baptism of one of Saul's children. In turn, Paloma is *comadre* to her brother and to his wife and also *madrina* (godmother) to the child. Saul and his wife are compadre and comadre, respectively, to Paloma's husband and to her.

Other factors compound this density of relations. First, Saul paid for Paloma's trip to the United States. Second, he was Paloma's foreman in the fields. Third, she lived in his home for her first three years in Brawley. Fourth, and finally, she participated in tandas that he organized. When friendship, affection, and love are added to the mix, as well as daily verbal, emotive, and material exchanges of multiple sorts, then this density translates into the necessity to follow basic rules of reciprocity of both a general and a specific sort. These can be used as "slantwise" relations to access needed resources.

Reciprocity of a *general* sort rests on the idea that no specific value is placed on that which is exchanged. For example, there is no specific value attached when Paloma takes care of Saul's child or cooks him a meal or when Saul selects Paloma to be a worker in the fields he oversees. Only in a general sense will these exchanges be paid back sometime in the indeterminate future. Reciprocity of a *specific* kind does have a value, such as the amounts of money exchanged in the tandas following specific timetables and rules about payments. The latter, in this case of the tandas, however, cannot occur without the general reciprocal obligations already established through various contexts and relationships.

Thus, the underlying value for all of these general and specific reciprocal relations and the "thickness" of the dense relations are all based on a culturally valued, glue-like concept: confianza, or mutual trust. Learned early in childhood and reinforced throughout the life cycle by ritual, material and nonmaterial exchanges, and the proximity of those involved, confianza is the key value that lets us understand Paloma's success. It also lets us understand, in part, her failure in her final financial transaction,

when she extended her confianza to a stranger, Mario García, simply
because he was an intimate friend of her brothers. The key is that this
repertoire of cultural practices and values are truly "slantwise" mediums
for access to institutions and economic domains and fields.

More Pathways to Success: Work, Rentals, Mortgages, Exchange, and Tandas

By 1994, Paloma had stopped working at Acosta Foods due to a wholesale immigration raid in which many of its employees were deported.
Her own status as a legal immigrant had not yet been confirmed, but her
second child was born in August, which helped solidify her prospects
for remaining in the country legally. Three months later, she separated
from her first husband. That year, she and her brother, with whom she
shared title to the home on Calle Hanson, decided to rent rooms out to
the ever-present agricultural workers. This was not unusual throughout
farming areas in the southwestern United States and in California's agricultural valleys. Brawley is centrally located in one, the Imperial Valley.
Throughout the town, people rent out modestly priced rooms, garages,
and even trailers standing in their backyards. Paloma was able to rent
out rooms to agricultural workers from her hometown. She had four
people living in each room. She also made lonche (lunch and dinner) for
all of them, and she charged $200 a month per person for this room and
board. Up to fourteen workers at a time lived in her home and garage.
On average, however, between March and November, a nine-month
period that coincides with the area's agricultural cycle, Paloma rented
to ten workers. Thus, for nine months of the year, she earned $18,000
in rental monies alone. She also participated in one tanda at $200 a turn
for eleven turns equaling $2,000. Additionally, she worked in the fields
with her brother. She arose at 3 a.m. to make taquitos for the workers.
Then she went to work in the fields and the packing sheds, returning in
the afternoon to make dinner for all of her renters.

She continued following this pattern through 1995. Additionally, she
began to work at the Fruit Salad Packing Company and participated in a
tanda organized by a woman named Marta. This $200 tanda had eleven
numbers. She alone paid for two numbers and shared another one with
her brother. Thus, in this tanda alone, she was able to garner $400 and
$200 respectively, for a total of $4,000 for her two numbers and $2,000
for the number she shared with her brother. Coupled with the rent from

boarders of $2,000 per month and borrowing $3,000 from her friend Esmeralda, who sold gold jewelry, she was able to pay for the tandas and save resources. She did this so successfully that, coupled with some borrowed money, she was able to pay a *coyote* to bring her mother, her sisters Lupe, Linda, Julia, Ronda, and her brother Eneos from Mexico.

By 1996, her sister Lupe had moved out and taken their mother with her, while Marga (another sister), Ronda, Julia, Eneos, and Orlando (another brother) all stayed at the house on Calle Hanson. Meanwhile, Paloma continued to work at the Fruit Salad Packing Company full time. On the weekends, she worked at the Seven Seas Restaurant, for $4.75 an hour for twelve hours each day, earning $60 daily plus $100 to $200 in tips and, occasionally, as much as $400, especially during the holidays. She continued to rent the garage and two of the bedrooms to between five and six people, and in 1996, she participated in six $100-turn tandas with two turns in each. The tandas operated in both the Fruit Salad Packing Company and the Seven Seas Restaurant. She took two turns each in six tandas at $200 each for eleven turns.

In sum, during 1996, she earned an average of $4,600 from renters, $12,000 from tandas, $5,760 in wages from the restaurant, and an average of $7,200 in tips. Thus, *not* counting her income from the Fruit Salad Packing Company, she was able to generate $29,560. The tanda money, of course, she had to pay back at each turn that was not hers. Yet, from all of these sources, she was able to accumulate this level of resources. Again, this is not unusual in many Mexican communities, especially for women who are very entrepreneurial.

Yet for Paloma, things were not easy. She had to use the money that she earned from her full-time job to cover her household expenses, to pay for medical care for her mother who had been hospitalized at least twice, and to pay back her friend Esmeralda for the $3,000 loan she had borrowed to bring her mother and siblings to the United States. During this period, Paloma remodeled the house at a cost of approximately $5,000, and her mother-in-law also moved into her refurbished garage.

In 1997, she continued participating in the tandas, collecting rent, and she even managed to buy a used Taurus for $3,000. She re-tiled her kitchen, living room, and bathroom at a cost of $2,000. The labor was provided as part of exchange relations between her brothers, her cousin, and friends.

By 1998, she began to work in Cherry King (a packing house) and continued working at the Seven Seas Restaurant during the weekend, from 6 a.m. to 10 p.m. on Saturdays and from 12 noon to 8 p.m. on Sundays. She again participated in six $150-turn tandas—two at Cherry King and four at Seven Seas—during the year. Thus, she saved an additional $9,000 from the tandas, as well as earning income from renters, wages, and tips. By this time, her brother Eneos had moved in with his wife and two children, so a total of eleven persons lived in her home, not counting her mother-in-law in the garage. She received money from Eneos for household expenses and rent.

In 1999, two important events occurred. In one, she seems to have suffered a setback, but in the other, she became involved in the lucrative selling and buying of gold bracelets. In 1999, a climatic freeze stopped production in the region, and Cherry King laid her off in November of that year. She then went to work at the Seven Seas Restaurant from 8 a.m. to 8 p.m., four days a week. She also continued to work in the fields with her brother, who was still a foreman.

She also participated in four tandas, from which she collected a total of $9,600 using two numbers. In December, she used this resource to invest in $5,000 worth of gold jewelry items, purchased in Los Angeles. She also received unemployment compensation for a short period, and she was able to sell her gold jewelry at a 100 percent profit.

Thus, in this period, she made a $5,000 profit, $2,800 per month at the restaurant with tips, $400 per month from her brother and family, and another $2,000 from her renters.

With this continuing source of income in the year 2000, she was able to participate in four tandas of $300 each, for a total of $12,000, which she saved. With those savings, she bought a $30,000 Dodge Ram with a down payment of $12,500. In this year, she was able to purchase $10,000 in gold jewelry by giving the seller two checks. The first was covered by savings from all the various sources already described; the second was a postdated check that the seller was not to cash for three months. Within those three months, Paloma sold a quarter of the jewelry at a 100 percent profit, thus making $5,000, which covered the postdated check. For the rest of the year, monies earned from this source were free and clear, although she saved $5,000 in order to buy the first installment of jewelry.

During this period, she sold the house in Mexico, which she had bought for 25,000 pesos thirteen years before, to her sister for 199,000 pesos, giving Paloma an 800 percent profit.

In 2001, she continued selling gold jewelry, earning between $5,000 and $7,000, and she participated in four tandas, each with $300 turns, from which she was able to recoup a total of $12,000. She also continued to work two jobs and collect rent. She was able to purchase a foreclosed triplex on West Downing for $99,000, with a down payment of $4,950. She immediately rented out each of the apartments, which covered the mortgage payment.

Thus, to sum up, by combining money from selling gold jewelry, renting rooms in her house, renting the triplex, working two jobs, and participating in tandas, she was able to purchase a second home on Buena Vista Drive and an apartment house for a total outlay of $166,000. By September 2005, these two properties were valued at $475,000.

By 2002, Paloma was in fact participating in two $300-turn tandas, one of eighteen turns and the other of twenty-five. She shared three numbers with her sister for a total of $900 per turn, or $450 each. Thus, in 2002, she collected a total of $16,200, and of that, she saved between $10,000 and $11,000. In 2003, she used these savings as part of the down payment for a fifth real estate investment: another house. Simultaneously, she was still selling the gold jewelry, working two jobs, collecting rent from the triplex, which covered that mortgage, and paying for her first home from money collected from her tenants—brother, cousin, sisters, and temporary renters.

In March 2003, as was mentioned, she purchased her third house, on West Upton, with a down payment of $13,447 from the saved tanda monies. She then rented the house on Calle Hanson to her brother and his family for $850 in rent, while her mortgage payment on that house was only $580 per month. She moved into the West Upton house with her new common-law husband, having divorced Manny, who now gave her child support of $330 a month, a year before. Seven months after the purchase of this third habitat, she was able to purchase yet a fourth house on Dorothea in Brawley.

She got the $22,500 down payment for the Dorothea house from three income-tax checks from her former husband, which she cashed for a total of $10,000, and from borrowing the balance: $5,000 from don Anastasio and $5,000 from don Benito. The remaining $2,250 came from savings from two tandas in 2003 in which she saved a total of $9,000. She used the rest of that money for upgrades to this home so that she could eventually rent it out.

By 2004, still combining tandas, working two jobs, selling gold jewelry, collecting rents on her houses on Buena Vista and Calle Hanson, and the triplex, she was able to save $16,200 and pay don Benito the

$5,000 owed. She also collected child support from Manny of $330 per month and had a monthly disability payment of $704. She was able to buy a 2000 Mercedes-Benz that only cost $9,600 because it had been crashed and rebuilt.

In January 2005, she refinanced two houses, one for $84,393 and the other for $96,752. With that, she paid the $5,000 owed to don Anastasio, put a $5,000 down payment on a 2003 Escalade worth $32,000, and, with the remainder, bought land in Brawley for $110,000. She simultaneously participated in a $300-turn tanda with twenty-five numbers, collecting on two numbers, for a total of $15,000 per turn.

In 2006, she borrowed on a line of credit for $99,999. With that and what was left from refinancing the two houses, she was able to purchase a trailer in Oregon for $85,000, paying $72,000 down, and she also made a down payment on a cherry orchard. Taking all the sources of income together—including rentals, selling gold jewelry, working two or more jobs, and participating in tandas from two to four times a year—it is very clear that between 1990 and 2006, Paloma had been able to parlay very limited resources into a position of real returns on her investments. She achieved this utilizing her hard work, ingenuity, and available capital resources from all sources. Clearly, she had established this pattern in Mexico years before. Up to this point, she was well on her way to whiteness.

In that year, a federal attorney indicted her for money laundering along with four other defendants.

Jail, Pleas, and Misprision

At almost every interview, one constant theme emerged: Paloma believed that all her economic activities were for the welfare of her two children. She stated incessantly that all the sacrifices she had made were so that her children did not want for an education, home, clothes, food, amenities, and certainly so that they could enjoy all the comforts of middle-class "white" living. Rolling tears, sobbing spasms, and head shaking from side to side only served to support what she reiterated over and over again: she had worked so hard just to make sure that her family was safe and did not have to worry about the future.

Yet in this place of incarceration where the majority of persons looked almost like her, it was probable that many, if not most, had landed in this white institution with some of the same motivations, but with alternate methods of employment. In fact, Paloma had not laundered money but had entered a deal to buy cherry orchards with Mario García when her brother convinced her that his good friend Mario needed a partner who could be trusted and that he was a man of confianza. Indeed, that is what she did by in fact leveraging her purchased houses, land, and triplex and her Mercedes-Benz, Cadillac, and Navigator to partner with García to buy Oregon land for $150,000. She could not obtain her half by the closing date for the deal, so he paid for it all. Paloma also signed the purchase papers as co-purchaser with Mr. García. Soon after, but before her arrest, she repaid Mr. García for her half.

The indictment of the four defendants, including Paloma, alleged that she was part of a large-scale drug importation ring headed by Mr. García, who also had a number of businesses in Brawley. The monies resulting from drug sales explained not only his wealth but also Paloma's accumulated wealth. Thus, all of her homes, automobiles, jewelry, and cash, as well as any accounts with money, were confiscated, and her children were forced to live with relatives. Her common-law husband, who was an undocumented Mexican citizen, was arrested at the same time as she was, and he was quickly deported.

For six months, Shelly introduced evidence and was able to show that, in fact, Paloma's wealth was earned in the manner I have described. (The attorney, however, did not introduce the information on the tandas, as will be explained below.) Additionally, a forensic economist supported the findings of how she had leveraged her holdings to accumulate the monies to buy the cherry orchard. This and other evidence presented to the judge before trial allowed Paloma to be separated from the others.

The federal attorney initiated a plea bargain, and in the process of developing it, Shelly consulted with a prominent judge from another district, who advised that given the backlash against immigration and all of the negative attention being given to the border that it was going to be impossible for Paloma to get a fair trial in the Southern California region. So, Shelley and Paloma made the decision to enter a guilty plea. The plea bargain required that Paloma plead guilty to one count of misprision of a felony. This involved her admitting her guilt by acknowledging that she knew money laundering was taking place but did not report it. It also included the forfeiture of her part of the cherry orchard, two of her homes in Brawley, her land purchase in the same community, and all of her automobiles. The government magnanimously agreed that she could farm and harvest the cherry crop in the year of her release and keep the income. However, she was forbidden to seek any loans for the purposes of purchasing land or homes during her probation.

What finally became of her purse and its $5,000 and the 24k gold bracelets and necklaces? The purse was found, but evidently the valuables had been distributed among a number of local, state, and federal arresting agencies. Finders keepers.

She received a sentence that was equivalent to her time already served and probation for a number of years. Her residency in the United States was not compromised. Her admission of guilt reads as follows, written in printed letters and in Spanish; it is translated here and slightly amended to mask the identity of the judge:

> Mr. Judge:
> My name is Paloma Rivera and I only want to ask your forgiveness for what I did. Because I only wanted to invest [sic]. Because I am a hard-working woman and I only thought of the best way of giving a better future to my children.
> Sincerely,
> Paloma

She had become partially successful for a price that she could not have ever imagined.

But there is one last anthropological tidbit to chew on. None of my tanda findings were presented before the judge, either when the decision was handed down to separate Paloma from the other defendants or during the plea bargaining. From Shelly's point of view, the concepts of tandas and rotating savings and credit associations would not be accepted because of their cultural foreignness and lack of an American reference and, in my words, their culturally organized relations based on confianza rather than a highly stereotypic individualized value of personal achievement. This is the great contradiction, in that Paloma's individual success is due to her communal participation in tandas, but this practice cannot be presented as a defense because it is culturally too foreign for either prosecutor or judge to understand.

As for Paloma, she said she learned a hard lesson, in that sacrifice and work for her children had not helped them. She vowed to spend much more time caring for them and keeping them happy inside of their extended families. In the final analysis, these nonsuccess domains, together with their possible slanty features and density of relations, are the only, mostly, predictive arenas for emotional success and human contact.

As for Shelly, she wrote to me: "So thank you again, my friend, for your assistance in this case. I don't know if we got absolute 'justice' (as if such a thing can be got in our current system), but we did significant damage control. I think she will be fine. I know she'll have no problem on probation."

Valentina

I first met Valentina Orozco at a private employment agency in southern Arizona. The agency was in a nondescript strip mall, which focused on providing domestic workers for private homes. This was certainly a "non-white" establishment, with mostly Mexican-origin clerks, Mexican-origin owners, and Mexican-origin clients. We two rather "white" academics—one Mexican, the other Puerto Rican—were seeking a person who could help us take care of the house, and as full-time academics with a thirteen-week-old baby, we knew we could not possibly manage without help. We interviewed a number of women, mostly Mexican, as well as an Anglo and one person of uncertain ancestry with tattoos on her yellowed fingers, hands, and arms.

Finally, at 3 o'clock in the afternoon, after pretty much interviewing everyone available, and with our struggling with an anxious infant, we struck gold with the last candidate, Valentina. She walked into the interview room with confidence. Well dressed in a pants suit, with her hair neatly brushed, she gave the appearance of someone always well groomed. After peeking at our daughter and smiling brightly, she sat down. She informed us that she had never worked before, but that she was raising three children, kept an immaculate house, and, in her present circumstances, wanted long-term work with a family that she could depend on and who could depend on her in return.

Her Spanish was tinged with the northerner's emphatic tone, and her eye contact was direct and balanced by frequent non-nervous smiles. That was it. We appraised her almost immediately as a strong, definitive, and confident person to whom we could entrust our house and, for part of the time, our child. We did not see letters of recommendation because she had none, but we measured her to be like many Mexican women who go against the stereotype: tenacious, courageous, and extraordinary, especially in times of distress. She explained that after separating from her husband, she had recently moved from Nogales, Sonora, to close to where we lived.

We found out over the next nine years, as Valentina helped us with the household and with our daughter, that she was a remarkable woman made of the same "right stuff" as Paloma. She eventually became our *comadre* when we asked her to serve as communion godparents to our child, so that ties between us became dense, as is expected. We carried on this very interesting double-helical relationship, in which she lovingly cared for our baby and our soon-to-be fourth grader, kept our house in order, and cooked the finest Mexican food imaginable, including my favorite flour "gorditas"—small, delicate paper-thin masterpieces that could be filled with just about anything or left empty to be gorged upon one after the other. Simultaneously, we many times did not know when and whether we worked for Valentina or Valentina for us. We paid her and she worked, but our relationship was not that of employer-domestic. We roared at her stories, and she accepted my silly male Mexican jokes and Sonoran *dichos* while she riposted with élan and elegance that left me silly many times. To my wife, she was counselor and advisor and older sister, even though they were the same age. They made each other laugh frequently. When things would begin to get out of hand because of the academic pressures of publication, who was to do what, a kid was suddenly taken ill, or the rubber chicken banquets that we were forced to attend, Valentina was there to support and to counsel and advise.

We would do the same for her when life was not as wanted and bad things happened.

When we moved back to California to take yet another academic job, Valentina remained in southeastern Arizona. She soon developed her own business and eventually recruited her sisters, cousins, and friends to clean quite an array of homes. The last time I saw Valentina, she was getting into her used Mercedes-Benz—a kind of statement of recuperation from all of the class, familial, and personal losses and gains she had undergone during those four years that we were all together, with all of us becoming a little more successful and its opposite.

Transborder Crossing over the Many Crossed. Valentina is a transborder person, as are most of the people in her kinship network. She was raised in the Mexican border town of Nogales, Sonora, which is bordered by the American town of Nogales, Arizona. The latter has a population of almost 21,000; the former more than 160,000. Before her more permanent migration to live in southeastern Arizona, Valentina had often traveled, visited, and stayed for short periods in numerous cities and towns in southern Arizona and California—at times visiting relatives, buying goods and services, and also accompanying her husband, who was a transborder salesman of many goods, from electrical items to restaurant supplies to wholesale vegetable produce and meats.[14] Both had less than a *prepa* (preparatory) or high school education, but this did not seem to limit either their initiative or their drive to succeed.

She had led a comfortable life, "slanting" often in order to achieve Mexican middle-class status in Nogales, Sonora. The family of five lived in a "modular" home, which initially began early in their marriage as a small concrete one-bedroom house. Over a period of twelve years, during which time her three children were born, it expanded to a spacious, four-bedroom home with living and dining rooms, and two bathrooms. It was constructed in a Mexican box style, with a sloping roof and large, grated windows. Flowerbeds surrounded the entire two-thousand-square-foot structure. Valentina was a full partner in building a comfortable life that included a secondhand late-model Ford as well as assorted marks of Mexican opulence—color television sets, dining room and living room ensembles, and well-appointed bedrooms. The entire house was floored in Mexican tile, and decorative tiles covered the bathroom and kitchen walls and sinks.

The house was situated on a large lot, a few blocks away from her father's own home and from the homes of brothers and sisters and other relatives. Her children blossomed, and their parents sent them to school "on the other side," to ensure they learned English fluently, since they had already mastered Spanish. They attended a Catholic elementary and middle school, and all finished high school in southern Arizona, except for the youngest, who was still in middle school when Valentina left Nogales. The three children were in fact *fronterizos*, almost born on the border, which was situated only a few miles from their homes.

They were—for all intents and purposes—a Mexican middle-class family, tightly embedded within the larger kinship relations of family and friends. This was the result of a combination of various "slantwise," as well as market, methods of achievement.

Slanting and the Formal Economy. Their household income emerged from a variety of formal, informal, and "gray" economies, with resources extracted from a variety of sources. First, Valentina depended mostly on her husband and his substantial income of 10,000 pesos a week from his sales from transborder transactions. Second, each transaction had hidden dimensions that, in a transborder context, are not unusual, with parts of the formal market products funneled to the informal and gray economies. For example, a hypothetical transaction began with Valentina's husband selling eleven boxes of electronics items to a customer in Nogales or Tucson. She and her husband would take a part of the contents of one box, keeping it as transaction costs. At the buyer's warehouse, the employees would take the rest of the contents of the partial box, report it as lost or damaged, and file an insurance claim. They would then give the customer the ten full boxes. In return, eleven boxes of frozen chickens were shipped back to Nogales, Sonora: ten delivered to one of her husband's customers, and the other distributed to warehouse employees, with Valentina and her husband deducting their own share of chickens. The boxes of chickens would be reported as "spoiled," but were actually sold to neighbors in Nogales, and the electronic items ended up in the local "swa" (swap) meets in Tucson.

These processes were such that after a period of time "orders" for particular items could be purchased at low prices, guaranteed to function or to be eaten, and the local shippers and businesses lost little in the actual transactions since it is expected that a percentage of loss would "normally" occur anyway. Valentina participated fully, as the accountant to her husband, taking "orders," announcing the availability of goods and products, and making certain that their own cut was taken and that those items sold on credit, as occasionally happened, were paid off before further credit was extended. She also accompanied her husband across the border to visit relatives and simultaneously ensure that their networks were stable and steady by visiting their partners in the gray markets. This gray business accounted for approximately 30 percent more over the 10,000 pesos he made weekly. Eventually, this became the single most important source of money for expanding the house itself, the purchase of household items, the children's clothing, and the yearly vacations north to Disneyland and the San Diego Zoo. All of these seemingly "white" strategies of income production, vertical mobility, and consumer purchasing could have continued indefinitely.

Alongside these activities were nearly hundreds of mini-transactions that occurred between Valentina's relatives and friends—favors and exchanges, and participation in tandas that crossed the border or were on or around the border. All pointed to success.

In 1992, a shattering event occurred. Valentina's husband had become enamored of a young waitress and had sired two children in the previous two years. For Valentina, there was no other recourse but separation and eventual divorce.

Around this time, her husband acquired a cocaine addiction that ensured his economic demise. This led to Valentina's fateful decision in 1994 to move with her three children from Nogales, Sonora, to southern Arizona. She moved to southeastern Arizona where her sister lived and began a new and precarious life. Her former husband lost all of it: his family, Valentina, his business, his home, the respect of his children. He eventually ended up serving time in jail for smuggling cocaine. What had been slanted became tilted on one end.

El cambio (The Change)

For Valentina, the border has been less a place to stop than a place to cross for the business transactions described above (less the cocaine). More importantly, it was a place to cross because of the strong ties to her sisters in southern Arizona and California. Her father, a U.S. citizen born in southern Arizona, had moved back to Mexico in his youth. He later worked as a *bracero*[15] in the 1950s in the very state in which he had been born. It was unusual for an American citizen to work as a Mexican national in the Bracero program, but he had access to all the Mexican documentation he needed through relatives in Nogales. Other brothers and sisters, like him, had lived on both sides—some returning from and others going to, depending on the economic circumstances of each side or sometimes just on a whim to get away from the daily grind of one side of the border or the other, or from irate husbands and wives, and even sometimes the law.

For Valentina, her husband's unfaithfulness was more criminal than his later cocaine addiction and imprisonment, but never, by implication or overt commentary, was she heard to speak badly of her children's father. As she said: "He had been a good man and cared for us all. But he was only a man."

Her three sisters and one brother, married to U.S.-born Mexicans, smoothed her passageways to jobs, institutions, medical care, and apartments. Most importantly, like the case of Paloma, they were the core of the dense households in Tucson. Since she was an "illegal," she had to use other means to establish her credentials, and these were mostly done through the use of her sister's identities, because as she often said, "Being a Mexican in their [non-Mexicans'] eyes blinds them to what we really are. They seem like they always have dark glasses on, even in the light."

But for the next four years, she worked hard to begin again. Like many women whose husbands have failed and who are double helical by the so-called illegality of citizenship, she operated at the fringes of the border economy by serving others. Yet, in this fringed edge, and buttressed by sisters and brothers on both sides, Valentina evened up the odds by combining cross-border "slanty" business, working in the informal service economy, working the swap meets, pooling monies, and participating in tandas (but never on Paloma's scale).

The Slanty Businesses and Transborder Funds of Knowledge.[16] Among the perks that transborder women especially enjoy are flexible knowledge and relationships that combine a deep association with fellow holders of social capital; highly functional information as to the limits and possibilities of documentation in relation to the legalities of border trade on both sides; an appreciation for the latest fashion trends and desired feminine objects and artifacts; the ability to quickly respond to changing situations vis-à-vis the authorities, which is passed on to following generations; and, certainly, the ability to plan for the future. From these relationships, women develop information, skills, and abilities, including the ability to conduct "slanty" businesses and to develop accumulated "funds of knowledge."

Valentina's responsibilities to her aging father in Nogales, the need to interact with her brothers and sisters who remained in Nogales, and the simple necessity to make a living in Tucson also demanded that she crisscross the U.S.–Mexico border at least once and perhaps twice a month. When she had been married, she crossed by showing her "passport," that is, a seventy-two-hour commercial visitor's card. Even after the divorce, this card continued to serve as the central means of going back and forth as long as all of her accompanying documents were in order. Given that she now lived in southeastern Arizona, how did she "slant" this piece of legality, her crossing card, to allow her not only to cross but also to reside in Arizona?

The Paper Mill. Valentina and her three children had to have at hand two sets of linked but unassociated legal, and semi-legal, papers that they would present in different spaces and domains. When crossing from south to north, or when renewing her "passport," she had to be ready at a moment's notice to produce documentation proving that she resided in Nogales, such as tax receipts, her voter card, utility bills, and property titles. For her children, the documentation included proof of school registration in Nogales; records of medical vaccinations; birth certificates; and, to be sure, baptismal, communion, and confirmation certificates issued by the Nogales Catholic Church.

On the U.S. side of the ledger, in order to stay in the United States, for daily interactions with authorities, and if examined at a U.S. Border Patrol stop, Valentina had to produce proof of residency, a credit record, and her children's school documents in order to establish a historical record of her legal right to medical care and sundry other things, such as employment, garbage collection, and the establishment of other utility services. In this case, she combined the use of social security numbers from close relatives' social security numbers or numbers of deceased persons to provide the bases for developing most of the documentation needed to create a seemingly legal record of civil standing in southern Arizona.

Therefore, Valentina had to keep in physically close proximity two sets of papers that were linked and yet legally in opposition. She placed each in a different purse, but in the heat of the moment, she occasionally got confused and opened the wrong one. Then, she would have to bluff her way through and fool the immigration official.

Being and Becoming a Border Warrior. There were other advantages to being a *fronteriza* (borderlander). After crossing so many times, and in the crush of automobiles and pedestrians crossing the line at peak periods in day, the immigration official, seeing her familiar face, usually waved her through. That was not the case at the checkpoints farther north. She suffered extreme tension, anxiety, and uncertainty when confronted with the officials at these checkpoints, which she had to offset with an exhibition of coolness, innovation, and élan. There is a level of response and aggressiveness that women like Valentina harness in such contexts that is not apparent to the untrained observer, but suffice it to say that it is akin to the cool detachment of a seasoned warrior. There is simply nothing that cannot be either defeated or deflated. And this skill is handed down to subsequent generations, including to her daughter Seline.

Seline, a precocious twelve-year-old when I met her, already carried herself like her mother, and having crisscrossed the border since she was four, she had already mastered the necessary skills to outwit, outsmart, and outmaneuver the intense and unremitting questions and tactics of the U.S. Border Patrol officers.

Among these are the practices of looking through a person's purse for proof that the crossing to the north is merely a return trip to home rather than a visit, and testing to see if questions asked in English are answered in English, which would indicate residence. Since Valentina and her children still maintained the façade that they lived in Nogales, attended school there, and participated in all of life's usual rituals in Sonora, any indication of residence in the United States would trigger a full-scale body and automobile search. Thus, in one instance, the border control officer at the Tubac checkpoint, which is fifty miles south of Tucson and twenty miles north of the border, found a photograph showing Seline and her cousins standing before a stop sign obviously situated in the United States. He turned to Seline and asked her in English if they were attending a party where they lived. Seline pretended not to understand what he asked, and she answered with an aspirated and quizzically reactive "¿Qué?" He tried twice more, then, tired of his approach, gave up, shrugged, and walked on. A second officer repeated the same question, but this time in Spanish. Seline had to shift languages, sort out the question, and not get caught agreeing that they lived in the United States. Her response was delivered in a convincing, forthright manner—all punctuated with a brilliant, confident smile of triumph while not communicating her mastery. The little warrior had learned well.

Going South. Crossing borders is reciprocal, and facing Mexican border officials is filled with different tensions, anxieties, and uncertainties. Two conditions are present. First, these officials can immediately spot a Mexican who lives in the United States. Even with Mexican border plates, automobiles have telltale indications of U.S. residency—from the shade of the color of the car to the age and type of tires. Second, these officials know that returning Mexicans often carry purchases of luxury goods that might present some possible gain for the official.

Valentina derives part of her income from cross-border tandas that she organizes. She also crosses American perfumes, whose import duties are normally quite high. The involvement in tandas does not pose a problem, but exhibiting too much wealth by wearing jewelry or ostentatious clothing immediately sets off a Mexican official's desire for unofficial tribute. Failing to declare the perfumes got Valentina in trouble when one official searched underneath her seat, guided by the smell of the merchandise. She therefore developed the novel practice of placing three or four meat burritos outside for three days to decay in the sunlight and acquire the right odor to mask the perfume smell when she crosses. She had done this at least three times with the same response of disgust by different border officials, until on her fourth try an official who had previously let her through caught her. The consequence was swift, with the confiscation of the perfume, confiscation of the car, and a $500 fine.

Slanting Mexican Justice. As a former Nogales resident—with kinship relations that are connected to Mexican middle-class networks, which themselves are interconnected to the webs of official and non-official privilege—as well as the spouse of a formerly important broker of cross-border goods, Valentina still has the potential for calling in favors or soliciting special assistance. Like the reciprocal relations of families, these relations extend out to friends of friends and relatives of relatives, into many different economic, political, social, and educational circles. Such circles are reinforced by having children attending the same schools across the border, cousins of cousins practicing law, border officials whose spouses are related to one of Valentina's aunts, and access to political actors whose own economic matters intertwined with her former husband's activities across the border and back. Such density of relations then governs the "slanting" of formal judicial actions and charges. Consequently, Valentina got her car returned and the charges were dropped, but she had to pay the aforementioned fine and a few dollars to her cousin's cousin, the lawyer.

Thus, "slanting" for Valentina has been a cross-border technique learned early, practiced often, and, like many such behaviors, out of sight and off the front stage of public recognition. For Valentina, cross-border living was good; she augmented her salary with these activities, participated in familial rituals and gatherings, and saw her eldest daughter marry a hardworking U.S.–Mexican carpenter, while her eldest son attended junior college, graduated with honors, and eventually became a successful warehouse manager. The youngest continued going to school and was an excellent student making high marks in mathematics and, of course, English.

Cross-Border Tragedies. As was seen in the case of Paloma, slanting cannot resolve everything. Life for many Mexicans, and certainly for Valentina, is a series of knots that she unties with practiced actions, such as making sure that her father was well in Nogales, that brothers and sisters were visited, and that her friends and their friends were treated with the proper social etiquette, aimed at maintaining and reinforcing social relations. Valentina insisted that her children not ignore their imprisoned father's plight. Mexican prisons are almost private institutions because families must provide money to make the prison survivable. In some cases, the money is used as a resource for even more illegal activities. Valentina's children did not go down that road, and they did everything possible to free their father with money, including hiring lawyers to prepare judicial pleas.

The husband was caught in an impossible knot, because his bosses were also part of those dense networks of judicial, educational, economic, and social ties, and his testimony could bring some of them down. So he said nothing to protect himself and paid the price of not going free because of the danger to others above him.

His children visited him to make him as comfortable as possible. At one point, they even pressured Valentina to borrow money on her house to see if they could get him released. She refused, but her son, with his own two children, and her daughter, with a little boy, continued the visits, especially at Christmas time when their father had been especially gracious and generous with gifts and affection.

They did this for five years until one very dark night in December when a SUV broadsided Valentina's son and daughter and tore their Toyota car and them to pieces. They had been visiting their father in the Hermosillo, Sonora, prison, and on their way back, they were struck as they crossed from one highway to another only a few miles from their home in Arizona. A part of Valentina also died that night.

Me levanto o me quedo (I Get Up or I Stay Down). Valentina grieved like only a mother can—one moment, struck dumb; the next, shrieking. But she persisted, and as she said, "Me levanto o me quedo." Six months later, she was the primary caretaker of her grandson, Seline was once again doing well in school, and her other two grandchildren were well cared for by their mother and grandmother. Eventually, she began taking care of other homes, hiring her sisters to assist her, and by the time we said goodbye, she had bought the Mercedes-Benz in which she rode away the last time we saw her.

Last Comments

Slantwise living, confianza, dense relations, affect, tandas, love, marriage, transborder living, and crossing borders cannot overcome the judicial and economic systems created to extract the maximum value from human beings. Both Paloma and Valentina tried their very best, but both were victimized, one woman directly by the American judicial system, and the other woman, indirectly, by the Mexican one. The Mexican system did not kill her children, but the circumstances increased the risk that her children would drive 220 miles, back and forth, to visit their father, who probably would have been in greater danger outside of prison than inside it. For both women, loss, disappointment, grief, and psychic injury became important parts of their daily lives, but none of these defeated them.

Nevertheless, participation in ROSCAs and similar confianza-laden activities has many positive implications and functions. And although tragic in the specific outcomes for these two women due to life's vicissitudes, as the next chapter illustrates, these practices have multiple functions whose importance for individuals and especially for those having to adapt to the dynamics of the Southwest North American Region cannot be underestimated.

5
Crossing Divisions and Social Borders
ROSCAs as Transborder Practices and Their Functions

This work so far has focused on broad theoretical assumptions that provide insights into how rotating savings and credit associations (ROSCAs) have emerged as important practices among many Mexican-origin populations. It has shown that ROSCAs are highly movable and cross the political borders of the Southwest North American Region. It has also developed the idea that Mexican-origin populations, like the practices themselves, have long crossed those borders, most recently because of this area's development as a central regional site. This centrality consists of a transborder economy, culture, social relations, and a multiple psychocultural identity, as described below. In part, the practice's capacity to endure, and the population's capacity to engage in the megascripts of the region, daily using "slanted" measures in their social and political lives, speak to the many functions ROSCAs fulfill. The ability of this population to skirt racialized statuses of gender and culture is due in part to the major ways in which ROSCAs fulfill a host of functions that have less to do with economic gain, although this is a most important function. Rotating savings and credit associations often crosscut divisions of class, cultural identity, and gender expectations. They crosscut and counter the social borders created by class and occupation and the insidious differentiation of racialized statuses, such as the commodity identity too often associated with Mexican-origin populations. They illustrate, in very specific ways, that Mexican-origin people are not mere "commodities." Instead, they are innovators and creators of a variety of means for reducing the uncertainty and indeterminacy of their daily lives. In a very specific manner, ROSCAs are functionally transborder in their ability to crosscut the differentiations that define Mexican-origin people as "the other," and they are counterpoints to this definition.

The Transborder Functional Dynamic

One of the most important functions of ROSCAs is that they help reinforce underlying cultural constructs within the Mexican population, both in and beyond the Southwest North American Region, and they are truly transnational and transborder. When I use the word "transnational" and "transborder," *at one level* I include only activities, events, behaviors, transactions, networks, and relationships in which people on both sides of the border participate in mutual fields and arenas in the Southwest North American Region and beyond.

However, *I also mean*, as previously discussed, those very useful practices and unseen ideas carried over from their points of origin and introduced into a new national setting, whether this involves people already accustomed to their use and ideational analogs, or people who encounter them as new knowledge learned in the new setting. As I have also stated, *there is a spatiality* that is not located in a single space, because many people live out "transnational and transborder lives" in which their "citizenship" is not the main locater for their existential sense of self; rather, it is tied to myriad points of cultural and physical places, emotional spaces, and cultural references on either side of the "border." For Mexican-origin populations living in and of the United States and those migrating to Mexico's northern border, "transnational living" has been an increasingly important phenomenon. This is especially true with the great demographic transitions between Mexico and the United States that have taken place from 1980 to the present, much of them an aftermath of the implementation of the North American Free Trade Agreement (NAFTA).[1]

Culturally and historically, Mexican-origin populations have lived transborder lives. Most of these individuals cannot be reduced to a category of citizenship or to their engagement in the transnational networks described above. In Ramón Saldívar's fine book (2006) on Mexican-American author Américo Paredes, who wrote texts focusing on border life, he quotes Paredes as saying he regards himself to be "a sociological phenomenon" because of his double cultural presence in both nations. Saldívar, extending Paredes's position, expands this as "a preposterous oddity existing both inside and outside of two discrete national realities" (161).[2] But I think it not as preposterous as either Saldívar or Paredes would suggest. Simply, events and history have prevented a single-tracked, citizenship-based personality development, in which our beings are tied only to an American civil life. The recognition that cultural personalities have multiple dimensions that cannot be reduced to simple unilineal identities has helped devastate the acculturation model. Mexican-origin populations in the United States live American civil lives, but this is contextualized within multiple transnational and transborder points of reference. Therefore, culturally these populations amass and discard layers of cultural skins that do not refer to only a simple cultural referent, such as citizenship. Transborder populations in the United States live with that referent, but they also live within and on many bordered aspects of themselves, which historically penetrated their very beings in a way that goes far beyond the reach of an imposed or acquired citizenship. Transborder populations gather in the midst of social relations as old as the Romans, worship in even older religions, and from recounted and lived experiences participate and are reminded of their transnational and transborder selves on a daily basis. And simultaneously, they die in American wars. It has been this way since the nineteenth century.[3] The rotating savings and credit association is but one other important, culturally functional practice that makes up one locus of the multiple layers of cultural references that Mexican-origin populations share.

Multiplicity of Functions

Rotating savings and credit associations let the poor and the wealthy, the working-class and the economically marginal groups, professionals and blue-collar workers, women and men, the elderly and children all adapt to the circumstances they face. Despite the heterogeneity across them, each of these sectors resides in a context that creates a variety of differentially distributed and culturally defined needs. "Adaptive ROSCAs" help meet the needs that each population has defined as essential to its continued existence. The cultural form of the ROSCA does not define the needs to be fulfilled, but rather, like any other cultural invention, it remains viable and important for behavior because of its flexible potential in diverse contexts. Even the more commercialized rotating credit associations (RCAs) that charge a fee or a free first turn in some ways are even more functional than the ones that do not—in the sense that the organizer has a vested interest in the RCA's success. Therefore, the participants have a higher probability of having their social and economic needs met, especially in the midst of economic limitations or hardship.

Similarly, RCAs, which I have defined as an institutionalized form that seeks to extend credit opportunities, also fill niches that are normally either avoided or simply not considered by a variety of class and cultural populations, especially in the Mexican-origin populations described here. The Internet revolution has partially accentuated the viability of RCAs.

Banks, for the most part, are brick-and-mortar platforms that offer more functions, but in filling market niches for credit, the FYGO and the Autofin types of RCAs are specifically tailored according to known cultural templates of trust and mutual trust. This form, extending credit via the Internet or through someone selling computers, household goods, cosmetics, and sundry other items, seems to evoke and psychologically intersect with the cultural template of the *tanda* or *cundina* networks of reciprocal relations. The announcement by FYGO (appendix B) clearly illustrates how companies and enterprises call up "structures of commonality" that are familiar and positively reinforced, and that resemble cultural outlines of known operational actions with positive outcomes.

Simultaneously, however, companies appropriate these local cultural forms and social behaviors, and they "dislocate" some of the local versions. On the other hand, as long as capitalist systems continue to scrape value from labor, goods, and materials, then inequality and stratification will continue, and local practices like the adaptive ROSCAs will remain viable forms that, although they do not make structural changes, nevertheless ease daily living and reinforce mutual trust and reciprocal relationships.

Class and Context

Economically Marginal Sectors

My data on economically marginal sectors in Ciudad Netzahualcoyótl and Los Angeles indicate that people of limited means have to pay exorbitant rates of interest to purchase consumer goods on credit. By belonging to ROSCAs, they can accumulate sufficient savings to purchase these goods while eliminating interest payments, thus avoiding further marginalization.

For those in economically marginal sectors, ROSCAs also serve other functions. By providing the wherewithal to purchase gifts and commensal items, they enable people to meet crucial ritual obligations. Fulfilling ritual obligations, such as those of *compadrazgo* (co-godparenthood), was the second most frequent (17 percent) use of ROSCA funds (fig. 2.7). Meeting one's ritual obligations expands assistance networks and increases social wealth. The act of accumulating money to meet these obligations selects for an increased number of social links and, with that increase, access to more favors. Each favor represents the possible reduction of a price in the marketplace, an increase in the number of tortillas received for a given expenditure, reduced prices in a clothing store, a discount on shoes, an introduction for a job, assistance in taking care of children, advice on medicine for a sick child, information about a desirable medical practitioner, the intervention of a political figure when a family member is jailed, access to a social security number and green card, or simply information about whom to avoid on a particular day. Each favor, in turn, is eventually returned. Rotating savings and credit associations contribute to the continuation and expansion of such reciprocal networks, and they thus increase the probability of cultural and biological needs being met under conditions of extreme scarcity. In economically marginal contexts, cooperation, not competition, selects for individual and group survival.

Working-Class Sector

Within working-class sectors, ROSCAs have similar expansionary social consequences. Although economic conditions are more comfortable than in economically marginal sectors, access and reciprocity still increase as a consequence of meeting ritual obligations. On the other hand, ROSCAs play crucial roles in occupational processes in both service and industrial working-class sectors. In the oil fields of Veracruz, for example, those engaged in *tandas* are generally regular, long-term employees. They are highly skilled, well-paid industrial workers, protected by a very strong labor union. Their fringe benefits are the envy of other Mexican industrial workers. Tanda participation is restricted to this regular workforce, which keeps out transient, temporary oil-field workers hired when production demands increase the need for labor. Thus, as an unintended function, the elite status of the regular oil-field worker is enhanced by his tanda membership.

Factory workers producing ceramics in West Los Angeles use various mechanisms to accumulate funds, including lotteries, games of chance, and the cundinas. Like the oil-field workers' tandas, these cundinas accentuate the elite status of certain workers. A $50 deposit, returned at the end of the cundina, is required, and only those people with relatively high wages can afford that entrance fee. Thus, as was the case with the Veracruz oil-field workers, the ceramic workers achieve greater social density through their involvement in tandas and cundinas, but as an unintended consequence, the practices also reinforce certain elitist patterns.

Yet, like the economically marginal populations, ceramic workers suffer from uncertainty and indeterminacy. For these workers, immigration raids are a constant source of uncertainty and a real threat to durable relationships. They also feel economic stresses, especially since there is little formal union organization; however, their skills are highly specialized and in great demand. Consequently, factory owners are quite willing to protect their workers' wages and offer benefits that are in some ways superior to union-organized factories. Thus, the cundinas serve not just as a monetary cushion for the ceramic workers but also as a mechanism of solidarity among them.

The consequences of ROSCAs for workers in labor-intensive industries like clothing manufacture are different from those in highly skilled craft sectors. Among clothing workers in the sweatshop-like factories of El Paso or Los Angeles, the competition for overtime piecework is intense. It takes place within sections devoted to certain specialized tasks, such as riveting jeans or attaching zippers, and involves relatively large numbers of workers. Because assembly line methods are used in the very large factories, like Farah in El Paso, Texas, competing workers must of necessity work side by side. It is likely that members of the same task section will cooperate in the operation of a tanda or *vaca* (in El Paso). Thus, although the overall structure of the factory demands incessant competition for overtime among members of the same task section, the ROSCA serves as one of the few means to generate cooperation. It crosscuts individual competitive divisions and thus acts to overcome the stress brought on by that competition and the low hourly wages. Its success in achieving solidarity can be measured by the fact that in these task sections, a few non-Mexican or non-Hispanic members also participated in ROSCAs.

Professional and Middle-Class Sectors: Women, Men, and Clubs

The specific context of residential and occupational middle-class sectors determines ROSCAs' variable consequences. Married women rely on the household allowances they receive from their husbands for their contributions to ROSCAs, but by their participation, they create circumstances in which they can spend money as they wish, that is, on other than household items. Dependency characterizes the relationships between middle-class-sector wives and husbands, just as it does between working-class-sector and economically marginal–sector couples. The husband's generosity in setting up his wife's allowance influences his power over her. The ROSCA enables wives to feel more secure and mitigates some of the uncertainty of dependency. Many women commented that "there is nothing like one's own" to enable one to make a decision. They compared this freedom to the constraints they felt in their role as dependent housewives. In some of the interviews, husbands were quite surprised to learn that their wives participated in ROSCAs. Some women kept this participation totally hidden, citing their husbands' propensities to influence how the fund share was spent.

Yet there were important consequences beyond the individual level for the professional and middle-class sectors. ROSCAs allowed many households living beyond their means in a consumer, credit-based context to get through the month without increasing their debts. As a consequence, they achieved some equilibrium between the resources actually available and debt. Such balance, although not resolving the basic problem of indebtedness, did alleviate stress within the household. It was not unusual for middle-class husbands to belong to occupational ROSCAs while their wives participated in residential ones. The combination of the two ROSCAs allowed couples to keep their heads slightly above water, thus reducing uncertainty.

There are still other consequences in middle-class contexts. Some women from a working-class or economically marginal background, having reached middle-class status through a job or a marriage, found their familial relationships strained, if not disrupted, by changing values and the acquisition of *pretenciosa* (pretentious) respectability. Pretenciosa is the cultural construct those from other sectors use to describe the middle-class sector. The construct refers to the disengagement of such people from relatives and friends in working-class or economically marginal networks. Visits between relatives become episodic, gift giving becomes haphazard or mechanical, and ritual obligations are seldom met between class-divided relatives. The result for many of these women is the impoverishment of historical family or friendship networks (see Vélez-Ibáñez 1978b).

The ROSCAs serve as important mechanisms enabling these women to associate with other women and generate "fictive friendships" (Moore 1978, 63). The usual pattern is for twenty or so women to gather on Friday afternoons between 4 and 8 p.m. to share information on children, husbands, households, television programs, and neighborhood improvements or changes. Besides providing the setting to distribute and collect funds for the tanda, these socially crucial meetings anchor women with others of the same sector in an association that functions in a manner reminiscent of the primary-group relations that changes in class status have disturbed. The consequences for these women go much beyond the intended club activities, creating reciprocal obligations normally found in primary relations. As an ample literature shows,[4] and data from this research verify, there is little doubt that structurally changed contexts stimulate people to seek out voluntary associations. In the aftermath of vertical mobility and the resultant value changes, people construct fictive relationships with others. The idiom of these relationships seems to have attributes of friendship, but they do not carry with them density, reciprocity, and affect, except in the context of tandas and clubs.

Because of class differences and perspectives, kin and long-term neighbors are likely unable to satisfy the affective needs of someone who has experienced social mobility. Yet affective needs, especially those involving personal security, can seldom be fulfilled by material success or upward vertical mobility alone. The fictive friendships forged in the club provide some measure of security. These new relationships, however, are based on the middle-class value of conspicuous consumption. The ROSCA's money-rotating mechanism allows this value to operate, but at the same time it guarantees flexible, mobile associational relationships. The very practice reinforces middle-class values of consumption, but it also integrates those values into a network of mobile and easily transferable social relations, which themselves demand conspicuous consumption both symbolically and concretely. Among upper-class women, the ROSCA generates the same sort of congruence between values and network relationships, except that the basic value articulated and integrated by the practice is not conspicuous, but rather sumptuous, consumption.

Participation in ROSCAs has other important consequences for professional and middle-class sectors. Among relatively high-level administrators in the Mexican national social security system, it was not unusual for ROSCAs of large amounts to be tied to office politics. These administrators' budgets were supervised by politically appointed bureaucrats, and each administrator was in direct competition with the others for budget allocations. The allocations served as signals the administrator could read to determine the political strength of his competitors. Yet all these competitors participated in the same ROSCA. Membership itself was also read as a signal of a competitor's strength. Since the supervisor and each administrator kept the administrator's budget allocation a well-kept secret, an administrator who did not participate in the ROSCA was considered to be in disfavor. The reasoning behind this belief was that a person in disfavor would have a lower salary, and thus could not afford a high-priced ROSCA and might not be able to finish the year-long cycle, the typical duration for these ROSCAs. The consequences for administrators participating in the ROSCA were positive, since a participant was likely to be regarded as being in control of his domain and in favor with the supervisor. Those not so regarded suffered more devastating office politics and further encroachments into what might otherwise have been funds allocated to their budgets. On the other hand, there were administrators with political acumen who were in disfavor, but they sacrificed a great deal in terms of their power in order to participate in the ROSCA. By obscuring their true circumstances, they kept competitors off balance.

Although the administrators were competitors in one context, as members of a ROSCA they cooperated in their obligatory relationships. This crosscut divisions resulting from competition and created alliances between departmental administrators and others in the struggles over budget allocations. The ROSCA assisted in integrative functions beyond those its participants intended. Most institutions operate not only according to the bureaucratic rules that define them but also according to informal mechanisms, like the ROSCA. In this case, the ROSCA served to stimulate crosscutting ties in one context—that of its own operation—and to loosen them in another—that of political competition. This "tying and untying" process is one means by which the social relations within the institution operate, and as an unintended consequence, it provides a dynamic impetus for the operation of the institution itself.

Networks of the Elderly

Among networks of elderly, retired bourgeois men and women in Mexico City, tandas are anchored in recreational activities. Canasta, pinochle, excursions, painting classes, museum visits, operas and symphony concerts, library visits, and occasional group vacations fill up the end of their life cycles. For the most part, these people have accumulated durable relationships and social credits, on which they draw during their recreational activities (Moore 1978). Social relations are expressed in shared laughter at the past and in favors, such as cheating for the other during canasta games, or buying popcorn for the other in a theater or park. These activities are anchored not only by accumulated social credits and durable social relations but also by the common reality of these individuals being near the end of their lives. The tanda provides material proof of the durable reciprocity of present and past relationships. Tandas commit those at the end of the life cycle to the future by placing in the distance the obligation to reciprocate with contributions. While the uncertainty of the future is made real by the deaths of those around them, their investment in the future, masked as an obligation, contradicts that uncertainty.

For the elderly in these bourgeois networks, the life cycle has also meant some withdrawal from interdependent relations with younger cohorts. Such networks are marked by their members' relative independence from either the economic or social necessity of maintaining dependent or interdependent relations with children, grandchildren, or institutions controlled by the young.

This is not the case for elderly people in working-class or economically marginal sectors who participate in tandas. Unlike the elderly bourgeois, they do not generally join age-homogeneous tandas. Their interdependence with the young—children, grandchildren, or friends—is necessary for most endeavors. One consequence for the working-class and economically marginal elderly is that interdependence relations between different age groups is maintained, thus preserving a sense of continuity throughout the life cycle.

Institutional Contexts

The complex reciprocal obligations generated among female civil service workers have already been mentioned. In these offices, gift giving, commensal activities, and economic cooperation in tandas replicate "normal social relations" (Goffman 1961, 6). New employees are integrated into the local-level complex of relationships outside of the institution's normative authority and power relations. Integration into the dynamics of social action within these partial institutions is made easier, and the integration softens the stresses created by the uncertainty of a new context. These contexts generate group obligations of reciprocity between old and new employees, and the tanda, gift giving, and commensal obligations equalize political relations between newcomers and those with seniority.

Although authority, seniority, and responsibility separate people in civil service contexts, the other relationships crosscut such divisions and create greater solidarity among the women. Hierarchy divides, but each member of the tanda is responsible for collecting the money in the week in which it is her turn to receive the fund share, which necessitates a recognition of equality by all concerned.

In private or public institutional settings, when employees from different task sections or departments participate in the same ROSCA, administratively defined divisions are crosscut by the ROSCA relationships. Even the highly specialized departments in the National Anthropology Museum, each of which has its own head (*maestro*), are crosscut by the ROSCAs. These ROSCAs also serve as information conduits between the departments, enabling them to share information on their budgetary and resource restrictions. The maintenance of a repair and construction schedule sometimes depends on the information channels kept open by ROSCAs or other reciprocal mechanisms.

In a more general sense, these crosscutting ties and dense interactive networks increase the probability that institutional information will be exchanged. In this way, employees improve their positions relative to opportunities that arise in other sections. According to informants in public and private institutional offices, wages for lower-level office workers are usually very low, so employee turnover is high. Changing jobs within the institution is, however, positively regarded since relations can be maintained across institutional divisions. The information exchanged during tandas and other reciprocity mechanisms provides a guide to intra-institutional opportunities. Thus, institutions in which tandas and other reciprocal mechanisms operate tend to retain their employees, and greater employee solidarity is created as an important, yet unintended, function.

General Economic Consequences

I have suggested that for economically marginal, working-class, and middle-class sectors, general scarcity of means and living beyond one's means are two important conditions under which ROSCAs are an adaptive tool. By eliminating interest charges from market relations, informal or intermediate ROSCAs are also very functional. However, even some of the most conspicuous examples of such interest-free consequences occur in the Volkswagen or Datsun tandas or RCAs. For example, in a Volkswagen tanda in the early 1980s, once a month, forty people each contributed a sum of money, which together totaled 88,000 pesos,

the price of a Volkswagen. A lottery then selected one person to receive
that fund share so that he or she could buy the car for cash. By avoiding
taking out a loan to buy the car, over a forty-month period, a person
saved almost 88,000 pesos in interest. This substantial savings freed the
participant to engage in other position-enhancing economic strategies.
By 2008, the price had doubled, but the functions remain the same, and
participants still gain all the favorable outcomes.

There are, however, other notable consequences. First, it is remarkable that people are willing to delay gratification, possibly for as long
as forty months. The willingness to delay gratification for such a long
period certainly testifies to the application of the *confianza* construct in
situations extending beyond the highly dense networks of relationships
in which it normally appears. Although participants understand that
they have a one-in-forty chance to be selected as the first Volkswagen
owner, they also know that they face thirty-nine chances of not being
selected. Although one's chances improve each time another car is allocated, this reliance on chance expresses a willingness to delay gratification. It is a remarkable achievement for these people to invest so much
confianza in the informal mechanisms for allocating the automobiles
and in the administrators in charge of the effort. The most remarkable
aspect of this, however, is the confianza they have in their good fortune,
which lets them put off ownership until luck decides in their favor. In
this case, economic maximization comes from avoiding interest charges;
the participants gamble on winning first, but because they are willing to
delay gratification for as long as the lottery system dictates, the bet seems
like a sure thing—there is no way to lose. In a sense, the participants are
investing in their own self-control and discipline. Most RCAs generate
in their participants a self-discipline not to spend, and most do it within
an obligatory savings relation.

Two other noneconomic contexts, in the formalist and functional
sense, exist.[5] In informal and intermediate quasi-commercialized ROSCAs
in which the first turn is free, a zero turn is taken, or a fee is charged, the
participants put in more than they take out. Commercialized ROSCAs
accounted for 42 percent of the dollar- and peso-denominated ROSCAs
sampled through 1982, but by 2008, that figure had risen to more than
60 percent. The question arises whether people in economically marginal,
working-class, or debt-ridden bourgeois sectors do, in fact, participate in
nonadaptive ROSCAs because their already strained resources would be
further depleted by the fees they pay to the organizer.

The answer seems to lie in the uncertainty of the context and not in the economic gain. For the most part, fees are charged in residential ROSCAs, but not in familial or occupational ones. However, sometimes even in occupational contexts, a fee or the first turn is charged because of the threat that participants will leave the job or, in the case of undocumented workers, face arrest by immigration authorities. Also, fees may be charged to offset the time and energy spent in organizing and carrying out these ROSCAs. Even noncommercialized ROSCAs appear frequently in areas of high population mobility. Since the major adaptive consequence of participation is the creation of reciprocal obligations, in a mobile context, the associations select for greater social stability rather than material gain. Second, highly mobile populations are likely to be alienated from institutional sources of credit or savings because they are unlikely to have established a credit history.

For less-mobile populations, the consequences can also be positively functional. The organizers' fees are no higher than the value of the service they provide. The organizers usually come to collect the members' contributions, and this means that the members do not expend energy dressing and feeding children and paying for transportation to a savings institution or to the organizer's home. This is a fair exchange for the fee paid to the organizer.

Corporate *mutualistas* and RCAs have intended and unintended economic consequences that are functionally positive. First, the payments are scheduled so that it is relatively convenient for people in many class sectors to have access to accumulated sums. Given the procedures necessary to establish credit in most lending institutions, it is easier, even though collateral is required, for an individual to join a mutualista than to be a customer of a lending institution. Second, the member has a chance of paying less than what he or she receives, thanks to the lottery system. In mutualistas with forty members, there are twenty chances that a person will pay more than he or she receives, and twenty chances that a person will pay less than what he or she receives. The economic consequences are distributed according to chance, with a 50:50 probability that a person will receive more than what was contributed (and vice versa). Third, each person has the same probability of becoming a borrower, although he or she will have to pay for the privilege of getting the fund share earlier, and the same probability of becoming a lender and profiting thereby. In essence, each person, in order to improve life's chances, becomes a risk taker. This single ingredient can be relatively adaptive in most urban environments in the long run. (In addition, of course, the participant is protected by the corporation's death-and-accident benefits.) Like deutero-learning of saving, taking risks in the mutualistas over extended periods generates a type of deutero-learning of risk taking, which is positively selected for in most urban environments. The last consequence of participating in such mutualistas is access to accumulated capital, which in times of inflation does not cost as much as the charges for having the first allotted number would suggest.

Interstitial Consequences and Dimensions

One of the most difficult tasks in anthropology has been to tie together analytically various levels of social domains. Wolf (1956), for example, pointed in that direction when he stated that anthropologists might properly concentrate their analytical energies on the interstitial connections between various levels of social action in complex social systems. Brokers, for example, are one such interstitial connection that has been studied by a variety of commentators (Bailey 1969; Blok 1974; Boissevain 1974; Fallers 1965; González 1972; Vélez-Ibáñez 1978a). Or, to state it a bit differently, how do we analytically connect the local with non-local and superlocal structures and relations?

The use of rotating savings and credit associations are one such interstitial connection made across various domains. Regional interstices, like those between Guadalajara in central Mexico and northern border towns like Ciudad Juárez, are bridged by merchant connections. Money from a ROSCA collected in Guadalajara is used as working capital for merchants who buy used American clothing in El Paso, which they sell in Guadalajara at a substantial profit. That same profit is used by the merchants to pay contributions to ROSCAs not just in Guadalajara, but in El Paso and Juárez as well. Merchants offset the costs of purchasing clothing and passing it through Customs by lodging and eating with relatives with whom they have already established tanda (*vaca* in El Paso) relations. (Notably, merchants who participate in ROSCAs in Guadalajara, Ciudad Juárez, and El Paso must also be able to shift the nomenclature they use, from *tanda* in Guadalajara to *quiniela* in Ciudad Juárez to *vaca* in El Paso, which illustrates the basic similarity of all ROSCAs.) Moreover, the geographic gap between central Mexico and the northern border areas is connected not only by the trade efforts of these merchants but also by the extension of confianza between networks of people in entirely different regions.

Similarly, transborder interstitial connections are more direct when generated by commuter cundinas, which occur all along the U.S.–Mexico border. As I have indicated, they are tied to the dollar-peso exchange rate, and the choice of currency depends on the participants' projections of fluctuations in the rate. Participants review the daily rate changes in order to ferret out any long-range trends. Their goal is to produce a profit by exchanging a dollar fund share for a peso share or vice versa. In making these calculations, multiple unintended functions ensue. First, people develop a very sophisticated knowledge of monetary-exchange systems. Second, they are part of an important knowledge base for local populations and often share predictions with each other to take advantage of falling or rising exchange rates. Lastly, each transaction contributes to the further development of local transborder skills and capacities often unavailable through formal institutions on both sides of the border. Banks do not share this type of information without a formal business relationship of some sort.

Most commuter cundinas are basically informal, with the organizer living in Mexico and the members in the United States. Needless to say, this kind of connection across national borders has to be based on quite-well-established confianza networks. The bridging of local-level interstices by commuter ROSCAs has yet to be explored in depth.

Interstitial connections between different social levels of activity and organization are among the most important. Connections between local-level kinship networks, institutional contexts, residential sectors, and class sectors are illustrated in figure 5.1, which shows the kinship network of a couple in Monterrey: José and Rosa López and their children, Ramón, Elías, Ana, Olea, and Evita. Each of the five children, in turn, has children, whose names are omitted, except for Olea's Petra and Elías's Rosa and Elías Jr. The diagram also shows the spouses of each of the five offspring and the connecting link to a second familial network of the same generational cohort: the Listo network.

The Listo network, all of whose members live in the squatter settlement of Colonia Paraíso, begins with Yspírito and Polo. Yspírito is a sister of Regina, who is Ramón López's wife. Thus, the affinal relationship between Regina and Ramón extends to the Listo network. Yspírito and Polo have seven children: Johnny, Norma, and five others not shown. Johnny has established intimate friendship and *compadre* relations with a third network composed of Carenas and Carlotta. As will be seen, each of the three networks is also connected to the others and to institutional sectors through tanda participation.

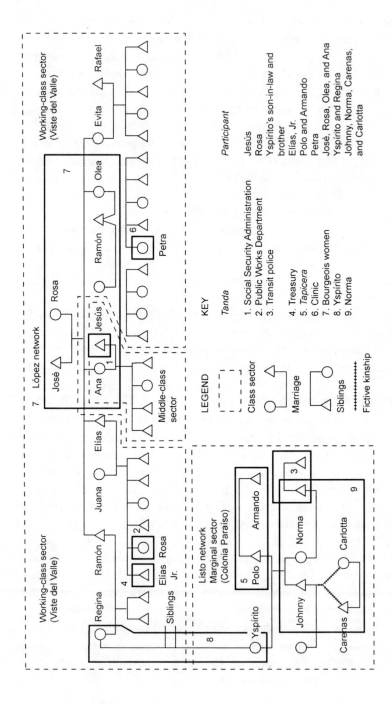

Figure 5.1 Interstitial connections. *Source:* Prepared by the author.

Each network, however, is also representative of different residential and class sectors. The López parents are working-class people who live in a residential area outside of Monterrey called Vista del Valle. It is home to working-class people who are employed year round, who have essentially steady incomes, and who have purchased homes constructed of relatively high-quality materials. Both José and Rosa participate in a joint tanda with their daughter Olea, who lives nearby with her children and four of her husband's by a previous marriage. In another tanda, Olea, José, and Rosa all share a number with Ana that is part of her bourgeois residential-sector network. Ana is the wife of a medical doctor, and she acts as the broker for her parents and sister in the residential tanda in which only bourgeois women participate.

This example is extremely important, for it points to the generalization of class divisions within the Mexican population, which can be produced by a job or marriage. Ana's relations with her nuclear family are strained. Visits are rare, José and Rosa serve as caretakers for Ana's home when she and her husband go on vacation, and ritual exchanges are mechanical and lack spontaneity. Yet, José, Rosa, and Olea, all working-class individuals, faithfully contribute to Ana's share in her bourgeois tanda. Interestingly, Ana socially discriminates against her relatives. This can be seen not only in their strained social relations but also in the fact that Olea's daughter, Petra—whom Ana describes as young, well dressed, and nice looking—is the only one allowed to deliver the tanda contribution to Ana's home. However, her husband works in the national health service, and his income is less than that of other husbands in the area. Consequently, although class restrictions keep José, Rosa, and Olea from participating directly in Ana's tanda, their indirect involvement makes it possible for her to cover the prohibitively large contributions. In order to enhance their standing, women who have joined bourgeois or upper-class sectors relatively recently may also participate by cooperating with working-class relatives, though I have not verified that. Because José, Rosa, and Olea participate in the same tanda with Ana, exchanges among kin across classes is possible. Olea's daughter Petra's visits and collection of money establish social connections across geographic space. Although geography and class separate, kinship and tanda reciprocity crosscut cleavages and differences.

Such interstitial connections also extend from working-class sectors to economically marginal sectors. Regina and Ramón, like José and Rosa, live in Vista del Valle. Regina participates with her sister Yspírito in the residential tanda in Colonia Paraíso, the squatters' settlement.

Consanguineous relationships between Regina and Yspírito are relatively strong, but the sisters are divided both by class and residence. Regina's participation in Yspírito's tanda bridges these interstitial gaps. Yspírito's husband, Polo, participates in *tapicero* (upholsterers) tandas with his brother, Armando. Within the same residential and class sector, Johnny, Yspírito's son, participates in his sister Norma's tanda within the third network of Carenas and Carlotta. Thus, a series of links connects Carenas and Carlotta to Johnny and Norma and then to Yspírito to Regina, and then, through Regina's in-laws, to the bourgeois Ana. This does not mean that any direct exchanges of information take place among these connections, but should the need arise, the possibility of mobilizing these connections exists.

Five institutional sectors are represented in these networks. Jesús, Ana's husband, is a medical doctor working at the headquarters of Mexico's Social Security Administration (which delivers free health care to the population), and Petra, Olea's daughter, works in the records office of one of the system's clinics. Elías Jr. is an office manager in the tax-collection branch of the Treasury Department, while his sister Rosa works in the Public Works Department. Yspírito's son-in-law and his brother are both policemen with the transit police. All of these people participate in office tandas. As has been suggested, exchange obligations normalize relations within institutions. Also, however, because of the deutero-learning, participation in institutional ROSCAs make it easier for spouses and relatives to participate in residential ROSCAs.

Both Elías Jr. and Rosa accumulate money from their salaries and tanda fund shares (fig. 5.2). Both contribute to their parents' (Juana and Elías) expenses, and their parents, in turn, provide money to their own parents, José and Rosa. José and Rosa, with Olea, then contribute money to Ana's bourgeois tanda. The fund share from the forty-women bourgeois tanda returns via Ana and is distributed to José, Rosa, and Olea.

As I have already suggested, these links to other class and institutional sectors can be mobilized as possible sources of assistance. For example, Carlotta once needed medical assistance, and Carenas asked his compadre, Johnny, for help. Johnny, in turn, mobilized his network, including his mother Yspírito and his mother's sister, whose husband, Ramón, is the brother-in-law of Jesús, the medical doctor. Since Carenas could not legitimately acquire medical treatment for Carlotta by means of workmen's benefits, Petra (Olea's daughter and Jesús's and Regina's affinal niece) were called upon to assist in the establishment of a medical record in the documents section of the local medical clinic where she worked.

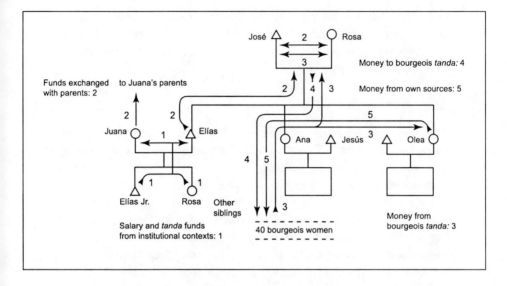

Figure 5.2 Circulation of funds. *Source*: Prepared by the author.

That particular clinic did not have the specialized treatment necessary, but by means of the documents acquired through Petra, Carlotta became eligible to receive the best medical treatment in Jesús's main medical office. Petra could not have accomplished this without the collaboration of her fellow office workers with whom she participated in dense network relationships that included a tanda, gift giving, and commensal activities. Thus, although people are divided by a number of cleavages, tandas help to bridge the gaps both directly and indirectly.

As we have seen, it is highly likely that as first-generation Mexicans in the United States participate in similar associations, the underlying element of confianza will continue to be an important construct in predicting others' behavior, structuring one's behavior with others, and maintaining a reflexive cultural reference to oneself.

In addition, unlike many previous generations of Mexicans migrating to the United States who could count on the security and protection of working-class neighborhoods, most Mexicans migrating today face the uncertainty of living in metropolises, which selects against the maintenance of social networks, cultural cohesion, and psychological security (Galarza 1981, 8–9). This social mobility "delocalizes"[6] the population, and thus ROSCAs provide a modicum of security in an uncertain context, while also reinforcing the construct of confianza. This promotes and reestablishes meaning in new contexts. Thus, for Mexicans in all contexts, the ROSCA and, equally important, the shared concept of confianza are very significant and adaptive at social, economic, cultural, and individual psychological levels.

After 9/11

Another important phenomenon has facilitated the reinforcement of the confianza construct in a most unintended manner. Since 9/11, crossing back and forth across the border has become highly problematic, especially so when a person does not have documents. Given that about six million undocumented Mexicans live in the United States, this very substantial population is more and more pressured to stay "below the radar." For example, various restrictive laws in Arizona have resulted in undocumented workers being charged as felons for smuggling themselves into the United States. Additionally, restrictions on hiring have certainly chilled the workplace for Mexicans, and nationwide, a generalized anti-Mexican political environment has appeared. With (re-)entry into the United States so much more difficult, expensive, and dangerous, many Mexicans no longer return to their homeland, opting instead to stay in the United States. However, they try to stay "below the radar," by not taking children to parks, recreation centers, or places where migrants congregate. Sheriff's officers in Maricopa County in Arizona have arrested entire families in these places, turning them over to immigration officials for deportation. Therefore, living underground demands that a migrant have complete and uncompromising confianza that others will not reveal the migrant's true legal status. Undocumented students, especially in universities, high schools, and elementary schools, must depend on the confianza of other students, their teachers, and administrators in order to keep them protected from police agencies and U.S. Immigration and Customs Enforcement (ICE) officials. This confianza can be maintained by ROSCAs in spite of the very long arm of the law.

Deutero-Learning: A Transborder Cultural Expansion

Saving to Save and Trusting Mutual Trust

One of the most important and unintended consequences of ROSCAs is what Bateson (1978) termed "deutero-learning." He stated that two types of slopes are expressed in all continuous learning: "The gradient at any point on a simple learning curve . . . we will say chiefly represents rates of proto-learning. If, however, we inflict a series of similar learning experiments on the same subject, we shall find that in each successive experiment the subject has a somewhat steeper proto-learning gradient, that he learns somewhat more rapidly. This progressive change in rate of proto-learning we will call 'deutero-learning'" (167).

To make the idea of deutero-learning clearer, Bateson (166) has likened it to what happens in an experimental setting in which a person "not only solves the problems set him by the experimenter, where each solving is a piece of simple learning, but, more than this, he becomes more and more skilled in the solving of problems." It can be inferred from my data that those individuals engaged in saving not only save but also, if rewarded, expand their notion of "saving." Not only do people expect mutual trust, but also, if rewarded, they expand the expectation of mutual trust. Thus, both saving to save and trusting mutual trust are deutero-learned constructs. As people internalize them, these truly transborder constructs come to occupy other cognitive spaces that are congruent to their maintenance with social practices, like engagement in dense social relations, growing up in cross-border households, participating in rituals, and sharing in funds of knowledge—all of which enhance daily living and the probability of greater social exchange.[7]

Ahorro para ahorrar (I save in order to save) is deutero-learned in that the habit or custom of saving expands at the moment an act representative of saving occurs or is expected to occur, regardless of the specific context. Participation in ROSCAs is one such act, as is the saving of the accumulated fund shares. Importantly, it is a transborder and transnational phenomenon and not situated within a single cultural reference of citizenship—Mexican or American. But how this is expressed (for example, in practice in the development of small businesses in which saving and borrowing are the linchpins for their creation) is a key element in their efficacy and continuous reproduction. In Arizona alone, 44 percent of all Hispanic businesses were owned by people of Mexican origin, and one in three Hispanic-owned businesses was started by undocumented immigrants. In almost any community in the Southwest North American Region and from Alaska to Hawaii, Mexican-origin populations open restaurants, garages, landscape services, domestic and community service groups, and hundreds of other small business ventures, all started from early savings practices, one of which is having learned to save to save.

Confianza en confianza (trust in trust) is similarly a transborder, deutero-learned construct in that the habit or custom of confianza expands at the moment an act representative of trusting occurs. But it also reinforces and expands the multiplicity of transborder identity. This construct expands to cross classes, political borders, and regional divisions, and it traverses any single citizenship identity based on a single cultural reference. Confianza en confianza emerges not just from ROSCA participation, but also is part and parcel of a much larger cultural experience that begins very early in the lives of Mexicans on both sides of the border.[8] Confianza en confianza can be considered somewhat more expansive than ahorro para ahorrar, since a series of reciprocal modes are expressed in other contexts including, for example, commensal, ritual, and social activities. Residential, occupational, and familial sectors all select for other reciprocal exchanges besides those emerging from the ROSCAs. Thus, it is likely that a wider deutero-learning process occurs for confianza than for saving.

In considering these two deutero-learning constructs, we should keep in mind that the details are inferentially derived from both observed behavior and my more formal data. The following descriptions of the details of each construct are validated by the data, but are not the data themselves. No single individual would be able to describe the constructs completely, but I infer that they exist from informants' statements, observed behavior, and the continuation of the practices themselves. This is a compromise between subconscious cognitive orientations that members of a group may share as equivalencies and a strictly inferential model that represents an abstraction derived from observed behavior. The constructs presented here are neither the predictive model used by others, such as Foster (1967), nor a description of a partial worldview of those who participate in rotating savings and credit associations.

Central Feature

The central feature of saving to save as a construct is not defined by the intentions or motives of those who join a ROSCA and make the effort to save. Nor are the meanings that workers, housewives, upper-class women, the elderly, corporate executives, or any others derive from ROSCA participation central to the construct of saving to save. Intention, motivation, and meaning vary with the contexts in which the associations appear. Instead, the essence of saving as an idea is that each person, regardless of context and regardless of intention or meaning derived, has placed his or her contribution in reserve. Saving to save is learned even by the upper-class women who spend their savings lavishly on one of their network members. The fact that these women agree to hold money in reserve until they accumulate enough is a savings activity regardless of intention. Nor does expenditure of the saved and accumulated money define the construct. On the other hand, if the money accumulated is itself further saved, then the savings process is reinforced and expanded. This is the only caveat to the proposition that neither intention nor the specific way in which the money is spent contributes to the formation of the construct of saving to save.

This construct also extends to the competing administrators and economists in the planning office who hold in reserve a portion of their income; their intention and the unintended consequences do not matter. The core of this proposition is very much like that postulated by Keynesian economics. The simple classical economic assumption about savings states "that savings always flow into investment at the going rate of interest regardless of the level of income" (Klein 1947, 79). Keynes, according to Klein, attacked the assumptions of this assertion and hypothesized that people can make other decisions in regard to what they do with incomes: "They may decide upon saving or consuming their incomes, and they may decide upon holding idle cash or non-liquid securities. Each decision requires an economic calculation. In the former case, individuals decide on the basis of their incomes how much they want to save. In the latter case, they must decide on the basis of alternative rates [of interest] whether they want to hold their . . . savings in the form of cash or securities" (123). Therefore, people must decide what to save out of their income for whatever reasons, and they must decide in what form to hold savings, that is, as money, stocks, bonds, or, as in the present study, as accumulated funds in rotating savings and credit associations. The rate of interest is as variable as the intention to participate, but nevertheless, the decision to set aside money in ROSCAs is an act of saving.

In addition, the specific reward derived from saving is as variable across all sectors as the intention, but in most cases, that specific reward will influence the rate of further expansion of the learned construct of saving to save. Thus, for the upper-class women, prestige rewards emerge from the reciprocal network which enhances their positions in that network. Again, for these women, the learned construct of saving has expanded. The rate of learning for them is probably lower that it is for someone who waits forty months for a Volkswagen, but nevertheless expansion occurs. To deny that upper-class women experience deutero-learning or to restrict their experience of it to specific stimuli or rewards would be to deny the concept itself. The degree to which, and how fast, the construct expands may be linked to the reliance on saving for meeting culturally constituted goals and biological necessities. The essence, therefore, of saving to save is that, regardless of specific intentions or rewards, the construct expands as an unintended consequence as people participate in ROSCAs.

Even when paying fees in *tandas muertas*, people learn because each saving activity proves rewarding: energy-consuming activities are avoided and social exchanges established. Each rewarded saving activity increases the rate of proto-learning. These savings will result in the deutero-learning of saving as a concept and its expression in behavior, so that saving to save as a cultural construct expands in use. Although participation in a fee-based ROSCA appears to be uneconomic, the experience still has important learning consequences.

Other elements of the construct "saving to save" can be inferred from an examination of the most frequent uses for the accumulated sums and by extrapolation from the congealed meanings contained in those uses. As will be recalled (see fig. 2.7), the most frequent use of saved money is for further saving, which also indicates a willingness to delay gratification. This shows that the idea of placing something in reserve as a value in itself is not only expansive but also implies a future-oriented outlook. In other words, a delay in the immediate gratification of a perceived need is an inherent aspect of placing something in reserve. The willingness of people engaged in tandas or cundinas to wait long periods for their fund shares illustrates this. Therefore, I suggest that both ROSCA participation as a saving venture and the use of the received funds for further savings imply the future-oriented outlook of the participants, regardless of their intentions or actual expenditures.

Many of the fourteen use categories in figure 2.7 imply a future-oriented outlook and planning strategies designed to increase the probability of meeting sociocultural and biological needs. The second most frequent use of funds was to fulfill ritual obligations, which indicates a desire to maintain and generate social relationships in the present and the future on a regularized schedule. A person's future is assured by meeting such obligations, since the other person in the exchange is required to provide a gift in return in the future. It is important to note, however,

that ritual obligations can also be used to expand existing social networks, and each expansion not only increases the absolute number of
social relationships but also "social wealth"—the favors and social credits accumulated for future use.

In terms of the strictly material benefits, each use of ritual obligations
also implies planning, direction, improvement, and a quest for future, as
well as present, stability. Each material artifact on which tanda or cundina
funds are to be spent is invested with values. Money spent on household
goods—the third most frequent use—expresses not only "consumer"
values but also those congealed in the physical presence of the goods.
As part of the home, these help to provide a platform for family stability: surrounding familial relationships with physical artifacts reflects the
desire to establish, stabilize, and strengthen them. Buying land, investing
money, and purchasing a home also indicate a future-oriented outlook
aimed at establishing familial or personal security.

Trusting Mutual Trust

Trusting mutual trust is the central construct in most informal and
intermediate ROSCAs in the Southwest North American Region and
beyond wherever Mexicans reside. My data support that. There is no
need to review the various figures illustrating the density of confianza
and the various mechanisms and processes used to establish it. It is also
unnecessary to review how the absence of fraud or default is evidence
of the profundity of confianza between participants, or to review the
multiple relationships shown in chapter 4 and the manner in which confianza enabled both Paloma and Valentina to operate within dense relations that are always susceptible to destruction by events and behaviors
beyond a person's control.

Confianza en confianza even extends to people who are strangers to
the other participants in a ROSCA. Not all members will have precisely
the same qualitative relationship with each of the other members. Thus,
people must project trust in mutual trust to those they do not know or
with whom qualitative relationships differ in density. Trust in the association organizer is necessary but not sufficient to establish confianza
in the operational stability of the entire enterprise. All relationships in
complex urban societies are segmented and partial, and even the best of
dyadic relationships between a ROSCA organizer and member—when,
for example, they are husband and wife—is based on partial equivalent

beliefs, since no two persons share the same beliefs, but only their equiva-
lences. Therefore, given the great stress on confianza as the single most
important mediator in social relationships, confianza en confianza is
likely to be an overriding cultural intersection shared by all concerned.
This includes not just Mexicans but also non-Mexicans, including Salvadorans, Columbians, Anglos, Filipinos, and sundry other populations
that participate in ROSCAs and that are subject to the dynamics of confianza en confianza. It is a kind of lingua franca of Mexican culture used
when people entrust their money, energies, needs, and goals to others.
It also shapes their general expectations toward those individuals who
are strangers to them. Because confianza en confianza is rewarding, the
construct has now expanded to become an overriding cultural intersection for most Mexicans and the many non-Mexicans who participate in
cundinas or tandas.

Trusting in the Trustworthiness of Self

A third important element is that confianza en confianza implies trusting
in the trustworthiness of self, which makes mutuality possible. It is not
accidental that ritual activities have been important in the expenditure
of ROSCA funds. As Erik Erikson (1963, 250) has suggested, "Individual
trust must become a common faith, individual mistrust a commonly
formulated evil, while the individual's restoration must become part of
the ritual practice of many, and must become a sign of trustworthiness
in the community." Without a firm sense of personal trustworthiness,
no such commonality of trust can be expressed in ritual. Mutual trust
is a trusting not only in the trustworthiness of others but also implic-
itly in the trustworthiness of self. In varying distributional frequencies
in urban Mexican populations, the trustworthiness of self is an internal
construct serving as the basis for potential social intersects.

   I use the phrase "trusting in the trustworthiness of self" to distinguish
the idea from the usual understanding of "self-trust" as self-reliance, which
is probably a form of complex narcissism. Self-trust and self-reliance are
indistinguishable in American usage, but self-reliance is not what Erikson
means by trust in oneself. What he calls "trust" coincides with the term
"confidence," but he prefers trust because there is more mutuality implied
in the term (1963, 248). "Trusting in the trustworthiness of self" implies
mutuality to a greater degree than either trust or self-trust. Like Erikson
with his notion of trust as a general state, I imply in the phrase "trusting

in the trustworthiness of self" the capacity of one's organs to cope with urges and the ability to consider oneself trustworthy enough so that those relying on one will not need to be on guard against possible machinations on one's part.

In summary, two basic elements are characteristic of confianza en confianza: first, it is a generalizable transborder construct extended to those with whom no social exchange has been established, and second, it reflects trusting in the trustworthiness of self. Thus, it establishes the basis for reciprocal exchanges in a variety of class, ethnic, and other contexts. Mexicans will seek out others with whom to have confianza because the construct itself, in its various forms and interpretations, functions as a cultural intersection for social interaction, and by providing coherent expectations of others, it has positive and adaptive consequences at a deeply psychocultural level. Mutual trust in others eventually reinforces trust in the trustworthiness of self. To trust others who are not known eventually reinforces trust in still others who are yet to be known. Both elements are expansive and increase in scope as long as they are adaptive and rewarded. To deny the learning consequences for such a construct among Mexicans is to deny the validity of learning theory.

Finally, I suggested that among the most important constructs learned from participation in ROSCAs was "saving to save" as a deutero-learned idea, as shown by the data. The population's willingness to save speaks to the fact that in so doing they have developed a strong sense of delaying gratification in order to plan for and fulfill future needs. Whether such constructs do in fact increase and expand is a processual and structural matter, not a motivational one, but it is certainly transborder and transnational. It is, however, tragic, and yet ironic and contradictory, that such a construct fits so importantly into the broad framework of the megascript of "success." Success does so by reinforcing achievement by saving for purchases, spending—within the economic confines of a system designed to extract as much value as possible coupled to the trappings of success—and lastly, by cognitively melding and adhering to the broader megascript of "success." This coupling of ideas, scripts, and material reality provides powerful cultural incentives to cross deserts, face back-breaking manual labor, wiggle in between immigration raids, and allow erasure of language by legislation.

6
Conclusions

From a transborder and transnational perspective, previous chapters have discussed the widespread use of rotating savings and credit associations (ROSCAs) by Mexican-origin populations. As I have indicated, this practice has expanded throughout many social sectors in the United States and Mexico. Its distribution across classes, occupations, and residential areas and its commercialization all speak to the expansion of the Mexican population throughout the Southwest North American Region and throughout rural areas, hamlets, suburban villages, towns, cities, and megacities in both countries. Changes in local, regional, national, and transnational economies, simultaneously facilitated by rapid communication and transportation, fueled this expansion. It is among the most important and largest demographic explosions in North America itself since the European migration of the nineteenth century to the eastern shores of the United States and the great shift of people moving from rural to urban Mexico in the late 1960s and early 1970s.

This development, as I have suggested, resulted in the creation of asymmetrical, but increasingly transborder, integrated economies. Here, postindustrial capitalism seeks untouched but available markets, and it transforms traditional agricultural, construction, mining, transportation, and assembly sectors. This transformation and the search for available new markets are the causal bases for the migration of Mexican-origin populations within and across political borders. Conversely, they are also the sources of Mexico's national dependence on remittances, which are crucial for local development in Mexico.

As I have shown and hypothesized, the Southwest North American Region is becoming a "central place" from and through which billions of dollars pass and millions of people traverse and settle, and settle and traverse. This region has a demographic dynamic that radiates east to New York, northwest to Alaska, south to Mississippi, and to Kansas, Indiana, and Iowa in the Midwest. Some parts of the region have seen the development of "Regions of Refuge," made up of thousands of people living in *colonias* on both sides of the border. In many cases, illegal settlers simply "invaded" the land, or they bought empty lots without getting legal title to them. No codes or regulations guided the development of these settlements, and many of them lack infrastructure, including potable water. These refuges offer the last desperate hope for possessing hearth and home (Vélez-Ibáñez 1996; 2004a).

Figure 4.1 illustrated the movement of the Mexican economy to its northern border. The ROSCA is but one transborder economic and cultural practice that constitutes part of the social and economic practices and relationships of the developing center. Coupled with the hundreds of transborder rituals, relationships, religious ideologies, child-rearing practices, businesses at multiple levels, and types of economy and social organization that radiate from and across the border region, ROSCAs provide an additional cultural platform for the emergence and reproduction of transborder culture.

As has been described, ROSCAs form from the networks of exchange that, at times, cross class divisions and cultural boundaries. Women participants, especially, reinforce the deutero-learned ability to save and to invest in social relations as part and parcel of the necessary mechanisms under which ROSCAs operate. Indeed, these networks and their accompanying ROSCAs are slantwise practices, as I have explained. In other words, these are innovations that utilize available social capital, relatively stable contexts (such as institutions, workplaces, neighborhoods, and now, Internet networks), and that skirt formal economic institutions in places where none exist or where social and economic obstacles make them closed to certain participants. Rotating savings and credit associations are the most handy, culturally congruent forms that "fit" the material—and certainly the social—needs of participating populations. These persons are positioned between the "interstices" of formal legal, economic, political, and social structures, and their participation in ROSCAs (prominently, the participation of women) crosscuts hierarchies of class, gender, and culture.

Equally importantly, however, ROSCAs contribute to the development of a transborder regional identity, which—when combined with all of the other constant reminders of the presence of the border—reinforces a multidimensional cultural approach and practice that inevitably transcends a single unitary format of national "citizenship." Daily, Mexican-origin populations practice both Mexican and American civic duties and obligations and lead civil lives on both sides of the border, but this is only one part of a plethora of cultural views, relationships, and practices that are uncoded and thus not within expected civic and citizenship cues, scripts, and behaviors based only on nationality. To illustrate this dimension, one only has to mention Valentina's daughter and her ability to linguistically and culturally shift codes and insert her own practiced behaviors in their place (chap. 5).

This book has also illustrated the various nomenclatures and types of ROSCAs that have developed, the importance of these associations, and the incipient development of commercialized associations, as well as their implications for saving. The expropriating features of an electronic financial system, like the FYGO that uses the cultural template of reciprocity in a completely market-oriented setting, also speaks to the manner in which local cultural patterns and practices become embedded within the arc of postindustrial capitalist ventures that I have termed rotating credit associations (RCAs) to differentiate them from true ROSCAs.

An examination of the social and cultural contexts in which ROSCAs appear showed how each context defined categories that served to fix people's relationships and that acted as social references. Various methods and boundaries that decrease the risks involved in lending, borrowing, and saving—so that fraud and default are rare—were analyzed. However, this work has also shown that a substantial part of the ROSCAs are increasingly semicommercialized through the institution of a fee paid to the organizer or the practice of having the organizer take the free first or "zero" turn. This has come about to guard against sudden withdrawal of participants or their refusal to pay their contributions. *Confianza* nevertheless is the central "cultural glue" that is crucial to the operation of ROSCAs, and in turn, they are but one means by which binding reciprocal obligations are maintained and expanded. Given the dynamics of the region and the unprecedented movement of Mexican-origin populations, both confianza and the ROSCA serve as key elements for reducing the uncertainty and indeterminacy of daily life.

As I have pointed out, numerous unintended and intended social, political, cultural, economic, and psychocultural consequences derive from ROSCAs, and the examples demonstrate that people using them are able to adapt to the structural demands of their various contexts. As Paloma and Valentina illustrate, however, indeterminacy and tragic failure cannot be avoided regardless of the existence of the most determined of cultural inventions and constructs, including ROSCAs and confianza. In Paloma's case, the anthropologist's work was not recognized as legitimate

because the identities from without concerning Mexican-origin populations are too often shaded, and they are defined as mere commodities, or
worse, as inferior, negative melanin bearers too exotic to be recognized.
Thus, confianza, exchange, reciprocity, and ultimately the ROSCAs were
considered by the defense attorney as too culturally exotic to be accepted
by the court, even if explained by an anthropologist—representing a
rather exotic discipline too often associated publicly with Indiana Jones.

The double helices created by history and economy capture transborder Mexicans, define them as commodities, and, on both sides of the border, burden them with judgments of "race." This generates personal and
group instability and indeterminacy. A second double helix is embedded
in the achievement megascript, which almost decrees sacrificing social
networks, exchange relations, familial affect, and children's well-being
as the quickest and most efficacious path to attain material success.
When these two helices combine, no cultural medium like ROSCAs nor
valued construct like confianza can solve the causative sources for their
necessity in the first place.

In the face of resulting uncertainty and indeterminacy, all such practices are local attempts to "fix" and regularize action and people. And
so it is in the transborder contexts in which such mutability is especially
pronounced and where the sudden turn of fortune may be just around
the corner. Here is where the world of accidents intersects with the daily
life of trying to live just a bit better. For Valentina, slantwise strategies,
tactics, and practices could do little to mitigate the slantwise transborder
tragedy of her children's constant negotiation of institutional barriers
and impediments and, ultimately, of their deaths.

Although the practice of the rotating savings and credit associations
and their developed networks probably promote well-being and survival, this does nothing to change the underlying forces that national
and transnational policies favoring postindustrial capitalism engender.
The great megascripts of "success" and "achievement" permeate the
daily lives of all transborder populations and, indeed, of all populations.
These scripts become normalized as being beyond question, not unlike
religion. Among Anglo Americans in the United States, individualism
rather than mutual trust has generated a heavy reliance on large-scale
institutional forms rather than on intense multiple networks to deal
with the resulting inequalities of distribution. But like Mexicans, they
suffer from the same changes, with those in the working class having
little recourse except to be the victims of downsizing and outsourcing,

especially as the world economy stresses the ability of national economies to deal with "economic cycles." Similarly, members of the Anglo middle class, like their transborder Mexican counterparts, face the uneasy prospect of living beyond their means, cleaning out their equity in the mortgage markets, while greater and greater wealth is scraped and lifted up to the 1 percent in the now intensely integrated Mexican and U.S. economies, particularly in the new center of economy and polity: the Southwest North American Region. Yet local Mexican-origin populations in this transborder world of economy, polity, culture, and region, nevertheless, must somehow challenge, develop, innovate, and adjust their contexts, spaces, structures, fields, and arenas of action.

In the present economic meltdown, will practices like ROSCAs and beliefs anchored in confianza become even more important to populations that are often at the edge of economic well-being and to other populations with over-extended credit? My guess is that such practices are among the few still in the hands of noninstitutionally dependent populations, and thus, more than likely, they will become even more important. Yet they cannot but contribute to the continuing efficacy of the megascripts that overlie them and the practices that make them possible. Such is making an impossible living in a transborder world.

Y Colorín Colorado, Este Cuento Se Ha Acabado.

Appendix A
Foreword to *Bonds of Mutual Trust* (Vélez-Ibáñez 1983) by Eric R. Wolf

Foreword

Anthropology has always been at its best when it could place seemingly ordinary features of everyday life in a new light, and deduce unforeseen implications from that examination. This is what Carlos Vélez-Ibáñez has done in his study of rotating credit associations among Mexicans and Mexican-Americans. He has not only shown the prevalence of this institution among different categories of that population, but he has demonstrated how much at variance are the resulting modes of behavior and thought from prevalent stereotypes of the shiftless poor or the distrustful Mexican. Participation in the rotating credit associations requires postponement of gratification, as well as prudential forethought. It also requires, as Vélez-Ibáñez shows, "trust in the trustworthiness" of fellow participants. Vélez-Ibáñez's account of how people save money through joining rotating credit associations is thus also an anthropological brief against myths that justify social discrimination by falsifying the picture of the victim.

Becoming accepted as an associate in one of these credit associations, and accepting others, depend on the cultural construct of *confianza*—the willingness to engage in generalized reciprocity with others. The concept derives from Marshall Sahlins, who saw it as a form of exchange in which gifts of goods and services are offered without the requirement of an immediate or equivalent return, in the expectation that prestations will balance out in the long run. Sahlins contrasted this form of open-ended reciprocity with "balanced reciprocity," in which a gift tended is immediately requited by a counteroffering of equal value. Confianza extended by the participants in a rotating credit association expresses the evaluation that offerings will continue over time, without an immediate calling in of shares extended. Trusting in each other's trustworthiness thus also expresses a shared sense that the self of each participant is culturally constructed to maximize long-term commitment and mutuality.

The social actors of Vélez-Ibáñez's account adapt to their economic circumstances, but they do not do so in the Darwinian sense of winning against competitors. Rather, they engage in their arrangements of mutual credit to meet biologically and culturally defined needs through the use of a cultural invention. The rotating credit association possesses this cultural referent, even while it can be used to meet the exigencies of widely varying circumstances.

Vélez-Ibáñez argues that confianza does not constitute a bundle of culturally uniform understandings, but rather is a "cultural intersect" allowing people of quite varied backgrounds and interests to communicate sufficiently to act in concert. He thus contributes to our theoretical perspectives on culture by using an action-oriented conception in place of the older views of culture as inert tradition handed down from the dead to the living. George Herbert Mead, Marcel Mauss, A. I. Hallowell, and Erving Goffman have all shown how the self is not given a priori, but is constructed socially and culturally. Vélez-Ibáñez's model, however, recalls the work of an earlier social scientist, Adam Smith, who understood that the search for utilities in the market was not carried on by atomistic maximizers, but by human beings whose behavior was constrained by what he called "propriety." Seven years before *The Wealth of Nations*, Smith wrote in his *Theory of Social Sentiment* that social interaction was governed by "sympathy," the great socializing force that ensued because each social actor, motivated by an "inner spectator" to maximize praise from others, strove to make himself praiseworthy in the eyes of the "real external spectators" who interacted with him. Sympathy gave rise to propriety, and only the desire for propriety made possible interaction in the market.

In showing how people construct notions of trustworthiness in the marketplace, Vélez-Ibáñez also points to a dimension of ethnicity that goes beyond current definitions of an ethnic category as a population occupying an ecological niche or acting as a political pressure group in competition with other economic or political groups. He suggests that economics and politics also involve notions of who can be relied on and the limits of such reliance. Sometimes the very strivings to build and maintain confianza go awry, as Vélez-Ibáñez shows in the ethnodrama. At other times there may be contradictions between the quantitative demands of the money economy and the qualitative demands of kinship, friendship, or neighborliness that underwrite the credit associations. Yet the picture of Mexicans and Mexican-Americans that Carlos Vélez-Ibáñez has painted is that of people active and innovative in the pursuit of their ends, comporting themselves with dignity to meet the cultural demands of confianza.

Eric R. Wolf

Appendix B
FYGO

FYGO Announces Public Launch of Beta Product

December 17, 2006 by Arizona Venture Capital

New online financial collaboration network makes it easier to borrow, lend, gift or repay and brings humanity and fairness back to finance.

Phoenix, AZ. FYGO, the leading provider of online financial collaboration networks, today announced the public release of its beta product. FYGO gives people the ability to leverage their own personal networks to borrow, lend, gift or repay.

At its core, FYGO enables groups to access and automate the lending process between friends and family. A secure Web site allows for an open exchange for people to easily lend or borrow initially $100–$2,000 and establish their own interest rate, duration and payback terms. At FYGO, users can create lending groups that can be accessed when the need arises.

"Everyone runs into short-term financial crunches at one time or another," said David Farias, founder and CEO of FYGO. "Until now, the options were limited to payday loans and credit cards that charge oppressive interest rates. FYGO provides a much fairer alternative by simply leveraging the relationships people already have and to develop new ones."

The process is designed specifically to be user-friendly, while at the same time employing best-in-class security and privacy measures. Those wishing to borrow or lend must go through an authorization process, including bank account verification and credit verification. The key to FYGO's process is the building of a personal network, which can be a group of friends, colleagues or family. Individuals build their network by inviting others to join. It is only within a network that one can make transactions.

"For borrowers, FYGO offers a new option to better manage your finances and a good way to increase financing options," noted Farias. "And for lenders, it's a great opportunity to help someone out in a more structured way than an I.O.U. This takes the emotion and awkwardness out of it; not to mention you can earn a fair return." Oh, and if borrowers do not pay, lenders can extend terms, forgive the loan or send to collections.

In addition to its person-to-person lending service, FYGO will offer the ability to manage funds through its "Virtual Treasurer" service. This can be used for dues management (i.e., alumni groups, football leagues, community events) or for personal purposes (i.e., event-planning, group travel).

FYGO's platform is patent pending.

About FYGO

FYGO is the leading provider of Trusted Financial Collaboration Networks, enabling consumers to conveniently lend, borrow, gift, repay, and conduct financial transactions online with people they know and trust. The company provides online services that allow people to create or join networks with people in their personal and professional lives. FYGO is based in Phoenix, AZ.

FYGO Press Contact:
Robert Wallace: rw@fygo.com
617.448.1885

http://azventurecapital.com/arizona-venture-capital/venture-capital-news/fygo-announces-public-launch-of-beta-product/

Appendix C
Six-Person, Thirty-Week Tanda

Table C1. Six-Person, Thirty-Week Tanda

Person	Turns	Contribution	Weekly Total	Weeks	Total Paid Out	Total Received
1	1–10	100	1,000	11–30	20,000	20,000
		5,000 from Person 2 (500 weekly for 10 weeks)				
		5,000 from Person 3 (500 weekly for 10 weeks)				
		5,000 from Person 4 (500 weekly for 10 weeks)				
		4,000 from Person 5 (400 weekly for 10 weeks)				
		1,000 from Person 6 (100 weekly for 10 weeks)				
2	11–15	100	500	1–10 16–30	12,500	12,500
		5,000 from Person 1 (1,000 weekly for 5 weeks)				
		2,500 from Person 3 (500 weekly for 5 weeks)				
		2,500 from Person 4 (500 weekly for 5 weeks)				
		2,000 from Person 5 (400 weekly for 5 weeks)				
		500 from Person 6 (100 weekly for 5 weeks)				
3	16–20	100	500	1–15 21–30	12,500	12,500
		5,000 from Person 1 (1,000 weekly for 5 weeks)				
		2,500 from Person 2 (500 weekly for 5 weeks)				
		2,500 from Person 4 (500 weekly for 5 weeks)				
		2,000 from Person 5 (400 weekly for 5 weeks)				
		500 from Person 6 (100 weekly for 5 weeks)				

(Continued)

Table C1.   (*Continued*)

Person	Turns	Contribution	Weekly Total	Weeks	Total Paid Out	Total Received
4	21–25	100	500	1–20 26–30	12,500	12,500

5,000 from Person 1 (1,000 weekly for 5 weeks)
2,500 from Person 2 (500 weekly for 5 weeks)
2,500 from Person 3 (500 weekly for 5 weeks)
2,000 from Person 5 (400 weekly for 5 weeks)
500 from Person 6 (100 weekly for 5 weeks)

Person	Turns	Contribution	Weekly Total	Weeks	Total Paid Out	Total Received
5	26–29	100	400	1–25 and 30	10,400	10,400

4,000 from Person 1 (1,000 weekly for 4 weeks)
2,000 from Person 2 (500 weekly for 4 weeks)
2,000 from Person 3 (500 weekly for 4 weeks)
2,000 from Person 4 (500 weekly for 4 weeks)
400 from Person 6 (100 weekly for 4 weeks)

Person	Turns	Contribution	Weekly Total	Weeks	Total Paid Out	Total Received
6	30	100	100	1–29	2,900	2,900

1,000 from Person 1 (1,000 weekly for 1 week)
500 from Person 2 (500 weekly for 1 week)
500 from Person 3 (500 weekly for 1 week)
500 from Person 4 (500 weekly for 1 week)
400 from Person 5 (400 weekly for 1 week)

Appendix D
Contract of Agreement

Contract of Agreement   Accion No.
                                            Serie:
                                            Plan:
                                            Grupo:

10,000 [50,000; 100,000; 150,000] Peso Mutualista

He quedado enterado de la existencia de una Asociación Civil con fines mutualistas con las siguientes caracteristicas:

DENOMINACION: Mutualista de Yucatán (pseudonym)

Domicilio: Mérida, Yuc.

Objeto: formar fondos de ahorro de $20,000.00 [50,000: $50,000.00; 100,000: $100,000.00; 150,000: $150,000.00] para cada uno de los Asociados que les permita adquirir o reconstruir bienes immuebles o y constituir gravámenes sobre ellos, y formar fondos de defunción e invalidez total permanente, por la misma cantidad, para el caso de fallecimiento o invalidez de un asociado.

Número de accíones: 40 [50,000: 50; 100,000: 50; 150,000: 50]

Valor de cada acción: $20,000.00 [50,000: $50,000.00; 100,000: $100,000.00; 150,000: $150,000.00] que es el importe del fondo de ahorro.

Duración: 327 [50,000: 394; 100,000: 394; 150,000: "393 semanas y cuoto complementaria de $162.00"] semanas.

Régimen legal: Código Civil del Estado de Yucatán y leyes relativas

Obligaciones para gormar los fondos de ahorro

I.—contribuir con 327 [50,000: 394; 100,000: "Todos los Asociados pagarán la cantidad de $212 semanales antes de resultar beneficiado con el fondo de ahorro"; 150,000: 393] aportaciones semanales de $54.00 [50,000: $106.00; 150,000: $320.00] cada uno.

II.—Contribuir con aportaciones semanales de $26.00 [50,000: $64.00; 150,000: $190.00] además de las anteriores, a partir de la fecha en que le corresponda al asociado recibir el fondo de ahorro, y ahorro, y durante el resto de duracion del plan de ahorro, o sean $80,000 [50,000: $170.00; 150,000: $510.00] semanales.

[100,000: "—Todos los Asociados paragon la cantidad de $340 semanales a partir de la fecha en que les corresponda recivir el fondo de ahorro."]

III.—Contribuir para formar los fondos de defunción o invalidez, a prorrata junto con los demás asociados con la parte proporcional que le corresponde de las cuotas faltantes del asociado o asociados fallecidos o invalidados.

[100,000: "—Todos los Asociados contribuirán a prorrata con la parte proporcional que le corresponde de las cuotas faltantes del asociado o asociados fallecidos o invalidados."]

IV.—Gastos: de estas cuotas se destinarán el 6% en las sencillas y el 8% en las premiadas par alas siguientes erogacio nes: Cobranzas y Administración (pago a cobradores, local, luz, teléfono, Contador Fiscal, Contador Privado, papelería y honorarios de los Directivos).

Fondos de defunción: $20,000.00 [50,000: $50,000.00; 100,000: $100,000.00; 150,000: $20,000.00]

Edad límite: de 15 a 60 años. Período de espera para que funcione el seguro: un año. [100,000: ". . . a partir del primer serteo."]

Seguro de invalidez total permanente: los coasociados cubrirán la cuota sencilla del accidentado o invalidado.

Asambleas iniciales cada diez semanas.

Quedó enterado asimismo de los presentes, después de dejar constituida la Asociación acordaron designer su Junta Directiva, la cual quedó constituida de la siguiente manera:

PRESIDENTE:

SECRETARIO:

TESORERO:

Enterado de todo lo anterior solicito que se me acepte como saociado, con todos sus derechos y obligaciones.

En espera de la respuesta favorable, acompaño a la presente solicitud, la cantidad de $50.00 [50,000: $75.00; 100,000: $150.00; 150,000: $200.00] para cubrir la parte proporcional que me corresponde en los gastos de organización legal de la Asociación y me es grato suscribirme como

Su atto. Y S. S.

Fecha _____

Nombre _____ Tel. Of. _____

Dirección _____ Tel. _____

Dirección para el cobro: _____

Días y forma de cobro: _____

El que premia primero, paga $26,000.00 [50,000: $66,340.00; 100,000: $132,680.00; 150,000: $197,692.00]

El que premia de ultimo, paga $17,062.50 [50,000: $41,764.50; 100,000: $83,529.00; 150,000: $125,922.00]

. . . .

Recibí del Sr. (a) _____
la cantidad de $50.00 [50,000: $75.00; 100,000: [*drops all wording but* "150.00
M.N."]; 150,000: $200.00] Cincuenta pesos 00/100 M. N.)
en concepto de Cuota de Inscripción del Grupo _____
de Mutualistas de Yucatán, A. C., quien se compromete a cumplir con los Esta-
tutos de la Sociedad.
Mérida, Yuc., _____ de 197_____
Director-Tesorero

Notes

Introduction

1. The idea of cultural scripts refers to the communicated way in which power becomes articulated and rationalized through multiple means of references, symbols, rituals, practices and expectations. These scripts are often contested, negotiated, or rejected or treated in a "slantwise" manner (see n. Hoefer, Rytina, and Campbell 2007), have many forms, and are often accepted as "natural." These scripts "underwrite local, institutional, or transnational relations of power and economy by seeming to cohere between the most abstract order of organization, such as the transnational corporation, and the local household, and correspond to the 'appropriate' definitions of the relations of gender, class, and ethnicity. Over time, these scripts become 'megascripts' at the most centralized and powerful levels—nations, transnational entities such as the World Trade Organization, and international bodies such as OPEC. Used in this way, 'culture' has a much more dynamic meaning than the common definitional sense. . . . The word 'script' allows for an interactive and changing process that involves both agency and internalization, both resistance and accommodation in the same space and place" (Vélez-Ibáñez 2002, 16).

2. Henry 1963.

3. There is an extensive and intensive literature on ROSCAs as key developmental and local operations in Asia, Africa, the Caribbean, the Indian subcontinent, and Latin America. I have included all of these works in a special bibliography that can be requested from the author. Their nomenclature reflects this heterogeneity and is included in the special bibliography.

4. Today, there are 44.7 million Latinos living in the United States (Pew Hispanic Research Center 2006). Almost 27 million are of Mexican origin, either born in or having migrated to the United States. This is a remarkable growth since 1930, when the census recorded 1.3 million Mexicans. Twenty years later, in 1950, the census reported 2.3 million people with Spanish surnames. By 1970, 9.1 million persons of "Spanish" origin were reported. In each period, approximately 75 percent to 90 percent of the population was of Mexican origin, having been born in either the United States or Mexico. Migration during the Mexican Revolution (1910–1920) added at least one million people of Mexican descent (Vélez-Ibáñez 2004c, 3–4). Between 1930 and 1950, only 83,000 Mexicans legally

immigrated into the United States, and the Mexican-origin population largely grew by natural births. Every region of the United States, from New York to Alaska and from Hawaii to Minnesota, has experienced the arrival of both native- and foreign-born Mexican-origin populations, especially after 1980. Particularly important has been the major growth in rural populations in the U.S. South and the southwestern United States. "The U.S. border population is growing three times as fast as the nation's. The population of Mexico's border municipalities is predicted to double in nine years." See U.S.–Mexico Border Health Commission n.d.

5. See Hawley 2007, 1. His detailed report cites the development of Volaris, Avolar, Alma, Viva Aerobus, Interjet, and Click airlines as having started up only since 2005. Other older carriers have been forced to lower their prices on routes shuttling migrants to the north.

6. Hoefer, Rytina, and Campbell 2007.

7. I use the term "Mexican-origin" to prevent a dehistoricization of both ancient and contemporary populations that have migrated from Mesoamerica to the southwestern United States. Beginning around 3000 BP, the arrival of hybrid corn, chili, squash, and beans, the result of either "down-the-line" trading or the direct migration of groups, is evidence of Mesoamerica's influence on the U.S. Southwest. See my discussion in Vélez-Ibáñez 1996, 20–35. Most recently, Jane Hill has taken a very different position "on the origin and history of Uto-Aztecan," and she argues that "speakers of the protolanguage were foragers who lived in upland regions of Arizona, New Mexico, and the adjacent areas of the Mexican states of Sonora and Chihuahua about 5,000 years ago" (Hill 2001, 913). She states unambiguously that "new lexical evidence supports a different view, that speakers of the protolanguage were maize cultivators. The Proto-Uto-Aztecan speech community was probably located in Mesoamerica and spread northward into the present range because of demographic pressure associated with cultivation. The chronology for the spread and differentiation of the family should then correspond to the chronology for the northward spread of maize cultivation from Mesoamerica into the U.S. Southwest, between 4500 and 3000 BP."

Coming from the north, the "Mexica"—the group from whose name the term "Mexican" is derived—were relatively new migrants to Mesoamerica. Most Mesoamerican populations trace their linguistic inheritance to Uto-Aztecan. The term "Mexican-origin" recognizes these ancient ties, migrations from south to north and north to south, the spread of the Spanish empire, the creation of the Mexican state in 1821 through the Mexican-American War, and the presence of native-born and migratory populations throughout the present-day U.S. Southwest.

8. See Campbell and Heyman 2007. Their actual approach is less economic than it is political. They are critical of the bipolar model used in many discussions concerning the agency versus domination opposites along an axis. They

emphasize acts that frustrate "the normal play of a given power relation by act-ing in ways that make sense in their own frameworks but are disconnected or oblivious to that power relationship's construction or assumptions" (2). I sug-gest that ROSCAs function in similar ways, in that they "take on" all normal-ized spheres of borrowing, lending, investing, and saving by creating their own spheres of slantwise action. The irony, however, as is discussed in later chapters, is that the formal economic sector has recognized the efficacy of ROSCAs, and it has appropriated their forms and functions.

Chapter 1

1. See Portes 2006.

2. Hayes-Bautista et al. 2007.

3. Conquered by the United States and acceding to the Treaty of Guadalupe Hidalgo on February 2, 1848, at the close of the Mexican-American War, the Repub-lic of Mexico was forced to negate its claim to Texas and to cede to the United States the region now comprising New Mexico, Arizona, California, Colorado, Utah, and Nevada. The territory turned over to the United States by Mexico consti-tuted about two hundred thousand square miles, or two-fifths of all her territory.

4. James Gadsden was a South Carolina railroad speculator who threatened Mexican negotiators with American armed force if they did not agree to the $10 million purchase price for Mexico's territory. See Vélez-Ibáñez (1996, 287, n. 53) for the actual ultimatum.

5. See chap. 4.

6. Such historical memory is easily accessed in most Mexican-origin house-holds. My father often reminded me of the Mexican presence, manifested not just in the Spanish that we spoke, his oral histories of criss-crossing the border, and first-hand stories of revenge and tragedy, but also in the small Sonoran twang in his American English learned on the streets of Tucson and in its pub-lic schools, such as Ochoa Elementary and later at "La High," as Tucson High School was known among Mexicans of the town.

7. The theme of "Lost Lands" in the southwestern United States ranges from nostalgia to Reyes López Tijerina's armed insurrection in the late 1960s in New Mexico. See Blawis 1971, Gardner 1970, and Nabokov 1969. Litigation concern-ing the four-hundred-year-old Atrisco Land Grant in New Mexico is still ongo-ing, mostly involving the failure to notify some 23,000 descendants of the sale of the grant.

8. See Alvarez for his pathbreaking monograph on the industrial basis of migration from south to north California, *Familia* (1987), and his transnational market study, *Mangos, Chiles, and Truckers* (2005).

9. See M. Smith and Bakker 2008 and Kearney 2004. Smith and Bakker clearly show how the Mexican government most recently became a transnational

electoral presence for both Mexican and American elections, while Kearney's work emphasizes the important role of Mixe community associations in the United States and the manner in which they carry out culturally constituted obligatory office functions from the United States through e-mail to Oaxaca. As well, through the use of the e-mail, Kearney has been able to develop a very large database of migration crossings since the 1990s and has developed a census for the villages included in his sample (private communication, Michael Kearney, 2009).

10. The White House emergency appropriations requested for security in 2006 alone were almost US $2 billion (White House 2006). Simultaneously, regional institutions are working diligently to create a North American identity in order to build North America as a community (North American Center for Transborder Studies 2008).

11. I view practices like the FYGO to be a hybrid blending of the strength of social network exchanges with straight lending practices and transborder origin and implementation. See appendix B for information on the FYGO.

12. See Campbell and Heyman 2007, 2.

13. As reported by Maria Luz Cruz Torres, based on her field research in Mazatlán, Sinaloa, and verified by my own observations of the same context.

14. See Bouman 1989, 58. Bouman states that 90 percent of the participants in the Bishi, the Indian version of the ROSCA, are men. Similarly, prior to the Chinese Communist Revolution, most participants in Chinese versions and their organizers were men, but afterwards, the gender participation reversed. See Tsai 2000, 143.

15. See Vélez-Ibáñez 1983, 12–15; 130–138.

16. See chap. 4 for a full discussion of the term "Southwest North American Region."

17. The early general literature on the topic focuses on the basic functions of such practices (Anderson 1966; Ardener 1964; Gamble 1944; Geertz 1962; Kerri 1976; Kurtz and Showman 1978; Lomnitz 1977); their degree of adaptability or nonadaptability (Cope and Kurtz 1980; Kurtz 1973; Kurtz and Showman 1978; Wu 1974); their incidence in various cultures and ethnic groups (Adeyeye 1981; Ardener 1964; Asiwaju 1979; Bonnett 1976; Geertz 1962; Light 1972; Miracle, Miracle, and Cohen (1980); the methods and techniques necessary for the collection of data (Ardener 1964); and their function as "middle-rung" developments in developing economies (Geertz 1962; Light 1972; Lomnitz 1977; Morton 1978; Wu 1974).

Another element should be considered in sorting out questions of a cross-cultural sort. Geertz (1962, 260) has admitted that in all cases with which he was familiar, such associations probably spread by diffusion. Yet he states that diffusion analysis does not contribute to our understanding of the social functioning of the associations themselves. From the point of view postulated here, whether practices emerge from a set of conditions or are diffused does not prevent the analysis of their intended and unintended social functions. Diffusion analysis may not provide causal explanations for the emergence of the ROSCAs cross-culturally, yet it can provide clues about what structural and cultural conditions must occur in their point of origin for such practices to spread. On the other hand, simple references to diffusion do not explain the spread of ROSCAs. Especially from the 1980s forward, they are part and parcel of transnational penetrations and the creation of supply chains from agriculture to labor—many of which head north from Mexico to the United States. Rotating credit associations are simply a capitalist version, in name and seeming values, of the ROSCAs, but in fact they serve as an important link in supply chains by financing the commercial products being rotated.

18. Rotating savings and credit associations exist worldwide, but are concentrated in Africa, Asia, and Latin America, with a few in the Pacific Rim region. It is notable that neither European nor Slavic peoples use this particular form. This list does not include versions in the United States nor in the Cape Verde Islands, which has a type of ROSCA consisting of labor exchange during crucial planting and harvesting seasons (Langworthy and Finan 1997).

"ROSCAs: What's in a Name?" (Global Development Research Center n.d.)

Africa
Benin: Asusu, Yissirou, Ndjonu, Tontine
Botswana: Motshelo, beer parties
Burkina Faso: Tontine, Tibissiligbi, Pari, Song-taaba
Burundi: Upato (in Kiswahili)
Cameroon: Jangi, Ujangi, Djana, Mandjon, Djapa, Tontine, Djanggi, Njanggi,
    Ngwa, Ntchw
Egypt: Gameya, Jam'iyya
Ethiopia: Ekub, Ikub
Gabon: Bandoi
The Gambia: Osusu, susu, esusu, Compin
Ghana: Susu, Nanamei akpee, Onitsha, Nnoboa
Ivory Coast: Tonton, Tontine, Moni, Diaou Moni, War Moni, Djigi Moni,
    Safina, Akpole wule, Susu, Aposumbo, Kukule, a tche le sezu, Komite,
    n'detie, m'bgli sika, Monu, mone
Kenya: Mabati, Nyakinyua, Itega, Mkutano ya wanwake, Mkutano ya wazee
Liberia: Esusu, susu, sau
Madagascar: Fokontany
Mali: Pari
Mauritius: Pool, Cycle, Sheet
Mozambique: Upato, Xitique
Niger: Adasse, Tomtine, Asusu
Nigeria: Esusu, Osusu, Enusu, Ajo (Yoruba), Cha (Ibo), Oha, Oja, Adashi
    (Haussa, Tiv), Bam (Tiv), Isusu (Ot), Utu (Ibo), Dashi (Nupe), Efe (Ibibios),
    Oku (Kalabari Ijawas), Mitiri, Compiri, Club (Ibo)

Congo, PR: Temo, Kitemo, Ikilemba, Kikedimba, Kikirimbahu, Likilimba,
    Efongo Eambongo, Otabaka, Ekori, Otabi
Senegal: Tontine, Nath
Sierra Leone: Asusu, Esusu
Somalia: Haghad, Shaloongo, Aiuto
South Africa: Chita, Chitu, Stokfel, Stockfair, Mahodisana, Motshelo, Umangelo
Sudan: Khatta, Sanduk, Sandook Box
Swaziland: Stokfel
Tanzania: Upato, Fongongo
Tchad: Pare
Togo: Soo, Tonton, Sodzodzo, Sodyodyo, Abo
Tunisia: Noufi, Sanduk
Uganda: Chilemba, Kiremba, Upato, Kwegatta
Zaire: Ikelemba, Osassa, Bandoi, Kitemo, Kitwadi, Adashi, Tontine, Bandal
Zambia: Icilimba, Upato, Chilenba
Zimbabwe: Chilemba, Stockfair, Kutunderrera

Asia
Bangladesh: Samity
Cambodia: Tontine
China: Lun-hui, Yao-hui, Piao-hui, Hui, Ho-hui, Foei-Tsjing
Hong Kong: Chinese types and Chit clubs
India: Kameti, Kuri, Chitty, Chit funds, Vishi, Bishi, Nidhi, Committee
Indonesia: Arisan, Paketan Daging, Paketan Kawinan, Mapalus, Bajulo julo,
    Jula-jula, Mengandelek
Japan: Ko, Kou, Miyin, Mujin, Musin, Tanamoshi
Korea: Keyes, Kyes, Mujin, Ke
Lebanon: Al-tawfir el medawar
Malaysia: Kutu, Kootu, Kongsi, Tontine, Hui, Main, Kut
Nepal: Dhikur, Dhituti
Pakistan: Committee, Bisi, Kistuna
Papua New Guinea: Hui, Sande
Philippines: Paluwagan, Turnohan
Singapore: Tontine, Kutu
Sri Lanka: Chit Funds, Cheetu/Sheetu, Sittu Danawa, Situ Mudal, Sittu Wendesiya
Taiwan: Hui
Thailand: Chaer, Hui, Hue, Pia Huey, Len Chaer
Vietnam: Hui, Hui Thao, Hui hue hong, Hui bac (ho), Yi hui
Yemen: Hacba

Latin America, Caribbean, and Pacifics
Bahamas: Esu
Barbados: Meetings

Belize: Syndicate, Tanda
Bolivia: Pasanacu
Brazil: Consorcio, Pandero, Syndicates
Curacao: Sam, Hunga sam
Dominican Republic: San
Guatemala: Cuchubal, Cuchuval
Guyana: Throw a box, Boxi money
Jamaica: Partners, (Throw a) Box, Susu
Mexico: Tanda, Cundina, Mutualista . . .
Panama: Pandero
Peru: Pandero
Surinam: Kasmonie
Tobago: Susu
Trinidad: (E)susu, Sou sou, Hui, Chitty
West Indies: Susu
Western Samoa: Pelagolagomai

19. The data in this work show that in both the United States and Mexico, ritual activity and gift giving are also important parts of ROSCAs. Rotating credit associations are also steeped in some ritualized behaviors, such as parties and gift giving. Yet, for ROSCAs especially, their functions cannot be reduced to the members' economic motives, although these are paramount. An important consideration in the analysis of the various forms of the associations found in this research is that without a willingness to engage in generalized reciprocal relations based on mutual trust, the associations could not function. As Sauliniers (1974) has shown in his analysis of urban reciprocal prestation systems in Zaire, education and long-term urban residence, which are usually indicators of modernization, contribute to the reinforcement, not the decline, of traditional prestation systems. Therefore, to consider the various forms of ROSCAs as institutions in which "traditional" populations learn "modern" attitudes of an economic sort does not seem to be a fruitful strategy. Cognitive learning does indeed occur, but in a different form from that postulated by Geertz (1962). The RCAs are much more in the market-exchange mode, and although confianza may be the initial value used to attract individuals to RCAs, they are in fact totally structured as commercial enterprises, whether they involve the rotation of computers, kitchens, or cars to participants.

20. See Cruz Torres 2004, 272–275. She establishes for the literature the first analysis and description of cundinas in a rural Mexican state. I also assisted in this work and provided the impetus for opening up the research question to include ROSCAs.

21. Ejidos in Mexico are post–Mexican Revolution farms organized along collective lines, in which land was held in common by a group of small-scale agriculturalists. They were formally recognized by the state under Article 27 of

the 1917 Mexican Constitution, but were later radically privatized by constitutional amendment in 1992 under the presidency of Carlos Salinas. For an excellent study of the historical changes in this area, see Cruz Torres 2004.

22. This is based on fieldwork observations of rural ejidos and "ranchos" in southern Sinaloa carried out during a number of summers from 2000 through 2004. But see Cruz Torres 2004, 132–137, for the best original fieldwork-based data, analysis, and description of multiple employment among men and women in the Sinaloa region.

23. See "The Anthropology of Money" (2004).

24. See Introduction, n. 3.

25. Camilo García Parra, now at the University of Veracruz, Xalapa, was my research assistant at UCLA in 1978–1979. He gathered intensive data using a questionnaire of his own design. Most recently, two people stand out as research assistants. Fausto Vásquez Flores, undergraduate sociology student at the Universidad Autónoma de Sinaloa, Mazatlán, was responsible for data gathering in Mazatlán for five months in 2005–2006. My stalwart graduate assistant, Irene Vega, was responsible for data gathering in San Luis Río Colorado, Sonora, and in Yuma, Arizona, as well as for contacting informants in Phoenix, Arizona, from 2005 into 2007.

26. In 1972, Thomas Weaver of the University of Arizona first suggested a possible relationship between the Chinese hui and the Mexican tanda. He reported that one of his students had uncovered hui among Chinese benevolent associations in Tucson, Arizona.

27. During the period that Plutarco Elías Calles served as president of Mexico (1924–1928), and later, when he was the power behind the throne (1929–1935), the Chinese were expelled from most of Mexico. Consequently, Chinese immigrants have settled permanently in only a few areas of the country.

28. During that work, I serendipitously discovered how consistently the Mexican ROSCA cropped up among urban Mexicans. See Wu (1974) for a description of the hui in New Guinea; Light (1972) for those in the United States; and Broady (1958) for those in Great Britain.

29. Katzin (1959, 440) has stated that Bernice Kaplan reported ROSCAs among Peruvian Indians, but I have been unable to find verification of this claim in the literature. However, Reymundo Paredes, a Peruvian anthropologist, has confirmed their existence among middle-class people in Lima. They are termed *panderos* and usually operate among family members or friends. In addition, he described the *pandero techo* (literally, roof association), which rotates homes, as well as panderos of cars rotated by Volkswagen automobile agencies. These last are analogous to the Mexican *tandas de casa* and *tandas de Volkswagen*. Paredes stated that the automobile panderos are advertised in Lima newspapers (personal communication, July 31, 1980). Panderos have also been reported in Brazil and Panama (De Wolfe 1982).

30. "Hola, hago cundinas de 10 numeros de edredones, colchas, artículos para cocina y baño de los libros Vianney y Concord" (Hello, I make 10-number cundinas for comforters, bed spreads, articles for the kitchen and bathroom from the Vianney and Concord catalogues). See http://us.clasificados.st/hogar/contacto/204862.

31. Baires 2008.

32. Recent work by Zarraugh (2007, 245) does not report any ROSCAs among thirty Latina and Latino entrepreneurs in Harrisonburg, Virginia. She states that although all are immigrants—with half coming from Mexico and the rest from El Salvador, Honduras, Cuba, the Dominican Republic, Uruguay, Argentina, and Puerto Rico—"no one mentioned using a ROSCA or tanda." In response, I would suggest that businesspeople rarely mention such participation overtly or directly, and it takes some digging about to ferret out that admission. Within household networks, many of these are in the hands of women, not men. The fear of being accused of participating in a pyramid scheme is many times the underlying reason for not admitting to participating in or organizing a ROSCA.

33. Voluntary cooperative associations, in which tanda-like structures were formed for different purposes, have, however, been numerous in Arizona, Colorado, and New Mexico. For example, in New Mexico, in the copper town of Hurley, Chicano miners in the 1920s formed cooperatives (Liga Obrera Mexicana) based on confianza in which forty or more miners and their families pooled relatively large amounts of money on a weekly basis. The money was used to open and maintain cooperative stores outside of the company town. Miners and their families thus circumvented the necessity of buying overpriced items in the company store, much as Mexicans today circumvent interest charges by forming tandas for Volkswagens and Datsuns. The history of the formation of voluntary associations by Mexicans north and south of the Río Bravo is a rich one.

34. California and Texas in 2005 comprised 34 percent of the 44.3 million Hispanics in the United States. Hispanics account for 15 percent of the total U.S. population. Almost half (48 percent) of all Hispanics live in Texas (8.4 million) or California (13.1 million). The county with the highest Latino population is Los Angeles County (4.7 million). Compare this with 1.3 million "Spanish speaking persons" in the entire U.S. in 1940; 2.3 million in 1950; 9.1 million in 1970; 14.6 million in 1980; and 22.3 million in 1990 (Center for Latin American, Caribbean and Latino Studies n.d.; Rivas 2007).

35. According to Jane Morse (2007), the El Paso and Ciudad Juárez metropolitan area includes some 2.6 million people and represents North America's fourth-largest manufacturing hub. Trade crossing through ports in the region amounted to $46.8 billion in 2006, according to statistics compiled by the El Paso Regional Economic Development Corporation. Northbound daily border crossings in 2006 tallied up to 42,648 private vehicles, 2,122 commercial trucks and 20,547 pedestrians. See Morse 2007.

36. See Schreiner 1999.

37. SICREA México Autofinancianmento.

38. SICREA México Autofinancianmento.

39. MexicaNet, n.d.

40. Mission Asset Fund Web site.

41. Baires 2008.

42. See *La Revista de Mérida* 1900; 1902; 1908. The 1900 article announced the formulation of a 100,000-peso fund that was to continue the first fund established in June 1898. Each contribution was worth 100 pesos, with protective beneficiary privileges for *socios* (members); a deduction was made to cover expenses. Each participant was provided with a legal title of association. From this description, it is clear the mutualistas antedate the twentieth century, and their mode of operation does not appear to have changed very much (see chap. 2).

Chapter 2

1. Diego de Vargas, the reconquerer of New Mexico in 1693, coined the term "españoles mexicanos" to describe the populations in the northernmost reaches of viceroyalty during the colonial period (Vélez-Ibáñez 1996, 37). There is no doubt that this population during the Spanish colonial and Mexican periods depended on the religious and secular construct of confianza for creating and maintaining familial relations through intermarriage, *compadrazgo*, labor and trade exchanges, and the holding of common water and land rights.

2. Blau (1964) has made the distinction between "social exchange" and "strictly economic exchange." He states that the former differs in important ways from the latter in that it is a nonspecific favor in which there is a general expectation of some future return whose exact nature is not stipulated in advance. An economic exchange, on the other hand, is an obligation that is specifically defined and is agreed to at the time the transaction takes place. Social exchange also differs significantly in that it generates feelings of "personal obligation, gratitude, and trust; purely economic exchange as such does not" (94). In addition, Blau says that social exchanges do not have an exact price in "terms of a single quantitative medium of exchange" and that this is a substantive fact (94–95). The problem with Blau's assertions lies in his use of definitional constructs such as "strictly economic exchange" and "purely economic exchange," two definitional requirements seldom found, even in the most capitalistic of market exchanges. Even in across-the-counter transactions, there has to be a diffusive quality attached to the medium of exchanges ("In God We Trust" is printed on all American currency and an all-seeing "Eye of Providence" appears on one-dollar bills): to the clerk who will guarantee the fairness of the exchange, to the person on whom one relies to provide information on the quality of the product, and to the product itself. Few transactions can really be understood to be

"strictly" or "purely" economic exchanges, without any diffusive qualities at all. I would assert that cultural values within the transactions as well as the contexts in which transactions occur will define the transaction.

3. Some studies suggest that the hormone oxycotin increases in women after childbirth, during nursing, and when stressed or tense. When combined with estrogen, it induces women to seek the company of others (Kosfeld et al. 2005, 435).

4. Inflation in Mexico has increased steadily since 1973. That year, the national retail price index rose by 12.2 percent. In 1974, wholesale prices rose by 21.9 percent and consumer prices by 23.7 percent. In the fiscal year ending March 1978, consumer prices rose by 17.5 percent (*Quarterly Economic Review of Mexico* 1979, 20). In 2008, the inflation rate was reduced to 3.76 (El Financiero en Liñea 2008). However, in 2005, 45 percent of the Mexican population was living in moderate poverty and 18 percent were living in extreme poverty. Therefore, the modest per capita income increase between 1980 and 2005 from $2,630 to $7,310 is still very problematic, and it reflects the increasing reliance on immigration to the United States as the basis for "parceling" out poverty and receiving benefits that have reached $25 billion in remittances in 2008 (Ratha and Xu 2008).

Even though there has been a reported consistent reduction in remittance receipts since mid-2007, and ". . . negative remittance growth early in 2008," most economists consider such decreases as "modest" (Inter-American Development Bank 2008a).

5. See appendix C for information on the online version of the Internet Social Lending Network.

6. Farias 2007.

7. Prestamos are a system of credit in which a lender provides an amount for fifty-five days of up to 5,000 pesos at a rate of 100 pesos a day. Depending on the cash income and outgo for these market women, they may even pay ahead of time in order to not get behind, but again, as in the case of the cundinas, calculated together, all the costs and earnings described in the text are part of the larger calculus that the women engineer. The lender earns 500 pesos from each borrower, so that if he/she has a ten-person network, the lender will make 5,000 pesos every fifteen days. The source of this data is the author's original field notes taken in 2006 in Mazatlán, Sinaloa.

Chapter 3

1. See Ávila 2005. Here, the process involved bringing together eight young male professionals between twenty-five and thirty years of age who remitted a part of their salaries each week and waited for their tanda prize of selecting from among seventy Argentine, Brazilian, and Venezuelan women who offered their carnal services for 2,000 to 3,000 pesos an hour.

2. The term "Hispanic" is used rather than Mexican because in most of the theater chains there are both managers and employees from Peru, Guatemala, and other Latin American countries who all participate in the ROSCAs. However, the great majority of both managers and employees are in fact Mexicans.

3. Projectionists seem to form their own ROSCAs across the theater chains because of their exclusive union status and skill. The rest of the associations are in the hands of the cashiers.

4. Light did not include any Mexican material in his work, probably because no published materials were available at the time he carried out his study. It would be interesting to see how he might have explained the presence of the cundinas or tandas in the U.S. Southwest; these are without the corporate structures he seemed to have thought were important for the development of the Chinese and Japanese ROSCAs.

5. See Silverman 1996.

6. Holt 2007. She explains some of the downsides to participating in a tanda:

- There are no legal guarantees that you will receive your money. You can't always trust the tanda organizer or participants to uphold the agreement and not run away with your money. Organizers sometimes put together a tanda because they are in need of cash.
- When you participate in a tanda, you don't receive interest for all the time you waited to get your money. You may need to wait for months to receive your money if you are the last in line.
- While people wait to receive their money, they may need to buy items for their home. Since they don't have the money on hand, they may buy these things through monthly payments and will end up paying more for them in the end.
- Even though people participate in tandas to save money, it's tempting for them to spend their money on things they don't need when it's their turn to receive the money.

    The best way to save money is by depositing your money in a savings account. You can open a savings account through a bank or credit union. Your money will be safe. Plus, you will earn a little extra money in interest.

7. Loera 2002.

Chapter 4

1. See U.S. Department of Transportation 2009c.

2. It must be emphasized that approximately 59 percent (over 7 million people) of the undocumented population are of Mexican origin, and about 40 percent, or more than 6 million people, have overstayed their temporary visas.

3. The Pew Hispanic Center tabulates the total unauthorized migrant population in 2009 as 11.9 million, of which 59 percent, or 7 million, were born in
Mexico (Passel and Cohn 2009)

4. See Hereford 2006.

5. For the Mexican side of the integrated economy, information on the movement from Mexico's central and southern areas to the north, and the source for
figure 4.1, see Robert W. Gilmer (2006). Also see chapter 1, n. 34 and 35 for the
U.S. demographic and economic changes.

6. See Galan 2000a and Vélez-Ibáñez 2004c. According to the Federal Reserve
Bank of Dallas (n.d.): "Colonias can be found in Texas, New Mexico, Arizona,
and California, but Texas has both the largest number of colonias and the largest colonia population. Approximately 400,000 Texans live in colonias. Overall,
the colonia population is predominately Hispanic; 64.4 percent of all colonia
residents and 85 percent of those residents under 18 were born in the United
States. There are more than 2,294 Texas colonias, located primarily along the
state's 1,248-mile border with Mexico."

7. U.S. Census Bureau n.d.

8. See Vélez-Ibáñez and Sampiao 2002.

9. "Whiteness" is one of the megascripts tied to success, hard work, sacrifice, ingenuity, innovation, and generally superior intelligence. Physical work
is not included, but rather is something to be avoided by education, mobility,
and success. This megascript is congruent with a general theory of profit gain,
scraping of labor value, and the conversion of energy from whatever source to
accomplish some material gain. But this is not the central analytic in this work.
There is a huge literature on the notion of "whiteness," which is much beyond
the purview of this work.

10. The examples cited here are actual. In order of discussion: (1) A number of
Internet sites feature caps, T-shirts, polo shirts, and even thongs for sale with the
logo "My Mexican works for less than your Mexican." (2) In the language example, this refers to a short, dumpy, frizzy-haired, badly blond-streaked matron at
a major department store in Scottsdale, Arizona, who berated my niece because
she was speaking Spanish to her non-Mexican mother from Puerto Rico. Since
she spoke no Spanish, the matron could not know that the rate of speech and
tilting chopping of the endings and the replacement of [l] with [d] was not from
Mexican Spanish. (3) The Aztec reference is to friends of mine who sartorially
garb themselves in blue Brooks Brothers suits, but who look like they could
replace Montezuma in a publicity shot. In one case, my friend is the chairman of
his own law firm. (4) The street corner reference, as well as the domestic servant
examples, are so numerous and occur on such a daily basis in the Southwest
United States and throughout the rest of the country that it is simply ludicrous
to take time to document it.

11. See Campbell and Heyman 2007, 2.

12. See Wolf 1956, 1065–1078.

13. All places and dates are changed, and the names have been replaced with pseudonyms to protect the identity of Paloma and Valentina.

14. According to the U.S. Department of Transportation (2009a), the number of Nogales pedestrian border crossings in 2009 was 4.2 million, a drop of 6.3 million from the year before of 10.5 million, an astounding drop, which is due to the economic conditions in the region.

15. The "Bracero" program was initiated in 1942 between the Mexican and U.S. governments in order to supply labor for the agricultural fields of the United States. Between 1942 and the program's demise in 1964 as the result of the ever-increasing introduction of mechanical agricultural implements, approximately 350,000 Mexicans worked throughout the United States.

16. The term "Funds of Knowledge" was coined by my colleague James B. Greenberg and myself in Véléz-Ibañez and Greenberg 1992. The term fills in the gap in much of the literature regarding the efficacy of the social and knowledge capital that migrants take with them to their new points of settlement from their point of origin and the manner in which such knowledge is used or discarded. These funds emerge basically through the life cycle from the labor, civil, social, emotional, and material experiences of individuals and households. They are used as the basis for creating fundamental elements and foundations from which future generations may emerge; they consist of a huge array of skills, information, techniques, and practices. Few attempts have been made to either catalogue them or insert them within learning environments, such as schools. See also Gonzalez, Moll, and Amanti 2005.

Chapter 5

1. See Portes 2006.

2. Saldívar 2006.

3. See Vélez-Ibáñez 2008.

4. See Anderson 1966; Anderson and Anderson 1958; Banton 1956, 1957; Baskuaskas 1971; Brandel-Srier 1971; Comhaire 1950; Dotson 1953; Doughty 1969, 1970; Frankenberg 1957; Freedman 1960/1961; Green 1969; Hamer 1967; Handleman 1967; Hausknecht 1962; Hogg 1965; Kapferer 1969; Kenny 1961, 1962; Leeds 1965; Levine 1962; Little 1965, 1967, 1971; Mangin 1959; Meillasoux 1968; Noble 1970; Norbeck 1966; Parkin 1966; Skinner 1974; Soen and de Camaramond 1972; Treudley 1966; Wallerstein 1966; and Wheeldon 1969. In addition, there is a vast literature on adaptive strategies such as voluntary associations. Cohen's excellent book (1974) is a case in point.

5. Polanyi (1957) and Dalton (1968) have suggested that the basic notions of economics, such as maximization (which assumes that individuals will make decisions rationally in order to achieve the maximum reward) should only be

used for market-exchange systems. Other systems organize exchange not on the basis of market maximization of scarce goods but rather on what both these authors regard as different modes of exchange, such as reciprocity or redistribution. It is therefore inappropriate to describe qualitatively different social institutions in terms based on market exchange. Polanyi's and Dalton's position is called the substantivist position: it argues that economic systems should be compared according to the mode by which the means of subsistence are organized and exchanged. The formalist position denies the validity of this approach and suggests that all economic systems can be fruitfully analyzed by the models of formal economics. Neither of the two approaches is quite acceptable to those espousing more radical approaches.

6. Delocalization is the process by which adaptive cultural systems are uprooted from their urban and rural contexts by structural and ecological changes. An area becomes "localized" once a population establishes meaningful patterns of social relations that assist in meeting the biocultural needs and goals of the population. I have developed this concept in relation to elderly Mexicans living in central Mexico (see Vélez-Ibáñez, Verdugo, and Nuñez 1981).

7. Vélez-Ibáñez 1996. See especially chapter 4, "Living in *Confianza* and Patriarchy: The Cultural Systems of U.S. Mexican Households" and Vélez-Ibáñez 1995.

8. See especially Vélez-Ibáñez 1993; and Vélez-Ibáñez and Greenberg 1992.

Glossary

ahorro (saving) Any form of saving activity

ahorro para ahorrar (saving to save) The deuteron-learned construct inferred from these data. The construct expands regardless of intent and use as long as rewards of some sort are generated. The construct includes future planning, goal orientations of stability, delayed gratification, and an interest in future generations.

amistad (friendship) One of the relationships of reciprocity important in maintaining dense "fixed" relations

asesor (consultant-broker) An individual who serves interstitial functions at different levels within many Mexican institutional sectors. Sometimes a broker, sometimes a confidant, and with or without portfolio, the asesor is necessary to many economic and political transactions. The term has an essentially positive connotation.

bolita (little ball) One of the terms used to designate a rotating credit association. The name is probably derived from the numbered balls in wire hoppers used in lotteries.

cacique (political leader) The traditional view of *caciquismo* is that it is an informal political method of control by a small association of individuals under one leader (Friedrich 1965, 190). Violence, verbal persuasion, and the use of collateral relatives are the principal methods of political control. It is also considered a transitional urban phenomenon restricted to evolving low-income settlements (Cornelius 1973, 150). I find that such leadership is neither specific to low-income areas nor transitory (Vélez-Ibañez 1978a).

caja de ahorros (a box of savings) Informal and formal credit unions, which are widely distributed throughout Mexico

chingar (to screw) The emic descriptor for exploitation, marginality, powerlessness, or the cause of disrupted social relationships. It is equivalent to the English "fuck." In its noun form, the word refers to a powerful individual. Some literature has used this emic descriptor to characterize Mexican personality, motivation, and relationships.

compadrazgo (co-godparenthood) An important Mexican fictive relationship that is ceremonially sanctioned and provides the impetus for network expansion in various contexts.

confianza (mutual trust) The Mexican cultural construct indicating the willingness to engage in generalized reciprocity. It may be open, processual, or closed.

confianza en confianza (trusting mutual trust) The deuteron-learned construct inferred from these data. The construct expands as long as reciprocity and exchange relations are maintained. The construct ultimately implies trust in the trustworthiness of self since mutual trust as an organizing intersect for social relations cannot be used without a sense of trust in the ability to cope with one's organs.

coyote (consultant-broker) An intermediary, but with a more negative connotation than asesor and carrying an implication that illegal or unethical activities are being negotiated

cuates (pals) Two or more intimate male friends

cuchuval (to raise a reunion) A Guatemalan variant of the rotating credit association, from the Quiche

cundina (from the verb cundir, to spread) One of the terms used to designate a rotating credit association: the second most frequently used term by our informants. It is found primarily in northern Mexico and the southwestern United States.

cundinero A person who organizes rotating credit associations on a part-time or full-time basis

ethnodrama A method of exposition of data couched within a reconstruction of events as similar to their unfolding as possible. Actors, roles, decisions, and cultural and structural constraints are emphasized. Such a technique is very much a part of situational urban analysis.

fictive friendship An interpersonal relationship in which the idiom of describing the relationship is "friendship," but in which the relationship is specific only to such contexts as clubs, institutions, and periodic events. Such friendships lack density, continuous reciprocity, and committed affect. Such relationships are more probable among urban peoples for whom mobility and flexibility are required as a consequence of complex wage structures. Academics, for example, because of the congruence between vertical and horizontal mobility, participate in such fictive friendship networks. Status changes, which are frequent among academics, require geographical movement in many instances. Fictive friendships serve a variety of social, affective, and professional needs, but are marked by their ease of transferability across institutions. See especially Moore (1978) for the seminal discussion of the term and the proper context for its use.

first turn The first turn may be the reserve asked by a specialist in order to ensure the timely distribution of the fund share. The turn may also, however, be provided to the organizer as a favor in return for organizing the association, but in this case it is not free.

flechazos (arrows) Verbal barbs used as a means of reducing someone's social prestige

free first turn The free first turn is the fee charged by a specialist and does not obligate the organizer to contribute to the association. Also known as *el cero* and first turn.

fuerte-pequeña (strong-weak) The former term refers to long-standing rotating credit associations, involving larger sums and more members than the latter

fund share The amount actually rotated to members of a rotating credit association

gente de rancho (people from ranches) The urban designation for rural persons, with a pejorative connotation of "country bumpkins"

hui (association) The Chinese version of the rotating credit association

Liga Obrera Mexicana (Mexican Worker's League) A mutual aid society composed of Chicano miners in Hurley, New Mexico, in the early 1920s

maquiladoras Labor-intensive light industry; sometimes used to describe sweatshops

muerta-viva (dead-alive) The former are rotating credit associations in which a specialist charges a fee, free first turn, zero, or a percentage. The latter involve no market relations and are therefore convivial and reciprocal.

mutualista One of the terms used to designate a rotating credit association. Designating both informally and formally organized types, the term is used only in Yucatán.

padrino politico (political godfather) A type of fictive friendship in which a person of influence becomes sponsor and protector for another seeking to enter institutional contexts in private, public, and labor sectors. While ritual relations generated through compadrazgo (co-godparenthood) may also bind the relationship between the padrino politico and those being sponsored, it is nevertheless often a single-interest, and always a dominant-subordinate, relationship.

pandero (perhaps a bulge) The Peruvian version practiced in Lima. Other types include *pandero techo* (roof associations) and automobile panderos.

paracaidista (parachutist) Land squatters

polla (pool, as in card games) A rotating credit association (RCA) fund or the participants in an RCA

pretenciosa(o) (pretentious) The term used by working-class women for middle-class persons

quincela (derivative of quincena, fortnight) One of the terms used to designate a rotating credit association

quiniela (betting pool) One of the terms used to designate a rotating credit association

regalos (gifts) A reciprocal exchange of gifts forming part of the tripartite exchange system of rotating credit associations, commensality, and gifts among women in various institutional contexts

rifa (raffle) One of the terms used to designate a rotating credit association

rol (roll) One of the terms used to designate a rotating credit association

ronda (round) One of the terms used to designate a rotating credit association

socio (member) The term used for members of mutualistas, also used in some of the tandas of Veracruz

tanda (turn) One of the terms used to designate a rotating credit association, the term found most often in this research

una union de confianza (a bond of mutual trust) An emic definition of the rotating credit association

vaca (cow) One of the terms used to designate a rotating credit association

vaquita (calf) One of the terms used to designate a rotating credit association

zero turn The fee charged by a specialist, also known as *el cero* or free first turn

Bibliography

Adams, Richard N.
1975   *Energy and Structure: A Theory of Social Power*. Austin: University of Texas Press.

Adeyeye, Samuel O.
1981   "The Place of 'Esusu Clubs' in the Development of the Co-operative Movement in Nigeria." Symposium on Traditional Co-operation and Social Organization and Enterprise, Intercongress of the International Union of Anthropological and Ethnological Sciences, Amsterdam.

Alvarez, Robert R.
1987   *Familia: Migration and Adaptation in Alta and Baja California, 1850–1975*. Berkeley: University of California Press.
2005   *Mangos, Chiles, and Truckers: The Business of Transnationalism*. Minneapolis: University of Minnesota Press.

Anderson, Robert T.
1966   "Rotating Credit Associations in India." *Economic Development and Cultural Change* 14: 334–339.

Anderson, Robert T., and Gallatin Anderson
1958   "Voluntary Associations and Urbanization." *American Journal of Sociology* 65: 265–273.

"The Anthropology of Money in Southern California"
2004   Exhibit, Department of Anthropology, University of California, Irvine. http://www.anthro.uci.edu/html/Programs/Anthro_Money/Exhibit2.htm

Aramoni, Aniceto
1961   *Psiocoanalisis de la dinamica de un pueblo*. Mexico City: Universidad Nacional Autonoma de Mexico.

Ardener, Shirley, and Sandra Burman, eds.
1964   "The Comparative Study of Rotating Credit Associations." *Journal of the Royal Anthropological Institute* 94: 201–209.
1995   *Money-go-rounds: The Importance of Rotating Savings and Credit Associations for Women*. Oxford, UK: BERG.

Asiwaju, Anthony I.
1979   "Colonial Approach to Rural Co-operative Production in West Africa, 1910–1960." Lagos, Nigeria: University of Lagos Central Research Committee.

Ávila, José Juan
2005   "Cambia internet formas de prostitución en el DF." *El Universal*, agosto 17. http://www2.eluniversal.com.mx/pls/impreso/noticia.html?id_nota= 23683&tabla=primera.

Bailey, Fredrick G.
1969   *Strategems and Spoils: A Social Anthropology of Politics*. New York: Schocken Books.
1971   *Gifts and Poison: The Politics of Reputation*. New York: Schocken Books.

Baires, Javier
2008   "Susu–Sociedad."   http://patersononline.net/potm/2008/03/02/susu -sociedad/.

Banco Compartamos
http://hoovers.com/company/Banco_Compartamos_SA_Institucion_ de_Banca_Multiple/rhshkxi-1.html

Banton, Michael
1956   "Adaptation and Integration in the Social System of Temne Immigrants in Freetown." *Africa* 26: 354–368.
1957   *West African City: A Study of Tribal Life in Freetown*. London: Oxford University Press.

Baskauskas, Luicija
1971   "An Urban Enclave: Lithuanian Refugees in Los Angeles." PhD diss., University of California at Los Angeles.

Bateson, Gregory
1978   *Steps to an Ecology of Mind*. New York: Ballantine Books.

Blau, Peter
1964   *Exchange and Power in Social Life*. New York: John Wiley and Sons.

Blawis, Patricia Bell
1971   *Tijerina and the Land Grants: Mexican Americans in Struggle for Their Heritage*. New York: International Publishers.

Blok, Anton
1974   *The Mafia of a Sicilian Village, 1860–1960*. New York: Harper and Row.

Boissevain, Jeremy
1974   *Friends of Friends: Networks, Manipulators and Coalitions*. New York: St. Martin's Press.

Bonnett, Aubrey W.
1976   "Rotating Credit Associations among Black West Indian Immigrants in Brooklyn: An Exploratory Study." PhD diss., City University of New York.

Bouman, Frits A. J.
1989   *Short and Unsecured Informal Rural Finance in India*. Delhi: Oxford University Press.
1995   "ROSCA: On the Origin of the Species." *Savings and Development* 19(2): 129.

Brandel-Srier, Mia

1971   *Reeftown Elite: A Study of Social Mobility in a Modern African Commu-
        nity on the Reef.* London: Routledge and Kegan Paul.

Broady, Maurice

1958   "The Chinese in Great Britain." In Morton H. Fried, ed., *Colloquium on
        Overseas Chinese*, 29–34. New York: Institute of Pacific Relations.

Buijs, Gina

1998   "Savings and Loan Clubs: Risky Ventures or Good Business Practice?
        A Study of the Importance of Rotating Savings and Credit Associations
        for Poor Women." *Development Southern Africa*, 15(1): 55–65.

Cabral, Carlose Dore, Esther Hernandez Medina, and Obed Vasquez

1999   "Mapping Dominican Transnationalism: Narrow and Broad Transna-
        tional Practices." *Ethnic and Racial Studies* 22: 316–339.

Campbell, Howard, and Josiah Heyman

2007   "Slantwise: Beyond Domination and Resistance on the Border." *Journal
        of Contemporary Ethnography* (February) 36(1): 3–30.

Carlos, Manuel L.

1973   "Fictive Kinship and Modernization in Mexico: A Comparative Analy-
        sis." *Anthropological Quarterly* 46: 75–91.

Carlos, Manuel L., and Bo Anderson

1981   "Political Brokerage and Network Politics in Mexico: The Case of a
        Representative Dominance System." In David Miller and Bo Anderson,
        eds., *Networks, Exchange, and Coercion: The Elementary Theory and Its
        Applications*, 169–187. New York: Elsevier.

Castillo, Franzika

2009   Notes from an interview of Sandra Rivera, Washington, D.C.

Center for Latin American, Caribbean and Latino Studies, CUNY Graduate Center

n.d.   "Growth of Hispanic Population of the US Compared with Growth
        of General Population, 1980–2000." http://web.gc.cuny.edu/lastudies/
        census2000data/Hispanic%20Population%20Growth%20Compared%
        20with%20General%20Population,%201980-2000.pdf.

Chang, Ching Chieh

1956   "The Chinese in Latin America: A Preliminary Geographical Survey with
        Special Reference to Cuba and Jamaica." PhD diss., University of Maryland.

Cohen, Abner

1974   *Urban Ethnicity.* London: Tavistock.

Comhaire, Sylvia

1950   "Associations on the Basis of Origin in Lagos, Nigeria." *American Catholic
        Sociological Review* 11: 234–236.

Cope, Thomas, and Donald V. Kurtz

1980   "Default and the Tanda: A Model Regarding Recruitment for Rotating
        Credit Associations." *Ethnology* 19: 213–231.

Cornelius, Wayne
1973   "Political Learning among the Urban Poor: The Impact of Residential
        Context." Sage Professional Papers Comparative Political Series. Beverly
        Hills, CA: Sage Publications.
Cruz Torres, Maria L.
2004   *Lives of Dust and Water: An Anthropology of Change and Resistance in
        Northwestern Mexico.* Tucson: University of Arizona Press.
Dalton, George
1968   "Introduction." In George Dalton, ed., *Primitive Archaic, and Modern
        Economics: Essays of Karl Polanyi,* ix–liv. Garden City, NY: Doubleday/
        Anchor.
de Bourbourg, Brasseur
1862   *Gramatica de la lengua quiche.* Paris: Auguste Duran Libraire.
De Vos, George
1975   "Ethnic Pluralism: Conflict and Accommodation." In George De Vos
        and Lola Romanucci-Ross, eds., *Ethnic Identity: Cultural Continuities
        and Change,* 1–37. Palo Alto, CA: Mayfield Pub. Co.
De Wolfe, Evelyn
1982   "Fund Pools Blocked by Postal Law." *Los Angeles Times,* February 21,
        part V, 11.
Dotson, Floyd
1953   "A Note on Participation in Voluntary Associations in a Mexican City."
        American Sociological Review 18: 380–386, 11 August.
Doughty, Paul L.
1969   "La cultura de regionalismo en la vida de Lima, Peru." *America Indigena*
        29: 949–981.
1970   "Behind the Back of the City: 'Provincial' Life in Lima, Peru." In William
        Mangin, ed., *Peasants in Cities: Readings in the Anthropology of Urbaniza-
        tion,* 30–46. Boston: Houghton Mifflin Co.
El Financiero en Liñea (Economía)
2008   "Revisan a la baja expectativa de inflación para 2008." February 19.
        http://www.elfinanciero.com.mx/ElFinanciero.
Embree, J. F.
1939   *Suye Mura: A Japanese Village.* Chicago: University of Chicago Press.
Erikson, Erik H.
1963   *Childhood and Society.* 2nd ed. New York: W. W. Norton & Co.
Fallers, Lloyd A.
1965   *Bantu Bureaucracy: A Century of Political Evolution among the Basoga of
        Uganda.* Chicago: University of Chicago Press.
Farias, David
2004   "Private Network Lending." Strategic paper, MBA Program/Managerial Eco-
        nomics, W. P. Carey School of Business, Arizona State University, Tempe.

2007   "Interview with David Farias—Founder, FYGO.com." http://www
        .pliwatch.org/podcast.

Federal Reserve Bank of Dallas, Office of Community Affairs

n.d.   "Texas Colonias: A Thumbnail Sketch of Conditions, Issues, Challenges
        and Opportunities." http://www.sos.state.tx.us/border/colonias/faqs
        .shtml.

Fei, Hsiao-tung, and Chih-i Chang

1949   *Earthbound China: A Field Study of Rural Economy in Yunnan.* London:
        Routledge and Kegan Paul.

Fei, Xiaotong

1939   *Peasant Life in China: A Field Study of Country Life in the Yangtze Valley.*
        New York: E. P. Dutton.

Festinger, Leon

1957   *A Theory of Cognitive Dissonance.* Stanford: Stanford University
        Press.

Foster, George M.

1967   *Tzintzuntzan: Mexican Peasants in a Changing World.* Boston: Little,
        Brown and Co.

Frankenberg, Ronald

1957   *Village on the Border: A Social Study of Religion, Politics, and Football in
        a North Wales Community.* London: Cohen & West.

Freedman, Maurice

1960/1961 "Immigrants and Associations: Chinese in Nineteenth Century Singa-
        pore." *Comparative Studies in Society and History* 3: 25–48.

Friedrich, Paul

1965   "A Mexican Cacicazgo." *Ethnology* 4: 190–209.

Fry, Richard

2006   *Gender and Migration Report.* New York: Pew Hispanic Center. http://
        pewhispanic.org/files/reports/64.pdf.

Galan, Hector

2000a   "The Forgotten Americans: Focus: *Las colonias.*" KLRU and PBS. http://
        www.pbs.org/klru/forgottenamericans/focus/howdevel.htm.

2000b   "Location of *Colonias* along the U.S.–Mexican Border." http://www
        .pbs.org/klru/forgottenamericans/images/texasmap.gif.

Galarza, Ernesto

1981   "Forecasting Future Cohorts of Mexican Elderly." In Manuel R.
        Miranda and Ramon A. Ruiz, eds., *Chicano Aging and Mental
        Health*, 238–248. Rockville, MD: Alcohol, Drug Abuse, and Men-
        tal Health Administration, U.S. Department of Health and Human
        Services.

Gamble, Sidney D.

1944   "A Chinese Mutual Savings Society." *Far Eastern Quarterly* 4: 41–52.

García, Ismael
2002   *Confeccionando desilusiones: Trabajadoras Mexicanas del la costura en Los Ángeles.* Culiacán, Mexico: Colección Nueva America del Norte, Centro de Estudios de la Globalización y el Desarrollo Regional.
Gardner, Richard
1970   *Grito Reyes: Tijerina and the New Mexico Land Grant War of 1967.* Indianapolis, IN: Bobbs-Merrill Co.
Geertz, Clifford
1962   "Rotating Credit Association: A 'Middle Rung' in Development." *Economic Development and Cultural Change* (April) X(3): 241–263.
Gilmer, Robert W.
2006   "Industrial Expansion Still Drives Growth on the U.S.–Mexico Border." El Paso Branch, Federal Reserve Bank of Dallas. http://www.glo.state.tx.us/energy/border/forum/13/reports_presentations.html.
Glick-Schiller, Nina
2003a   "The Centrality of Ethnography in the Study of Transnationalism Immigration." In Nancy Foner, ed., *American Arrival: Anthropology Engages the New Immigration*, 99–128. Santa Fe, NM: School of American Research Press.
2003b   "Transnational Theory and Beyond." In David Nugent and Joan Vincent, eds., *A Companion to the Anthropology of Politics*, 448–467. Malden, MA: Blackwell.
The Global Development Research Center
n.d.   "What's in a Name?" http://www.gdrc.org/icm/rosca/rosca-names.html.
Goffman, Erving
1961   *Asylums: Essays on the Social Situations of Mental Patients and Other Inmates.* Garden City, NY: Doubleday/Anchor.
Goldschmidt, Walter F.
1976   "The Rural Foundation of American Culture." Gregory Foundation Memorial Lecture, Columbia, MO.
González, Nancie
1972   "Patron-Client Relationships at the International Level." In Arnold Strickon and Sidney M. Greenfield, eds., *Structure and Process in Latin America*, 179–209. Albuquerque: University of New Mexico Press.
Gonzalez, Norma, Luis Moll, and Cathy Amanti
2005   *Funds of Knowledge: Theorizing Practices in Households and Classrooms.* Tucson: University of Arizona Press.
Green, Vera M.
1969   "Aspects of Interethnic Integration in Aruba, Netherlands Antilles." PhD diss., University of Arizona.
Grupo Autofin
        http://www.autofin.com.mx/casas.asp.

Grupo Autofin México
> http://www.grupoautofin.com/InterProdCasa.asp.

Hamer, John J.
1967   "Voluntary Associations as Structures of Change among the Sidamo of Southwestern Ethiopia." *Anthropological Quarterly* 60: 73–91.

Handleman, Don
1967   "Leadership, Solidarity and Conflict in West Indian Immigrant Associations." *Human Organization* 26: 118–125.

Hansen, Roger D.
1971   *The Politics of Mexican Development.* Baltimore: Johns Hopkins Press.

Hausknecht, Murray
1962   *The Joiners: A Sociological Description of Voluntary Association Membership in the United States.* Totowa, NJ: Bedminster Press.

Hawley, Chris
2007   "Migrants Filling Mexican Flights." *Arizona Republic*, October 12, 1–3.

Hayes-Bautista, David E. A., Cynthia L. Chamberlin, Branden Jones, Juan Carlos Cornejo, Cecilia Canadas, Carlos Martinez, and Gloria Meza
2007   "Empowerment, Expansion, and Engagement: *Las juntas patrioticas* in California, 1848–1869. (Report)." *California History* (December 22). http://www.accessmylibrary.com/article-1G1-173276434/empowerment -expansion-and-engagement.html.

Henry, Jules
1963   *Culture against Man.* New York: Random House.

Hereford, Jesse
2006   "The U.S.–Mexico Border: Integrated Economies." *Economic Development America*, Spring. http://www.eda.gov/EDAmerica/spring2006/ integration.html.

Hernandez, Esther, and Obed Vasquez
1999   "Mapping Dominican Transnationalism." *Ethnic and Racial Studies* 22(2): 316–339.

Hewes, Gordon W.
1953   "Mexicans in Search of the Mexican." *American Journal of Economics and Sociology* 13: 209–223.

Hill, Jane
2001   "Proto-Uto-Aztecan: A Community of Cultivators in Central Mexico?" *American Anthropologist* 103(4): 913–934.

Hoefer, Michael, Nancy Rytina, and Christopher Campbell
2007   "Estimates of the Unauthorized Immigrant Population Residing in the United States: January 2006." Washington, D.C.: Office of Immigration Statistics Policy Directorate, Department of Homeland Security. http://www.dhs.gov/xlibrary/assets/statistics/publications/ill_pe_2006 .pdf.

Hogg, Thomas Clark
1965   "Urban Migrants and Associations in Sub-Saharan Africa." PhD diss., University of Oregon.

Holt, Alejandra Okie
2007   "The Risks of Using 'Tandas' to Save Money." http://www.thebeehive .org (no longer available).

Honigmann, John J.
1970   "Sampling in Ethnographic Field Work." In R. Naroll and Ronald Cohen, eds., *A Handbook of Method in Cultural Anthropology*, 121–139. New York: Columbia University Press.

Inter-American Development Bank
2008a   "Economic Downturns, Inflation Hit Remittances to Latin America: IDB Fund Forecasts Money Transfers Made by Migrants Will Decrease in Real Terms." http://www.iadb.org/news-releases/2008-10/english/economic -downturns-inflation-hit-remittances-to-latin-america-4779.html.

2008b   "IDB Estimates of 2008 Remittance Flows to Latin America and the Caribbean: Remittances Contributing Less to Regional Family Income for First Time." Washington, D.C.: Inter-American Development Bank. http://idbdocs.iadb.org/wsdocs/getdocument.aspx?docnum=1662094.

Itzigsohn, J., C. D. Cabral, E. H. Medina, and O. Vazquez
1999   "Mapping Dominican Transnationalism: Narrow and Broad Transnational Practices." *Ethnic and Racial Studies* 22(2): 316–339.

Kapferer, Bruce
1969   "Norms and the Manipulation of Relationships in a Work Context." In J. Clyde Mitchell, ed., *Social Networks in Urban Situations: Analyses of Personal Relationships in Central African Towns*, 181–244. Manchester, UK: Manchester University Press for the Institute for Social Research, University of Zambia.

Katzin, Margaret F.
1959   "Partners: An Informal Savings Institution in Jamaica." *Social and Economic Studies* 8: 436–440.

Kearney, Michael
1986   "From the Invisible Hand to Visible Feet: Anthropological Studies of Migration and Development." *Annual Review of Anthropology* 15: 331–361.

2004   *Changing Fields in Anthropology: From Local to Global.* Lanham, MD: Rowman & Littlefield.

Kenny, Michael
1961   "Twentieth Century Spanish Expatriates in Cuba: A Sub-culture?" *Anthropological Quarterly* 34: 85–93.

1962   "Twentieth Century Spanish Expatriates in Mexico: An Urban Subculture." *Anthropological Quarterly* 35: 169–180.

Kerri, James N.

1976   "Studying Voluntary Associations as Adaptive Mechanisms: A Review of Anthropological Perspectives." *Current Anthropology* 17: 23–47.

Kim, Eleana

2003   "Wedding Citizenship and Culture: Korean Adoptees and the Global Family of Korea." *Social Text* 74 (21[1]): 57–81.

Klein, Lawrence R.

1947   *The Keynesian Revolution.* New York: Macmillan.

Kosfeld, Michael, Marcus Heinrichs, Paul J. Zak, Urs Fischbacher, and Ernst Fehr

2005   "Oxytocin Increases Trust in Humans." *Nature* (June 2) 435: 673–676.

Kurtz, Donald F.

1973   "The Rotating Credit Association: An Adaptation to Poverty." *Human Organization* 32: 49–58.

Kurtz, Donald F., and Margaret Showman

1978   "The Tanda: A Rotating Credit Association in Mexico." *Ethnology* 17(1): 65–74.

Langworthy, Mark, and Timothy J. Finan

1997   *Waiting for Rain: Agriculture and Ecological Imbalance in Cape Verde.* Boulder, CO: Lynne Rienner Publishers.

Leach, Edmund R.

1967   "The Language of Kachin Kinship: Reflections on a Tikopia Model." In Maurice Freedman, ed., *Social Organization: Essays Presented to Raymond Firth*, 125–152. Chicago: Aldine Pub. Co.

Leeds, Anthony

1965   "Brazilian Careers and Social Structure: A Case History and Model." In Dwight B. Heath and Richard N. Adams, eds., *Contemporary Cultures and Societies of Latin America*, 379–404. New York: Random House.

Levine, Donald N.

1962   *Wax and Gold: Tradition and Innovation in Ethiopian Culture.* Chicago: University of Chicago Press.

Levitt, Peggy, and N. Glick-Schiller

2004   "Conceptualizing Simultaneity: A Transnational Social Field Perspective on Society." *International Migration Review* 38: 1002–1039.

Lewis, Oscar

1959   *Five Families.* New York: Basic Books.

1961   *Children of Sanchez.* New York: Random House.

1968   *La vida.* New York: Random House.

Light, Ivan H.

1972   *Ethnic Enterprise in America: Business and Welfare among Chinese, Japanese and Blacks.* Berkeley: University of California Press.

Little, Kenneth

1965   *West African Urbanization: A Study of Voluntary Associations in Social Change*. Cambridge: Cambridge University Press.

1967   "Voluntary Associations in Urban Life: A Case Study in Differential Adaptation." In Maurice Freedman, ed., *Social Organization: Essays Presented to Raymond Firth*, 153–165. Chicago: Aldine Pub. Co.

1971   *Some Aspects of African Urbanization South of the Sahara*. Reading, MA: Addison-Wesley Modular Publications.

Loera, Martha Eva

2002   "Las Rifas o Tandas, Arma de dos Filos." Gaceta Universitaria, Mexico City, October 28, p. 9.

Lomnitz, Larissa

1971   "Reciprocity of Favors in the Urban Middle Class of Chile." In George Dalton, ed., *Studies in Economic Anthropology*, 93–106. Anthropological Studies 7. Washington, D.C.: American Anthropological Association.

1977   *Networks and Marginality*. Translated by Cinna Lomnitz. New York: Academic Press.

Lomnitz, Larissa, and Marisol Pérez

1974   "Historia de una familia de la Ciudad de Mexico." Paper presented at the annual meeting of the American Anthropological Association, Mexico City.

Lynch, Tim

1996   "DSN Trials and Tribble-Actions Review." Psi Phi: Bradley's Science/ Fiction Club. Bradley University. 8 October 1997. http://www.bradley .edu/campusorg/psiphi/DS9/ep/503r.html.

Madsen, William

1962   *The Mexican American of South Texas*. New York: Holt, Rinehart and Winston.

Mahler, Sarah J., and Patricia R. Pessar

2004   "Gender Matters: Ethnographers Bring Gender from the Periphery toward the Core of Migration Studies." *International Migration Review* 40: 27–56.

Mangin, William P.

1959   "The Role of Regional Associations in the Adaptation of Rural Migrants to Cities in Peru." *Sociologus* 9: 23–25.

Mansell Carstens, Catherine

1995   *La finanzas populares en Mexico, lasel redescubrimiento de un sistema financiero olvidado*. Mexico City: Centro de Estudios Monetarios Latinoamericanos / Editorial Milenio / Instituto Tecnoloìgico Autoìnomo de Mexico. http://www.cmmayo.com/aboutcatherinemansellcarstens.html.

Meillasoux, Claude

1968   *Urbanization of an African Community: Voluntary Association in Bamako*. Seattle: University of Washington Press.

MexicaNet
n.d.   http://www.mexicanet.com/CENTRO/MERCADO/MENU.HTML.
Miracle, Marvin P., Diane S. Miracle, and Laurie Cohen
1980   "Informal Savings Mobilization in Africa." *Economic Development and Cultural Change* 28: 701–724.
Mission Asset Fund
        http://www.missionassetfund.org/
Mitchell, J. Clyde
1969   "The Concept and Use of Social Networks." In J. Clyde Mitchell, ed., *Social Networks in Urban Situations: Analyses of Personal Relationships in Central African Towns*, 1–50. Manchester, UK: Manchester University Press for the Institute for Social Research, University of Zambia.
Moore, Sally Faulk
1975   "Epilogue: Uncertainties in Situations, Indeterminacies in Culture." In Sally Faulk Moore and Barbara G. Myerhoff, eds., *Symbol and Politics in Communal Ideology, Cases and Questions*, 109–143 . Ithaca, NY: Cornell University Press.
1978   *Law as Process.* London: Routledge and Kegan Paul.
Morawska, Ewa
2001   "Immigrants, Transnationalism, and Ethnicization: A Comparison of This Great Wave and the Last." In Gary Gerstle and John Mollenkopf, eds., *E Pluribus Unum? Contemporary and Historical Perspectives on Immigrant Political Incorporation*, 175–212. New York: Russell Sage.
2004   "Transnationalism." In Mary C. Waters and Reed Ueda, eds., *Harvard Encyclopedia of the New Americas*, 149–163. Cambridge, MA: Harvard University Press.
Morse, Jane
2007   "U.S.–Mexico Border Officials Balance Security, Commerce Needs: Technology Helps Minimize Delays, Detect Contraband." Washington, D.C.: U.S. Department of State. http://www.america.gov/st/washfile -english/2007/September/20070924141658ajesromo.7344171.html.
Morton, Keith L.
1978   "Mobilizing Money in a Communal Economy: A Tongan Example." *Human Organization* 37: 50–56.
Murphy, Robert
1971   *The Dialectics of Social Life.* New York: Basic Books.
Nabokov, Peter
1969   *Tijerina and the Courthouse Raid.* Albuquerque: University of New Mexico Press.
Noble, Charles
1970   "Voluntary Associations of the Basukuma of Northern Mainland Tanzania." PhD diss., Catholic University of America.

Norbeck, Edward
1966   "Rural Japan." In William A. Glaser and David L. Sills, eds., *The Government of Associations: Selections from the Behavioral Sciences*, 72–78. Totowa, NJ: Bedminster Press.
North American Center for Transborder Studies
2008   "Border Officials Cross Talk." June 1(1): 2. Tempe: Arizona State University.
Orbach, Michael K.
1979   Making Extraordinary Decisions in Ordinary Ways: Decision-Making as a Natural Process. Unpublished ms.
Parkin, D. J.
1966   "Urban Voluntary Association as Institutions of adaptation." *Man*, n.s. I: 91–94.
Passel, Jeffrey S., and D'Vera Cohn
2009   "A Portrait of Unauthorized Immigrants in the United States," Pew Hispanic Research Center, April 14. http://pewresearch.org/pubs/1190/portrait-unauthorized-immigrants-states.
Paterson, New Jersey
        http://patersononline.net
Paz, Octavio
1961   *The Labyrinth of Solitude: Life and Thought in Mexico*. New York: Grove Press.
Penny, D. H.
1968   "Farm Credit Policy in the Early Stages of Agricultural Development." *Australian Journal of Agricultural Economics* 12: 32–45.
Pew Hispanic Research Center
2006   *From 200 Million to 300 Million: The Numbers behind Population Growth.* October 10, 2006. http://pewhispanic.org/files/factsheets/25.pdf.
Polanyi, Karl
1957   "The Economy as Instituted Process." In Karl Polanyi et al., eds., *Trade and Market in the Early Empires*, 243–270. Glencoe, IL: Free Press.
Portes, Alejandro
2001a   "Conclusion: Theoretical Convergences and Empirical Evidence in the Study of Immigrant Transnationalism." *International Migration Review* 37: 874–892.
2001b   "Introduction: The Debates and Significance of Immigrant Transnationalism: The Place of 'Esusu Clubs.'" *Global Networks* 1(3): 181–194.
2002   "Theoretical Convergencies and Empirical Evidence in the Study of Immigrant Transnationalism." *International Migration Review* 37: 814–892.
2006   "NAFTA and Mexican Immigration." Border Battles: The U.S. Immigration Debates, Social Science Research Council, July 31. http://borderbattles.ssrc.org/Portes.

Price-Williams, Douglas, and Manuel Ramirez III
1974   "Ethnic Differences in Delay of Gratification." *Journal of Social Psychology* 93: 23–40.
Quarterly Economic Review of Mexico
1979   *Annual Supplement* 20.
Ramírez, Santiago
1959   *El Mexicano: Psicologa de sus motivaciones.* Mexico City: Editorial Pax–Mexico.
Ratha, Dilip, and Zhimei Xu
2008   "Migration and Remittances: Top 10." Migration and Remittances Team, Development Prospects Group, World Bank. http://siteresources .worldbank.org/INTPROSPECTS/Resources/334934-1199807908806/ Top10.pdf.
La Revista de Mérida
1900   "Caja de ahorros monte piedad de Yucatán sociedad coperatie." Feb. 9, 3.
1902   "Caja de ahorros monte piedad de Yucatan sociedad coperatie." June 12, 6.
1908   "Caja de ahorros monte piedad de Yucatán sociedad coperatie." February 25, 3.
Rivas, Jorge M.
2007   "U.S. Census Figures Show that Hispanics Are Increasing Their Clout." http://www.associatedcontent.com/article/318538/us_census_figures _show_that_hispanics.html.
Rubel, Arthur
1965   *Across the Tracks.* Austin: University of Texas Press.
Sahlins, Marshall
1969   "On the Sociology of Primitive Exchange." In Michael Banton, ed., *The Relevance of Models in Social Anthropology*, 139–241. ASA monograph 1. London: Tavistock.
Saldívar, Ramón
2006   *The Borderlands of Culture: Américo Paredes and the Transnational Imaginary.* Durham, NC: Duke University Press.
Sauliniers, Alfred H.
1974   *The Economics of Prestation Systems: A Consumer Analysis of Extended Family Obligations with Application to Zaire.* Ann Arbor: Center for Research on Economic Development, University of Michigan.
Schreiner, Mark
1999   Formal ROSCAs in Argentina. Unpublished paper, Microfinance Risk Management and Center for Social Development, Washington University, St. Louis, MO.
Schwartz, Theodore
1968   "Beyond Cybernetics: Constructs, Expectations, and Goals in Human Adaptation." Paper prepared for Symposium 40, The Effects of Conscious

Purpose on Human Adaptation, Wenner-Gren Foundation for Anthropological Research, Burg Wartenstein, Austria.

SICREA México Autofinancianmento
http://www.sicrea.com.mx/

Silverman, Amy

1996   "Nothing for Money." *Phoenix New Times*, June 13, 1996. http://www .phoenixnewtimes.com/1996-06-13/news/nothing-for-money/.

Skinner, Elliot

1974   *African Urban Life: The Transformation of Oaugadougou.* Princeton, NJ: Princeton University Press.

Smith, Michael Peter, and Matt Bakker

2008   *Citizenship across Borders: The Political Transnationalism of El Migrante.* Ithaca, NY: Cornell University Press.

Smith, Robert C.

2006   *Mexican New York: Transnational Lives of New Immigrants.* Berkeley: University of California Press.

Soen, Dan, and Patrice de Camaramond

1972   "Savings Associations among the Bamileke: Traditional and Modern Cooperations in the Southwest Cameroon." *American Anthropologist* 74: 1170–1179.

Suninistros, Sistemas y Servicios de la Laguna, S.A. de C.V.
http://escoon.tripod.com/

Treudley, Mary

1966   "The Transformation of Peasants into Citizens." In William A. Glaser and David L. Sills, eds., *The Government of Associations: Selections from the Behavioral Sciences*, 59–62. Totowa, NJ: Bedminster Press.

Tsai, Kelle S.

2000   "Banquet Banking: Gender and Rotating Savings and Credit Associations in South China." *The China Quarterly* 161(March): 142–170.

U.S. Census Bureau

1979   *Persons of Spanish Origin in the United States: March 1978. Population Characteristics.* Washington, D.C.: U.S. Government Printing Office.

U.S. Census Bureau, Foreign Trade Division

n.d.   "National Trade Data; State Export Data." http://tse.export.gov/ ITAHome.aspx?UniqueURL=cfos0145a0qr0x45arrgn4na-2007-11-21 -13-39-13.

U.S. Department of Transportation, Research and Innovative Technology Administration, Bureau of Transportation Statistics

2009a   "Border Crossing/Entry Data." http://www.transtats.bts.gov/Fields .asp?Table_ID=1358.

2009b   "U.S. Border Crossings/Entries by State/Port and Month/Year." http:// www.transtats.bts.gov/bordercrossing.aspx.

2009c   "U.S. Border Crossings/Entries by State/Port and Month Year." http://
www.transtats.bts.gov/BorderCrossing.aspx?Sel_Fields=Pedestrians.
Author's compilation of statistical information; selection for pedestrian
field.

U.S.–Mexico Border Health Commission

n.d.   "Demographic Profiles of the Border." http://www.nmsu.edu/~bhcom/
bhcomm-demog.html.

Vélez-Ibáñez, Carlos G.

1978a   "Amigos politicos o amigos sociales: The Politics of Putting Someone
in Your Pocket—Strategies of Power among Brokers in Central Urbanizing Mexico." *Human Organization* 37: 268–277.

1978b   "Youth and Aging in Central Mexico: One Day in the Life of Four Fam-
ilies of Migrants." In Barbara Myerhoff and André Simic, eds., *Life's
Career—Aging: Cultural Variations on Growing Old*, 107–161. Beverly
Hills, CA: Sage Publications.

1980   "Mexican/Hispano Support Systems and *confianza*: Theoretical Issues
of Cultural Adaptation." In Ramon Valle and William Vega, eds., *Hispanic Natural Support Systems: Mental Health Promotion, Perspectives*,
45–54. Sacramento: California Department of Mental Health.

1982   "Social Diversity, Commercialization, and Organizational Complexity
of Urban Mexican/Chicano Rotating Credit Associations: Theoretical
and Empirical Issues of Adaptation." *Human Organization* 41: 107–120.

1983   *Bonds of Mutual Trust: The Cultural Systems of Rotating Credit Associations among Urban Mexicans and Chicanos*. New Brunswick, NJ: Rutgers
University Press.

1993   "Ritual Cycles of Exchange: The Process of Cultural Creation and
Management in the U.S. Borderlands." In P. Frese, ed., *Celebrations
of Identity: Multiple Voices in American Ritual Performance*, 119–143.
Westport, CT: Bergin & Garvey.

1995   "Funds of Knowledge in Urban Arenas: Another Way of Understanding
the Learning Resources of Poor Mexican Households in the U.S. Southwest and Their Implications for National Contexts." In Judith Freiden-
berg, ed., *Anthropology of Lower Income Urban Enclaves: The Case of East
Harlem*, 749: 263–280. New York: Annals of the New York Academy of
Sciences.

1996   *Border Visions: Mexican Cultures of the Southwest United States*. Tucson:
University of Arizona Press.

2004a   "The Commoditization and Devalorization of Mexicans in the Southwest United States: Implications for Human Rights Theory." In Carol
Nagengast and Carlos G. Vélez-Ibáñez, eds., *Human Rights: The Scholar
as Activist*, 153–168. Washington, D.C.: Publications of the Society of
Applied Anthropology.

2004b   "The Political Ecology of Debt among Mexican Colonias in the South-western United States." In Hotze Lont and Otto Hospes, eds., *Livelihood and Microfinance: Anthropological and Sociological Perspectives on Savings and Debt*, 129–151. Delft, The Netherlands: Eburon Publishers, 2004.

2004c   "Regions of Refuge in the United States: Issues, Problems, and Concerns for Mexican-Origin Populations." *Human Organization* 63(1): 1–20.

2008   "Fronterizo and transborder existences y lo que le paso a Paloma." Spring Seminar on Transnational Artistic and Cultural Production, Lennox Seminar, Trinity University, San Antonio, Texas, January 26–27, 2008.

Vélez-Ibáñez, Carlos G., and James B. Greenberg

1992   "Formation and Transformation of Funds of Knowledge among U.S. Mexican Households." *Anthropology and Education Quarterly* 23(4): 313–335.

Vélez-Ibáñez, Carlos G., and Ana Sampiao

2002   *Transnational Latina/o Communities: Politics, Processes, and Cultures.* Lanham, MD: Rowman & Littlefield.

Vélez-Ibáñez, Carlos G., Richard Verdugo, and Francisco Nuñez

1981   "Politics and Mental Health among Elderly Chicanos." In Manual R. Miranda and Ramon N. Ruiz, eds., *Chicano Aging and Mental Health*, 118–155. Rockville, MD: Alcohol, Drug Abuse, and Mental Health Administration, U.S. Department of Health and Human Services.

Wallace, Anthony F. C.

1961   *Culture and Personality.* New York: Random House.

Wallerstein, Emanuel M.

1966   "Voluntary Associations." In James S. Coleman and Carl G. Rosenberg, Jr., eds., *Political Parties and National Integration in Tropical Africa*, 318–339. Berkeley: University of California Press.

Weaver, Thomas, and Theodore Downing

1977   *Mexican Migration.* Tucson: Bureau of Ethnic Research, Department of Anthropology, University of Arizona.

Wheeldon, P. D.

1969   "The Operation of Voluntary Associations and Personal Networks in the Political Processes of an Inter-Ethnic Community." In J. Clyde Mitchell, ed., *Social Networks in Urban Situations: Analysis of Personal Relationships in Central African Towns*, 128–180. Manchester, UK: Manchester University Press for the Institute for Social Research, University of Zambia.

White House, The

2006   "Fact Sheet: President Requests Funds To Strengthen Border Security." http://merln.ndu.edu/archivepdf/hls/WH/20060518-6.pdf.

Wolf, Eric R.

1956   "Aspects of Group Relations in a Complex Society: Mexico." *American Anthropologist* 58: 1065–1078.

1959   *Sons of the Shaking Earth.* Chicago: University of Chicago Press.

Wu, David Y. H.
1974   "To Kill Three Birds with One Stone: The Rotating Credit Associations
        of the Papua New Guinea Chinese." *American Ethnologist* 1: 565–584.
Zarraugh, Laura H.
2007   "From Workers to Owners: Latino Entrepreneurs in Harrisonburg, Vir-
        ginia." *Human Organization: Journal of the Society for Applied Anthro-
        pology* 66(3): 240–248.

Index

About the Author

Carlos G. Vélez-Ibáñez is Motorola Presidential Professor of Neighbor-hood Revitalization and Chairman of the Department of Transborder Chicana/o and Latina/o Studies and Professor of Transborder Chicana/o and Latina/o Studies and School of Human Evolution and Cultural Change at Arizona State University. An Emeritus Professor of Anthropology of the University of California, Riverside, Dr. Vélez-Ibáñez received the 2010 Outstanding Support of Hispanic Issues in Higher Education Award by the American Association of Hispanics in Higher Education, the 2004 Robert B. Textor and Family Prize for Excellence in Anticipatory Anthropology awarded by the American Anthropology Association, and in 2003 the Bronislaw Malinowski Medal presented by the Society for Applied Anthropology as well as a number of other awards. He is the recipient of several fellowships including Fellow of the Center for Advanced Study in the Behavioral Sciences, Stanford, in 1993–94 and Fellow of the American Association for the Advancement of Science, 1999. In 2011, he will begin serving as the Director of the new School of Transborder Studies.

LaVergne, TN USA
11 October 2010
200366LV00003B/2/P